CW01261704

Masséna at Bay

Masséna at Bay

The Lines of Torres Vedras to Fuentes de Oñoro

Tim Saunders

Pen & Sword
MILITARY

First published in Great Britain in 2021 by
PEN & SWORD MILITARY
an imprint of
Pen & Sword Books Ltd
47 Church Street
Barnsley
South Yorkshire
S70 2AS

Copyright © Tim Saunders, 2021

ISBN 978-1-39900-132-8

The right of Tim Saunders to be identified as the author of this work has been asserted by him in accordance with the Copyright, Designs and Patents Act 1988.

A CIP catalogue record for this book is available from the British Library.

All rights reserved. No part of this book may be reproduced or transmitted in any form or by any means, electronic or mechanical including photocopying, recording or by any information storage and retrieval system, without permission from the Publisher in writing.

Typeset by Concept, Huddersfield HD4 5JL.
Printed and bound in England by CPI Group (UK) Ltd, Croydon CR0 4YY.

Pen & Sword Books Limited incorporates the imprints of Atlas, Archaeology, Aviation, Discovery, Family History, Fiction, History, Maritime, Military, Military Classics, Politics, Select, Transport, True Crime, Air World, Frontline Publishing, Leo Cooper, Remember When, Seaforth Publishing, The Praetorian Press, Wharncliffe Local History, Wharncliffe Transport, Wharncliffe True Crime and White Owl.

For a complete list of Pen & Sword titles please contact
PEN & SWORD BOOKS LIMITED
47 Church Street, Barnsley, South Yorkshire, S70 2AS, England
E-mail: enquiries@pen-and-sword.co.uk
Website: www.pen-and-sword.co.uk

Contents

Acknowledgements vi
Introduction vii
  1. The Storm Clouds Gather 1
  2. The Lines of Torres Vedras 23
  3. Winter at Santarém 55
  4. Withdrawal to the Rio Mondego 81
  5. Pursuit to Spain 101
  6. Combat of Sabugal, 3 April 1811 133
  7. Back on the Border Lands 153
  8. Fuentes de Oñoro, 3–4 May 1811 175
  9. Fuentes de Oñoro, 5 May 1811 189
10. Aftermath 221
Appendices
    I: Wellington's Memorandum for Lieutenant Colonel Fletcher 231
   II: Wellington's Orders for Operations against Guarda 235
  III: Wellington's Orders for Sabugal 237
  IV: Wellington's Orders for Fuentes de Oñoro 241
   V: Masséna's Orders for 5 May 1811 247
 VI: Order of Battle, Fuentes de Oñoro 249
Notes 253
Index 261

Acknowledgements

This book was written during the 2020 COVID-19 lockdown when the archives and libraries that would normally be the starting-point for research were firmly closed. However, in the great digital leap forward of the year, I have been amazed at quite how much documentation can be found online with a bit of determined digging. To the forums and online libraries that I have used, many thanks. Also very helpful are the considerable number of Peninsular memoirs and diaries that are available through publishers and researchers such as Gareth Glover. As strict lockdown receded, the skeleton staff in sundry regimental museums gave me access to their unique knowledge. I am grateful to one and all.

As usual I have been helped and encouraged by friends and colleagues with historical advice and the battlefield guide's knowledge of the ground out in the Peninsula. I particularly thank fellow guide and historian Rob Yuill who helped significantly and loaned me books from his extensive Napoleonic library.

Napoleonic living historians have again played a significant part in helping me understand the army's Peninsular War drill and tactics. The insight they provided has enabled me to go into greater detail, with a clear understanding and ability to interpret those passages in accounts that I for one have tended to pass over quickly.

As before, images of this period that are correct in every respect are but few, and again, museums' help in selecting pictures is much appreciated. The living historians who posed illustrative photographs for me have been unstinting with their patience, understanding and their time. I am most grateful to those groups who have allowed us to use images from their archives. I also owe a significant debt of gratitude for the continuing support of Major (Retired) Nick Haines of the Green Jackets and that great artist Christa Hook, whose accurate paintings are not only detailed but evocative even when reproduced in black and white.*

Finally, to the team at Pen & Sword: Heather, Matt, Pamela and Noel, once again my thanks for nursing this project to fruition.

Tim Saunders
Warminster, 2020

*To see more of Christa's work and commissions please visit
http://www.christahook.co.uk.

Introduction

The 1810 French invasion of Portugal, commanded by Marshal André Masséna, has been well covered by historians. Conversely, the shock revelation of the Lines of Torres Vedras barring the French Army of Portugal's way to Lisbon via numerous combats and the Battle of Fuentes de Oñoro, through to Masséna's dismissal from command, has been frequently and unjustifiably glossed over. Starting with the Lines of Torres Vedras, which were at the heart of Wellington's peninsular strategy from October 1809 until 1812, this is the story of Wellington while he was still forging his peninsular army, refining his own art of war and is a period when the outcome of the struggle in Iberia was still very much in doubt.

In this book I have as far as possible continued my practice of letting the officers and soldiers of both armies who fought in the campaign, its combats and battles, tell their own story, taking them from Wellington's lines just a few miles from Lisbon, across Portugal to the borders of Spain and victory over Marshal Masséna. The doubts expressed in letters home and diaries during the 1810 invasion in the face of a powerful French army steadily melt away and a growing confidence is observed as the enemy was bundled back to Spain in the early spring of 1811.

The pursuit of Masséna's army, however, reveals that Wellington's army had much to learn in the conduct and coordination of its marches and the commissariat was still unable to supply the army as it advanced. Wellington wrote increasingly pithy instructions on both subjects as he grew progressively frustrated with the senior commanders, a number of whom he regarded as having been foisted on him by Horse Guards.

Some thirty-eight maps are included in the book, but to help readers follow the action on modern topographic maps or indeed follow the campaign on the ground, I have changed all but the most familiar place names to their modern spellings. I have also, as is my normal practice, used the ranks of individuals as they were during 1810–11.

Chapter One

The Storm Clouds Gather

'The hideous leopard contaminates by its very presence in the peninsula of Spain and Portugal. Let us carry our victorious eagles to the Pillars of Hercules.' [Napoleon]

Despite his victory at Talavera during the high summer of 1809, the newly-ennobled Lieutenant General Viscount Wellington faced a growing threat from Napoleon. It was generally expected that the master of Europe would turn his attention to the insult to his imperial dignity that was the British army in the Peninsula. Following the Battle of Wagram and the collapse of the Fifth Coalition, there were no pressing military reasons why the emperor could not personally lead the 100,000 men he was preparing for the third French invasion of Portugal.[1] Civil practicalities in France, however, intervened. Issues with money, law, national administration and a new wife saw him handing over command of the Army of Portugal to a reluctant Marshal André Masséna, one of the few in the marshalate capable of independent action without Napoleon's supervision.

Created Prince d'Essling following his success in the 1809 Danube campaign, Marshal Masséna was tired and recovering after a fall from his horse, and at 55 he was ageing somewhat. According to Major Marbot, an aide-de-camp (ADC) on Masséna's staff, another reason for Masséna's reluctance to take command was that he was concerned that his senior subordinates would resent him being placed in command over them.[2] In short, he did not want the command, but even though he was visibly no longer 'Masséna of the flashing eyes' of his younger days, 'the spoilt child of victory' was prevailed upon by Napoleon to take to the field again. His task in invading Portugal was to 'throw the leopard into the sea' and reinstate his master's Continental System,[3] thereby bringing Britain to her knees via her economy. The system, however, leaked badly, especially at the extremities of Europe where Portugal continued to trade with Britain.

To help persuade Masséna to take the command, Napoleon promised to give him an army of 100,000 men, everything he needed in terms of matériel, that he would be 'lacking nothing in supplies' and that he would have freedom of action. Fatally for the marshal and the Army of Portugal, Napoleon kept none of these promises.

British Peninsular Strategy

In March 1809, as preparations were being made to return to the peninsula and reinforce Sir John Craddock's small British army left in Lisbon, the then

Marshal André Masséna, Prince d'Essling, commander of the Army of Portugal.

Lieutenant General Sir Arthur Wellesley wrote in a 'Memorandum on the Defence of Portugal':

> I have always been of opinion that Portugal might be defended, whatever might be the result of the contest in Spain; and that in the meantime the measures adopted for the defence of Portugal would be highly useful to the Spaniards in their contest with the French.
>
> My opinion was, that even if Spain should have been conquered, the French would not have been able to overrun Portugal with a smaller force than 100,000 men; and that as long as the contest should continue in Spain

Lieutenant General Viscount Wellesley.

> this force, if it could be put in a state of activity, would be highly useful to the Spaniards, and might eventually have decided the contest.
>
> The British force employed in Portugal should ... not be less than 30,000 men, of which number 4,000 or 5,000 should be cavalry, and there should be a large body of artillery.[4]

Ensign Leith Hay[5] wrote of the significance of the presence of a British army in the peninsula in 'giving confidence to the Spanish cause, protracting the struggle, forming the nucleus of future strengths to be marshalled against him [Napoleon]. It was this influence which he especially wished to destroy.'

In addition to the size of the British contingent, Wellesley recommended reforming the Portuguese army.[6] He wrote in his memorandum:

> My notion, that the Portuguese military establishments, upon the footing of 40,000 militia and 30,000 regular troops, ought to be revived ... It is obvious, however, that the military establishments of Portugal cannot be revived without very extensive pecuniary assistance and political support from this country.

Under Marshal Beresford and a leavening of British officers in the chain of command, the Portuguese army was rebuilt.

The experience of attempting to work alongside his other ally, the Spanish, in offensive operations during 1809 had been a salutary experience for Wellesley. They had consistently failed to live up to their promises and Wellesley, complaining to Lord Castlereagh, wrote that it '... has opened my eyes regarding the state of the war in the Peninsula.' Deciding 'not to have anything to do with the Spanish [way of] warfare', he wrote to Marshal Beresford that his plan 'is to remain on the defensive'.

In on the defensive, Viscount Wellington recognized the unique position of Lisbon as the heart and soul of Portugal and if it remained in Portuguese hands, the invader would not have achieved his aims. In addition, he believed that as long as the British army remained in Portugal it would be able to perform the role outlined above by Leith Hay. To ensure that the army could stay in the country, Wellington ordered the construction of defensive lines across the 25 miles of the Lisbon Peninsula. These defences, the Lines of Torres Vedras, were both a refuge for the allied armies and the defences of the city. Consequently, they lay at the very heart of Wellington's strategy during 1809 and 1812.

Of course, not everyone was happy with the cost of the war in the peninsula or its prospects. Even one of Wellington's own divisional commanders was what Wellington described as a 'croaker'. Major General Thomas Picton shared the views of Whig politicians and many soldiers serving in the peninsula when he wrote:

> We shall affect nothing worth talking of in Portugal. We may delay the entire occupation of the country for some months, but certainly not much longer, and that too with a considerable degree of risk: for if we protract our opposition too long we may experience, I understand, very considerable difficulty in bringing the Army off: for should the enemy, which we cannot prevent, get possession of the left Bank of the Tagus, opposite Lisbon, our ships of war and Transports must quit the Harbour, and in that case our communication with them will become extremely difficult and precarious.

Thanks to some extraordinarily effective operational security, even Picton was clearly not aware of Wellington's strategy or the extent of the Lines of Torres Vedras.

The Army of Portugal

In early 1810, there were more than 250,000 French troops in the peninsula keeping Napoleon's brother King Joseph on his throne in Madrid. The marshals and generals who commanded them, however, were committed to holding down their own fiefdoms and staving off attacks by Spanish guerrillas. In addition, they were famously unco-operative, being jealous of each other and the spoils of Spain

A French centre company infantryman.

they could garner. This meant that Masséna and the Army of Portugal were effectively on their own facing 40,000 British and Portuguese troops under Wellington's command. It would appear from French estimates that Napoleon dismissed the newly-raised Portuguese army as irrelevant.

The army that Masséna joined in Salamanca during May 1810 consisted of Marshal Ney's veteran VI Corps and General Junot's VIII Corps, totalling not the 100,000 men, including the Imperial Guard, originally considered necessary by Napoleon, nor the watered-down promise of 70,000 but fewer than 50,000. On his arrival Masséna made it clear to his headquarters staff: 'Gentlemen, I am here against my own wish: I begin to find myself too old and too weary for active service.'[7] As he feared, his senior subordinates were already resentful at being placed under the command of a senior marshal rather than Napoleon. Ney and Masséna were old enemies and the situation was made worse by Ney being 'furiously jealous' at being superseded as commander of the Army of Portugal. Despite some fine words of loyalty, from the start Masséna's corps commanders were in a state of almost open dissent and were reluctant to follow his orders.

The Army of Portugal had a hard core of veterans, particularly in Ney's VI Corps, but to bring that corps up to 27,000 strong, the marshal had been reinforced by a division of recruits. The other smaller corps was even more heavily reinforced by additional battalions of inexperienced levees formed by regiments at their depots across France. Napoleon assembled these battalions into formations for service in the peninsula, having carefully kept his Grande Armée veterans in France or garrisons in Germany. Those understrength units already in Spain were reorganized into provisional regiments of cavalry or battalions of infantry. Consequently, the French army preparing to invade Portugal in 1810 was not of the same quality as those that had delivered victory after victory to Napoleon elsewhere in Europe.

In contrast with the campaign season in central Europe, Masséna's campaign started later in the year for the simple reason that Portugal was one of the poorest parts of Europe and large areas of the country had already been impoverished by the previous French invasions. By 1810 the French had learned that their preferred tactic of living off the land, which allowed them to move fast, unencumbered by slow-moving supply trains, did not work in the peninsula. Napoleon had appreciated that the army would inevitably have to increase its reliance on magazines and convoys. The difficulties of extemporizing a logistic system deep in Spain and being unable to significantly resupply by sea meant that logistic support would be minimal. Consequently, the invasion of Portugal would have to wait until the Portuguese harvest had been gathered in.

Of the three practicable routes into Portugal, only the northern route had not been previously used and offered greater foraging opportunities for French units. Wellington had, however, appreciated this and moved most of his command north to Beira, leaving General Hill to cover the southern routes. His estimate was confirmed by secret correspondents who reported the arrival of

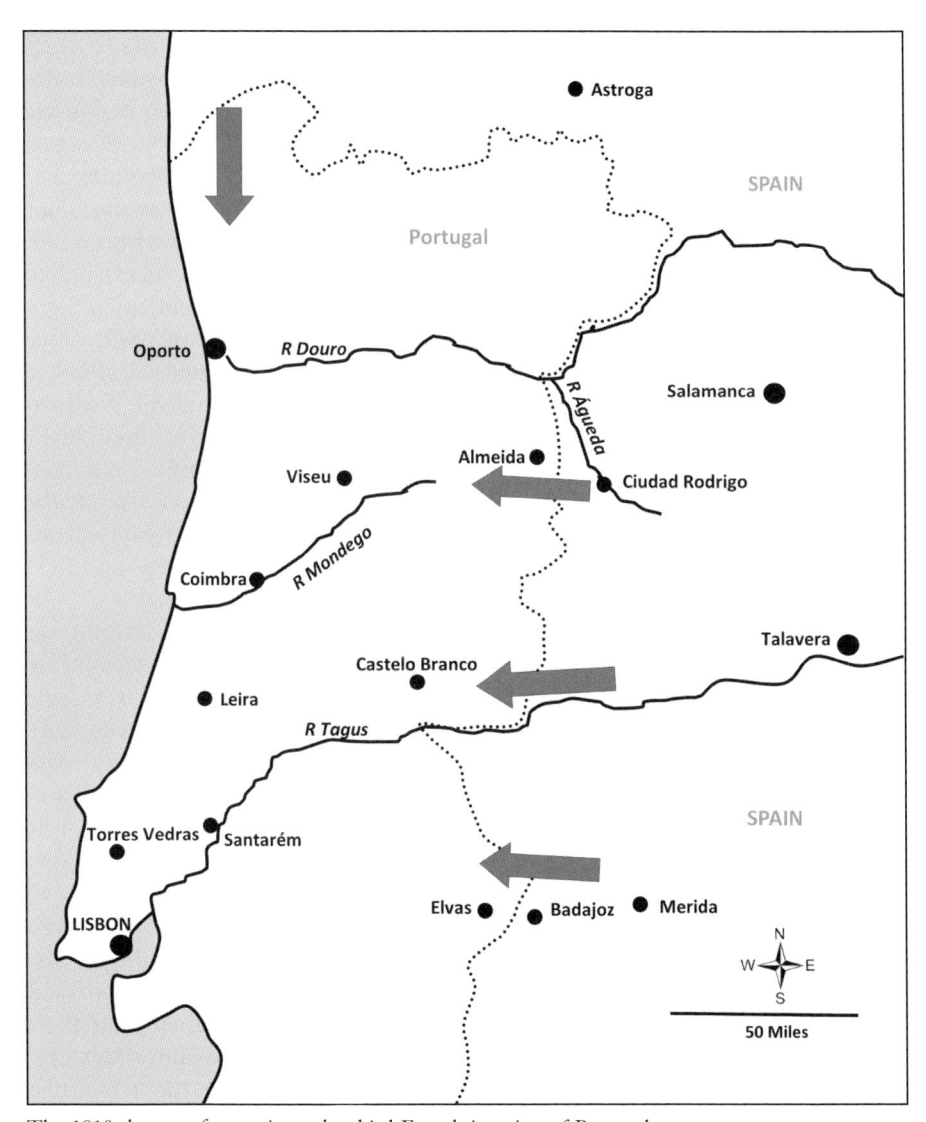

The 1810 theatre of operations: the third French invasion of Portugal.

reinforcements, preparation of magazines and the concentration of divisions at Salamanca.

On whichever invasion route was to be taken into Portugal, Napoleon knew that the Spanish and Portuguese border fortifications, all of which were still in allied hands, would have to be taken. Consequently, Masséna was well provided with an appropriate number of engineers and a substantial train of siege artillery. This is in contrast to other parts of the Army of Portugal, which were in many cases barely adequate.

The Spanish Army

The treacherous way the French had occupied Spain and usurped the throne in 1807 and the brutal manner in which the Dos de Mayo Rebellion in Madrid in 1808 was suppressed had outraged the Spanish. On top of this, foraging and systematic plundering brought about popular resistance in the form of a burgeoning level of guerrilla warfare. Napoleon's irritation at his commanders' failure to subdue the Spanish provinces was growing and, as the war went on, it is said that the only ground that the French held was a musket shot from where their soldiers were standing.

Following the Junta's disastrous campaign during the autumn of 1809, which was crowned by the defeat at Ocaña in November, the various Spanish armies had withdrawn into southern Estremadura, Andalusia, Galicia and Valencia. However, as the 1810 campaign season opened, King Joseph and Marshal Soult made the mistake of ignoring Wellington's growing army and advanced south into Andalusia and secured the wealth of Seville, along with the destruction of the Central Junta. By 3 February General Alburquerque and the remnants of his army had withdrawn into the fortress of Cadiz.[8] Overall, the Spanish-held enclaves were further reduced.

In response to this situation, Wellington's strategy enunciated when he was given command of the army in the peninsula in early 1809 still applied. He explained that it was not the job of the British to beat the French but to keep sufficient of them occupied so that the Spanish could continue fighting. The Peninsular Army, even at its largest, including its Portuguese contingents, was never large enough to defeat all of the French armies in the peninsula.

Maintaining a British army in Portugal was key to providing time for the Spanish to reorganize and train, but with the remains of their armies pushed into the extremities of Spain, the local juntas looked to their own interests. They used all available resources for their own defence and were reluctant to co-operate with the orders of the Central Junta.

On the occasions when the British army met their Spanish counterparts at Astorga at the beginning of the retreat to Corunna and during the Talavera campaign, the woeful state of the great country's army was a shock to the British soldiers. Their uniforms were ragged; many were shoeless and virtually starving. Of course, when the British withdrew back to Portugal after Talavera they were reduced to a not dissimilar state, with the commissariat having failed and Spanish promises proving to be hollow.

The Peninsular Army

By the turn of the year the army had been reinforced to a strength of nearly 30,000 but the failure of the Walcheren Expedition, where the ravages of malarial typhus laid so many low, meant that drafts to replace casualties were scarce. Similarly there were few units to deploy to the peninsula and increase the overall size of the army. Nonetheless, by the summer of 1810 Wellington had, for

A contemporary image of a Spanish guerrilla and Spanish grenadiers.

instance, 3,000 cavalry under General Cotton, but this was still half the number of Masséna's mounted arm.

At the beginning of 1810 the Anglo-Portuguese army consisted of six divisions with a seventh two-brigade division being added before the Battle of Buçaco under the command of Major General Leith. Later in the autumn, while in the Lines of Torres Vedras, the 5th Division was brought up to strength when a further British brigade arrived. To help introduce new battalions and brigades, Wellington attempted to retain veteran units and to mix them with newly-arrived battalions in order to produce steady formations, with the example of an experienced unit to follow.

Unlike the French army the British, operating in allied countries, relied on a commissariat to supply them with all their necessities. Most of the army's needs were imported by sea, but locally-procured food and forage would be paid for with cash or by issuing promissory notes. There was rarely a shortage of food in Lisbon or in the magazines, but delivering it to the battalions was altogether more challenging as the peninsula was bereft of decent roads. Local carts and waggons and the necessary draft animals were not available in the quantities required, so the brigades of mules and muleteers were the backbone of Wellington s logistic system. As will be seen, this tended to work well during static phases of the campaign, such as at in the Lines of Torres Vedras and before Santarém, but when on the march over extended distances the commissariat frequently failed to deliver food to the divisions leading an advance. On such occasions when no food was delivered to troops for more than two days, operations had to be halted. The Portuguese commissariat was responsible for feeding their own army but, starved of cash and resources, Wellington had to divert British rations to them to prevent wholesale desertion due to hunger.

By 1810, almost a year into the programme of raising a new Portuguese army, there were some 33,000 infantry and somewhere in excess of 4,000 (mounted) cavalrymen, supported by around 40 artillery pieces.[9] Of this force at the time of the Battle of Buçaco in September, some 24,500 were with Wellington's army as a part of his 7 divisions or in the 3 independent brigades.[10] The remainder, plus the forty-eight regiments of militia, were still in training or in garrisons across the country.

The 1810 Campaign Begins

With detailed instructions having been issued by Napoleon, the preliminary moves to take the Spanish border fortress of Ciudad Rodrigo got off to a slow start. This was not just because of the timing of the Portuguese harvest but because of the state of the roads, which made filling magazines at Salamanca and moving the battering train forward both manpower-intensive and slow. Ciudad Rodrigo was invested on 26 April, but the normally poor Spanish roads in the early spring of 1810 were made worse due to it being a particularly cold and wet year.[11] When the French eventually broke ground before Ciudad Rodrigo on 15 June, the rocky Tesón feature was full of water and their trenches regularly flooded, slowing progress. A further delay to the invasion was occasioned by the harvest being almost a month later than normal.

The French had hoped that Ciudad Rodrigo would fall quickly, but an unexpectedly stout defence by its governor General Herrasti and the 5,500-strong garrison[12] meant that a full twenty-six days of digging and battering had to be undertaken. By the time Ciudad Rodrigo capitulated on 10 July, the siege had taken a total of ten weeks and the sundry delays provided Wellington between a month and two and a half months more crucial time to prepare for the invasion.[13]

With the crops barely ripe, the French began to press forward on 14 July. They advanced past the small Spanish border fortress of La Concepción, which was slighted as they approached, and on across the frontier into Portugal, where the fortress of Almeida was their next objective.

On the night of 23/24 July Ney made an unauthorized advance with his VI Corps under the cover of fog and fell upon General Craufurd's Light Division, which was Wellington's corps of observation deployed just south of Almeida. Craufurd, usually so aware of the enemy's likely movements, despite

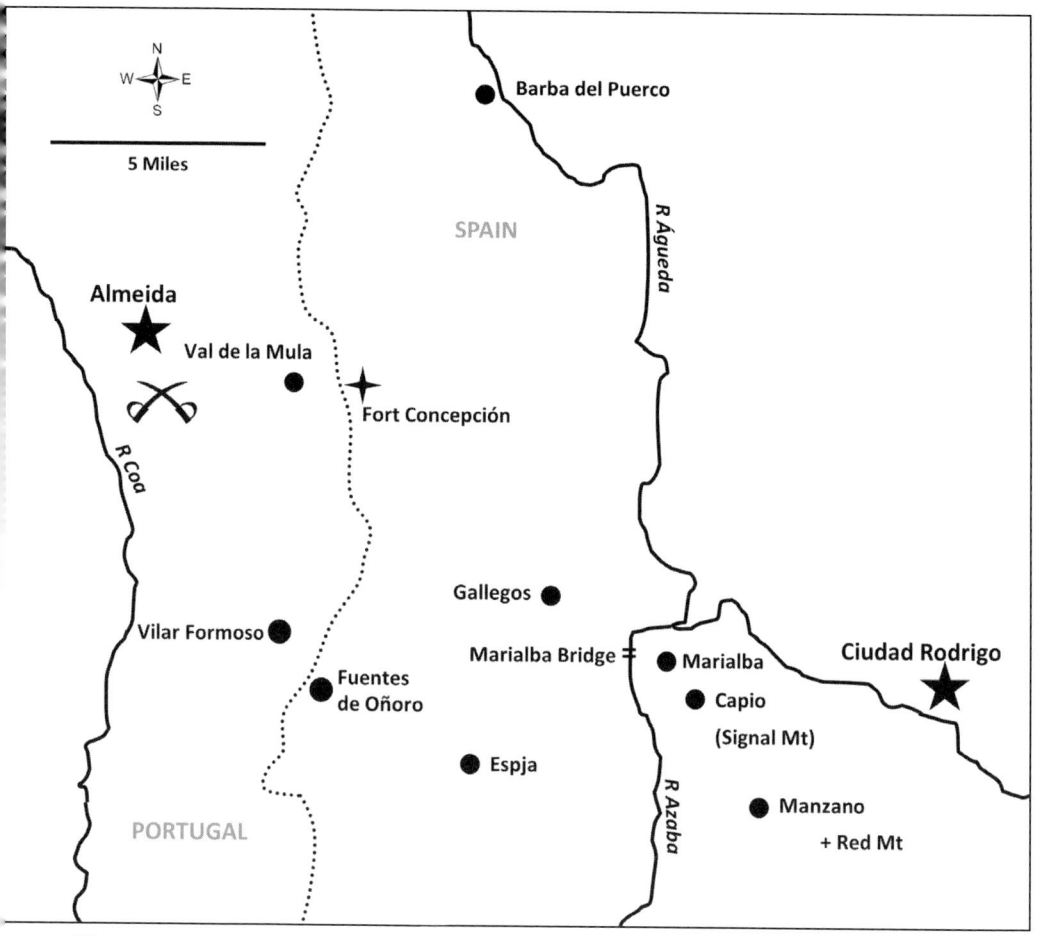

The area of operations between Ciudad Rodrigo and the Côa.

Wellington's concerns, had remained in a vulnerable position east of the Rio Côa, with just a single bridge to his rear. Consequently, in considerable danger and under great pressure, the battalions of the Light Division fought their way back across the river, suffering losses of some 308 men in what many of the division regarded as an unnecessary action.[14] Ney, however, was unable to force a crossing of the Côa and maintain his pressure on the Light Division, which along with Picton's 3rd Division was able to withdraw 15 miles into Portugal.

Both Craufurd and Ney were roundly criticized by their respective commanders for the combat on the Côa: Ney for committing his corps to an unauthorized general action and Craufurd for his reluctance to withdraw when the situation clearly demanded it. Both, however, retained their commands.

The tempo of French operations remained slow in the aftermath of the fall of Ciudad Rodrigo. It took six days to bake bread and replace the considerable amount of ammunition and siege materials that had been used at Ciudad Rodrigo before besieging Almeida. Consequently, even though that fortress had been enveloped by Ney's advance, it wasn't until 15 August that the French were able to break ground. After ten days of digging, the batteries opened fire and after just

The site of the breach in the defences of Ciudad Rodrigo.

The gateway to Almeida.

thirteen hours of bombardment a lucky shell detonated the fortress's magazine and the Portuguese garrison duly surrendered on 28 August.

Having to secure his line of communications and garrison both Ciudad Rodrigo and Almeida, Masséna needed reinforcement and summoned Reynier's 18,000-strong II Corps north to join him. Having boosted his strength to 65,000, Masséna began the advance into the heart of Portugal on 15 September. His aim was to reach Lisbon as quickly as possible, initially via, as Wellington had expected, the valley of the Rio Mondego.

Now was the time for Wellington to put his strategy of denial into place. He was under no illusion that the French, after years of victory across Europe, could with sufficient numbers drive the British from the peninsula, as they had done to Sir John Moore's army at La Corunna only the previous year. Unless, that is, special measures were taken. The first of these were instructions for what would today be known as a 'scorched earth policy', which had been reluctantly approved by the Portuguese Regency Council. Wellington wrote: 'Send round to the people that they must retire from the villages, and let the magistrates know that if any of them stay, or if any of the inhabitants have communication with the enemy, they shall be hanged.'

In addition to abandoning villages, stocks of food were to be removed and any standing crops destroyed, along with mills for grinding corn. Deputy Assistant Commissary Schaumann wrote:

> ... the Portuguese Government published another proclamation, calling upon the inhabitants of Almeida and the surrounding country to leave their houses and estates and to remove their portable effects into the mountains. And now again everybody begins to take flight. Much wine, corn and straw were offered to me for sale, and the cornfields were cleared of crops.[15]

Wellington's aim was to draw the French, still largely reliant on foraging, deep into Portugal. Here, firstly the work of starvation would wear them down and secondly dispersal to seek food would make them vulnerable to attack by the *ordenanza* and by a vengeful population.

Based on inadequate maps and some terrible advice by eighteen renegade Portuguese officers whose knowledge of the area was negligible, Masséna was diverted from a bad road in the Mondego valley onto what soon became obvious was little more than a mountain track. After several days of manoeuvring, French intentions became apparent to the allies when they crossed to the north of the Rio Mondego. Wellington could see that Masséna was heading for Viseu, bypassing the Ponte de Murcela defences on the Rio Alva where the British were believed to be preparing to fight in a strong position.[16] He would therefore probably attempt to cross the Mondego further downstream at Coimbra before turning south towards Lisbon.

The Army of Portugal reached Viseu on 19 September, but had to halt there for six days to allow the supply train, baggage and artillery to catch up. The poor, rocky roads had already damaged vehicles and repairs had to be made to wheels

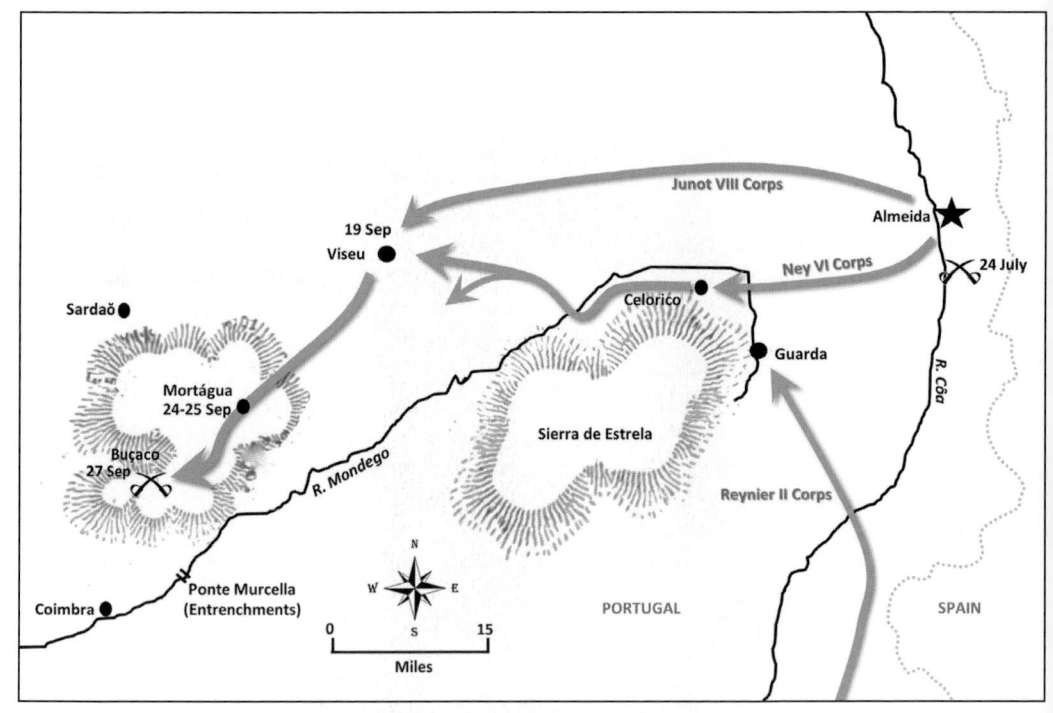

The French advance into Portugal.

and axles. The pause at Viseu, however, gave Wellington time to concentrate north of the river and plan to fight on advantageous ground where the French superiority in numbers of cavalry would be negated.

Battle of Buçaco Ridge

As he withdrew into Portugal, Wellington, unable to publicly explain his strategy, had come under increasing pressure from both the Portuguese Regency Council and politicians in London to fight, and by taking the mountain road from Viseu to Mortágua, Masséna had provided a favourable opportunity. The 10-mile long, 1,000ft-high Buçaco Ridge was a classic Wellingtonian defensive position, standing square across the French army's route.

When Masséna resumed his march on 25 September, it was again slow due to the dreadful road the army had taken, and further delays were attributed to the marshal being accompanied by his mistress. The presence of Henriette Leberton,[17] wife of another officer, as an 'additional aide-de-camp' had caused resentment since their arrival in May, but during the siege of Ciudad Rodrigo she had remained at Salamanca. Now she was accompanying Masséna, and one of his ADCs, Major Marbot, hinted that delays in marching, poor decision-making and a lack of proper reconnaissance prior to Buçaco was the result of Masséna's concern for 'Madame X', as she was known by the marshal's staff.

The position that Wellington occupied at Buçaco was anchored on a walled convent, left of centre, at the point where the Mortágua to Coimbra road climbs across the ridge. There was a rough track along the crest of the ridge, which the engineers improved to enhance mobility along the front, and a further, lesser

A portrait believed to be of Henriette Leberton.

road from Ameal crossing the ridge further to the right. As usual Wellington deployed his divisions, totalling 50,000 men and sixty guns, behind the ridge out of sight of the French, less his piquets.

On the evening of 26 September Ney's cavalry patrols reported the presence of the allies at Buçaco. The marshal's assumption was that they were Wellington's rearguard and that they would withdraw as usual when pressed. The following day Masséna joined Ney at the foot of the ridge and concluded that this was indeed the rearguard and decided to attack the following morning once the army had closed up to the foot of the ridge.

Masséna, unaware of the extent of Wellington's dispositions, planned to turn what he believed to be Wellington's right flank via the Ameal track with Reynier's II Corps. Once he was up on the ridge, Ney's corps would advance up the road to Buçaco Convent towards the northern end of the ridge and pursue the rearguard.

A thick mist delayed the French advance at dawn on 27 September 1810 and hampered development of their knowledge of Wellington's deployment. At 0600 hours Reynier's corps began to advance with Heudelet's division marching up the Ameal track and onto the crest where they were surprised by the 74th Foot and two Portuguese battalions, supported by a dozen guns of Picton's 3rd Division. The resulting exchanges of volley fire in this area continued for most of the

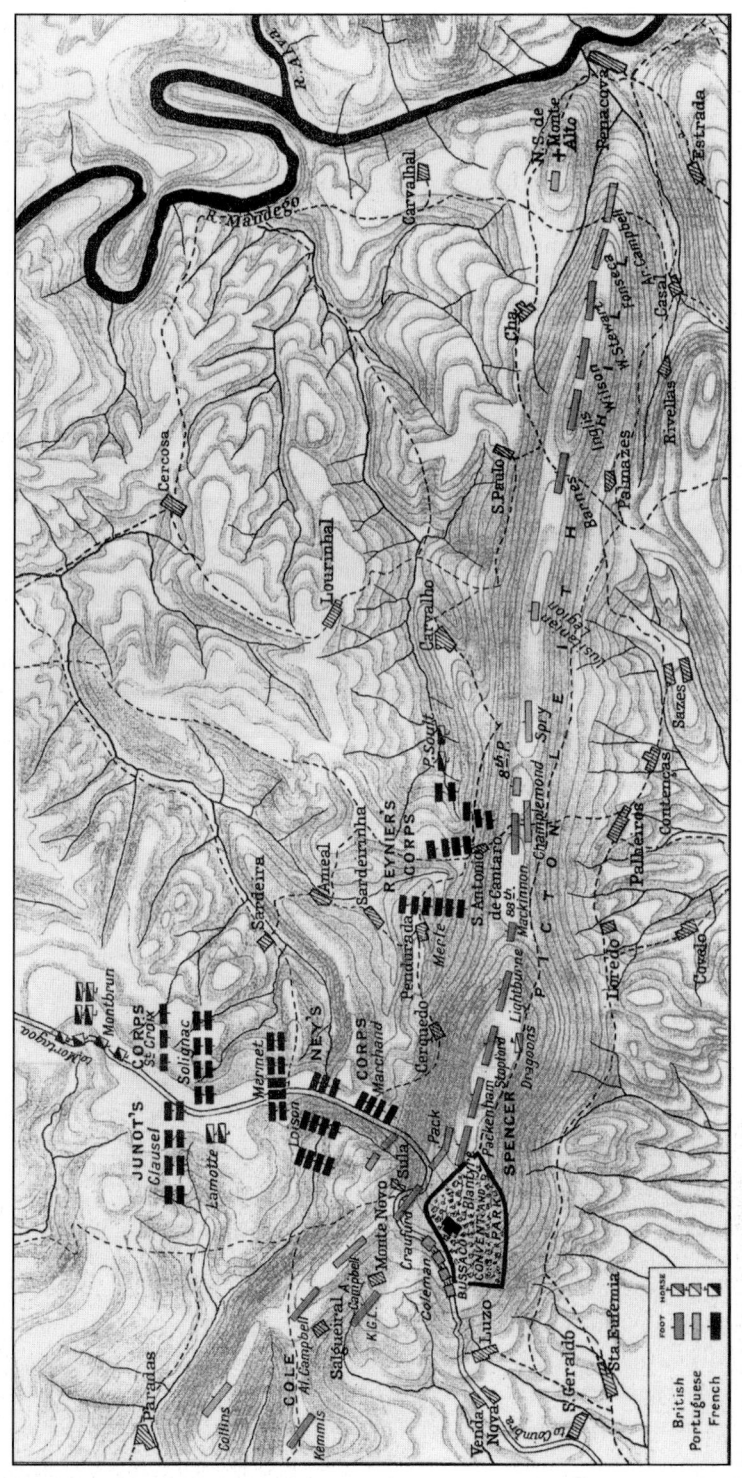

Oman's map of Buçaco Ridge.

battle with neither side being able to gain advantage. Merle's division reached the crest further to the north, where they were engaged by the 88th Connaught Rangers. Brigadier Mackinnon had seen the enemy column scaling the ridge and redeployed the battalion to meet it, along with several companies of the 45th Foot. Having fired their volleys, they cheered and charged, sending the French back down the ridge. Meanwhile Brigadier General Foy renewed Heudelet's attack and succeeded in reaching the crest of the ridge where he remained until driven off by a counter-attack by the 5th Division.

Ney, still down in the valley shrouded in fog, heard the sound of fighting on the ridge, thought that Reynier must have succeeded and ordered his VI Corps' advance up the main road. Loison's division advanced in column, with its left on the road driving back the heavy screen of skirmishers provided by the Light Division, which they believed to be the main defensive line. Consequently, when they reached the ridge, they were confronted by a well-timed surprise attack from a concealed position by the 43rd and 52nd Light Infantry, supported by Caçadores. Climbing out of a sunken road, they formed, volleyed into the head of the column at a range of just 25 yards and charged with the bayonet, driving Ney's men back down the ridge. Marchand's division, advancing alongside Loisin's, was brought to a halt by Pack's Portuguese brigade. One of the great advantages of Buçaco to the allied cause was in giving confidence to the newly-reformed Portuguese army.

With the failure of the attack, Masséna's subordinates refused to continue the battle and cavalry patrols were dispatched to the north to find a route that turned the ridge on the British left. Wellington's army remained in position overnight

Buçaco Ridge and the village of Sula before the trees!

but the following morning, seeing that the French had found the road via Sardão, which would outflank them, they withdrew towards Coimbra.

At Buçaco Ridge the allies inflicted a significant reverse on the Army of Portugal, but what turned a French reverse into a serious matter was the effect on the morale of Masséna's men. Of even greater importance was the impact of their defeat on the French corps commanders, which significantly undermined their confidence to face Wellington. *Chef de Bataillon* Pelet, Massena's senior ADC, even suggested that the marshals were for withdrawing back to Spain but were overruled by Masséna in a rare flare of his former ability.[18]

The Withdrawal to the Lines

Wellington's army marched for Coimbra, with the Light Division providing the rearguard, and passed through the city and across the Mondego on 30 September. Craufurd's rearguard remained north of the river with Anson's cavalry brigade, but on 1 October they were once again in contact with the French and the Light Division fell back into Coimbra, which in the optimistic aftermath of Buçaco was still in the process of being belatedly abandoned by its people. Captain Ferguson of the 43rd Light Infantry wrote of the condition of the refugees:

> It was a distressing sight to see the inhabitants of that large town obliged to abandon their houses and property and fly for their lives; many of the better class, accustomed to every luxury, obliged to travel on foot night and day, suffering every description of misery, until they arrived at Lisbon: many died from want and fatigue. The miseries of war never struck us so forcibly; we felt for the poor creatures, but it was not in our power to relieve them. We were hard pressed by the crowd, and with difficulty made our way through them to Condeixa and escaped.[19]

Even though the Portuguese had been ordered to deny food and any sort of comfort to the French, the Light Division found themselves destroying the contents of the large magazine that had been formed at Condeixa. In the context of a poorly-conducted withdrawal, the commissariat officers had issued items to those who could carry them away. Lieutenant Kincaid of the 1st 95th Rifles stated that 'They handed out shoes and shirts to anyone that would take them, and the streets were literally running ankle deep with rum ...'[20] Unable to take away or distribute the stores, they had to be destroyed. According to Captain Ferguson the items included '... cavalry equipments, hospital supplies, tea, brandy, shirts, shoes, trowsers [sic], and tobacco – and after a most disagreeable service, without rest, we had to resume the march at daybreak.'

Having secured the crossing of the Mondego, the French halted for three days, firstly to restore order among the hungry soldiers of VIII Corps, which had dissolved into wholesale looting. When that was accomplished, further delay was due to organizing the defence of Coimbra and collecting such food that had not been wasted by the looters. This delay allowed the Light Division and cavalry to break clean and to continue the 90-mile march south unmolested for several days.

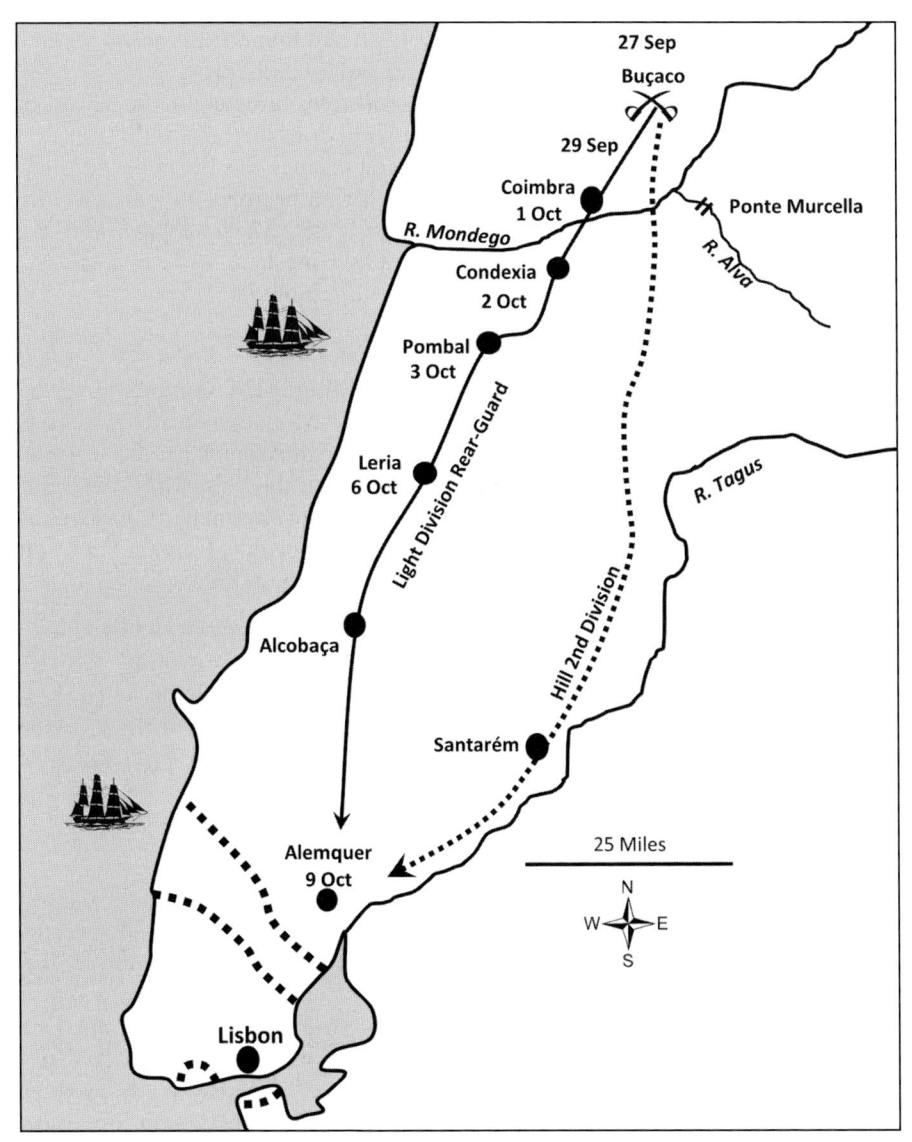

The withdrawal to the Lines of Torres Vedras.

Masséna had some 2,500 sick and wounded, which as the Army of Portugal resumed its march on Lisbon, he left in Coimbra with a small guard. As soon as the French divisions had marched, Colonel Trant's force of Portuguese irregulars re-entered Coimbra. It is often claimed that the French wounded were 'massacred' by the Portuguese but, in reality, the majority were taken prisoner.[21]

British retreats during the Peninsular War invariably presented an unedifying sight to observers and that from Coimbra to the Lines of Torres Vedras was sadly

A portrait of an officer of the 43rd Light Infantry.

no exception. Commissary officer August Schaumann recorded: 'The retreat to the fortified lines, over a stretch of thirty leguas, presented a sad spectacle. The roads were littered with smashed cases and boxes, broken waggons and carts, dead horses and exhausted men.'

Even the Light Division had its share of stragglers, but these were newly-arrived unseasoned troops. Kincaid explained that 'Marching is an art to be acquired only by habit':

> It was generally the fate of troops arriving from England, to join the army at an unhappy period – at a time when easy stages and refreshment after the voyage was particularly wanted and never to be had. The marches at this period were harassing and severe, and the company with which I had just

arrived were much distressed to keep pace with the old campaigners – they made a tolerable scramble for a day or two, but by the time they arrived at the lines the greater part had been obliged to be mounted. Nevertheless, when it became Masséna's turn to tramp out of Portugal a few months after, we found them up to their work.[22]

The provost marshal and his men were all there to attempt to keep order among the stragglers left behind on the road committing outrages. Lieutenant Kincaid continued:

> We retired this day to Leiria, and, at the entrance of the city, saw an English and a Portuguese soldier dangling by the bough of a tree – the first summary example I had ever seen of martial law.
>
> A provost-marshal, on actual service, is a character of considerable pretensions, as he can flog at pleasure, always moves about with a guard of honour, and though he cannot altogether stop a man's breath without an order, yet, when he is ordered to hang a given number out of a crowd of plunderers, his *friends* are not particularly designated, so that he can invite anyone that he takes a fancy to, to follow him to the nearest tree, where he,

Light Infantry on the march.

without further ceremony, relieves him from the cares and troubles of this wicked world.

While the divisions marched, the cavalry rearguard and occasionally piquets of the Light Division kept the French at a respectable distance. The final occupation of the Lines was, however, a scramble with the Light Division in Alenquer on 9 October believing the cavalry vedettes were still deployed to the north. Cotton had, however, unknown to Craufurd's battalions, already withdrawn into the Lines. When the French unexpectedly appeared, the division's well-practised ability to be quickly under arms with baggage loaded saved them. Ferguson commented 'no bad consequences occurred, with the exception of some officers losing their baggage, and several their dinners which were left cooking at the fires for the French to regale themselves with.' It was, however, the Portuguese element of the division that stood their ground:

> While the Army retired on the lines, the 3rd Caçadores distinguished themselves particularly at Alenquer, where, owing to a heavy rain and thick fog, the enemy succeeded in entering the village unobserved. Here the Caçadores promptly formed, and taking possession of a height commanding the bridge, held it against a division of the enemy, until that part of the Army occupying Alenquer had time to form and retreat to their respective stations.[23]

On the night of 10 October 1810, it was a very wet Light Division that approached the Lines of Torres Vedras at the end of another retreat.

Chapter Two

The Lines of Torres Vedras

'The great object in Portugal is the possession of Lisbon and the Tagus, and all our measures must be directed towards this object.'

[Wellington to Fletcher[1]]

It is clear from Major Marbot's account of the French advance south from Coimbra to Lisbon that Marshal Masséna and his staff had recovered from the shock of Buçaco Ridge. With the prospect of successfully 'driving the leopard into the sea' and arriving in a city, morale was high despite continual rain. The anticipation of success, combined with poor maps that failed to show the hills that stood between them and Lisbon, led to the French failing to appreciate that their fortunes were about to change dramatically.

Thanks to Wellington's outstanding operational security, the first inkling that the French had of the existence of the Lines of Torres Vedras was from Portuguese civilians and prisoners of war between 7 and 9 October. They spoke of defences at Alhandra, covering the coast road to Lisbon and at Bucelas, where the main road cuts through a pass in a chain of hills. In addition, a poor and probably partially-marked map was captured by Reynier's corps, showing defences. The French were expecting to fight a battle before Lisbon but it appears that in the optimism of the time, the intelligence was interpreted as being the presence of minor field fortifications at key points, and nothing to be overly concerned about.

Concept and Construction

The retrenched positions covering Lisbon, known under the denomination of the Lines of Torres Vedras, have gained so much celebrity, as having formed the barrier from which the tide of French conquest first receded, and moreover possess so many peculiarities of defence, and are so free from the objections usually urged against lines, that some observations on their nature, construction, and mode of occupation, can scarcely fail to be interesting to professional and other officers seeking military information.

So wrote Captain Jones, the Royal Engineer who superintended the construction of the Lines on behalf of his commander, Colonel Fletcher, after that officer went forward to join the army in the spring of 1810. He went on to outline, in the frank terms of the day, the reasons for their construction:

The determination to commence these works may be dated from the battle of Talavera. The offensive movements which led to that action having put to

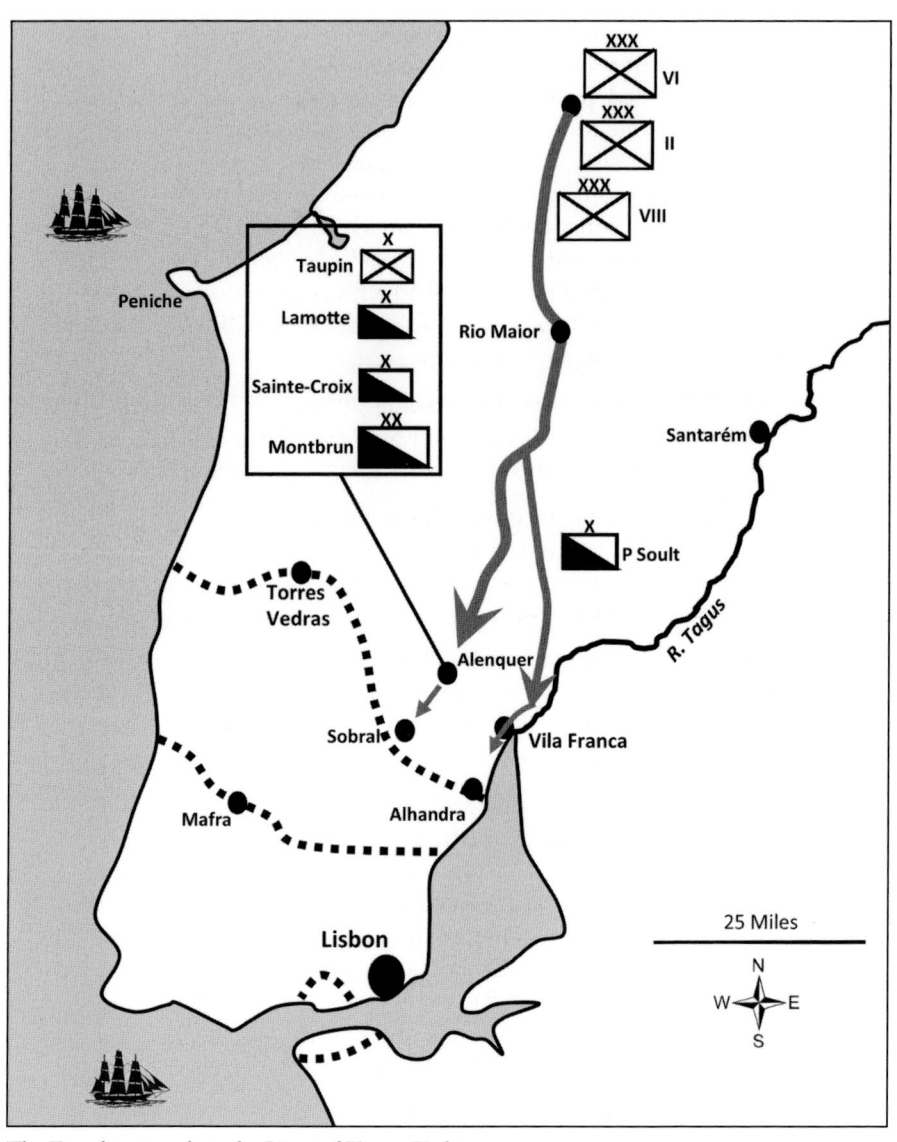

The French approach to the Lines of Torres Vedras.

the test the value of Spanish cooperation, and having fully demonstrated the utter inefficiency of their armies, from want of organisation, want of discipline and skilful officers, it became apparent to the Duke of Wellington that the contest would, in the next campaign, devolve on the small body of veteran British and newly-raised Portuguese troops under his command, and a defensive system of warfare ensued. To prepare for a final struggle was thenceforward the great object of consideration; and as the hope of successfully defending an extended and open frontier, like that of Portugal, against a very superior and highly skilful enemy, could scarcely be entertained, it was decided to seek out some position in the lower part of Estremadura, not liable to be turned or passed, and having an assured communication with the sea, which should command all the approaches to Lisbon, and which position, being retrenched in the strongest manner, would offer a point of concentration for the whole of the defensive forces of Portugal, army, militia, irregulars, etc. where they might, in conjunction with the British, be victualled and supplied with ammunition for any period of time, whilst occupying a most favourable field for deciding the fate of the capital and kingdom in a general action.

Early in 1810 Wellington was under increasing pressure from the government at home 'not to lose the army', as the inevitability of a substantial French invasion of Portugal had become all too obvious. Lord Liverpool wrote to Wellington:

I should apprise you that a very considerable degree of alarm exists in this country respecting the safety of the British army in Portugal ... I have no difficulty in stating that you would be rather excused for bringing the army away a little too soon than remaining in Portugal a little too long.[2]

Not only was the Peninsular army Britain's last hope, but the political ramifications of a repeat of the previous year's evacuations from Corunna and Walcheren would spell disaster for an already weakened administration. Consequently, Wellington had to repeatedly reassure government along these lines:

All the preparations for embarking and carrying away the army, and everything belonging to it, are already made, and my intention is to embark it, as soon as I find that a military necessity exists for so doing. I shall delay the embarkation as long as it is in my power and shall do everything in my power to avert the necessity of embarking at all. If the enemy should invade this country with a force less than I think so superior to ours as to create a necessity of embarking, I shall fight a battle to save the country, for which I have made the preparations; and if the result should not be successful, of which I have no doubt, I shall still be able to retire and embark the army.[3]

Wellington, however, as part of preventing word of the Lines leaking into the press, stopped short of explaining exactly what those preparations were.

The idea behind the concept of the Lines of Torres Vedras is still debated with the Portuguese pointing out that Major José Maria das Neves Costa came up with the concept in 1808 and his plans were passed to Wellington the following year. On the other hand, Wellington was familiar with the hills, having marched through them on his way to Lisbon following the Convention of Cintra in 1808. Wherever the idea came from, it was Wellington's strategy and orders, British money and oversight but above all, in the heat of the Iberian summer of 1810, the sweat of Portuguese labourers that brought the Lines into existence.

The Earl of Liverpool, Secretary of State for War and the Colonies in Spencer Perceval's government.

Almost exactly a year before the Lines were occupied, in October 1809 with his army back in Portugal after Talavera, Wellington travelled to Lisbon. In the company of Lieutenant Colonel Fletcher, Major General D'Urban and Vice Admiral Berkeley, he visited the hills north of Lisbon to plan the Lines.[4] Captain Jones explained the significance of the location on the Lisbon peninsula:

> ... they derived their strength and value primarily from their peninsular situation on the sea, which precluded the possibility of an enemy manoeuvring on, or turning their flanks, and assured their rear being constantly open for

Colonel Fletcher, Wellington's chief engineer.

the defenders to receive supplies and reinforcements; secondly, from the unusual degree of natural strength of the ranges of hills and ravines forming their front; and lastly from the judgement with which the engineer connected the several strong features of the country into an equally defensive line. Art and labour were judiciously exerted to improve natural advantages, to strengthen and cover the weak points, to diminish the length of accessible front, to block up the approaches, to facilitate the movements of troops within, and to cramp and confine the movements of those without.

On 20 October Wellington issued a twenty-one-point memorandum to Fletcher covering his concept and instructions for the construction of key works (see Appendix I for a full transcript of the memorandum). Reflecting the government's concern over the army's evacuation, Wellington noted that 'There is another also connected with that first object, to which we must likewise attend, viz. – the embarkation of the British troops in case of reverse.' To that end a safe point of embarkation at São Julião's Bay to the west of Lisbon was established and garrisoned by British infantry and Royal Marines. Here a handful of battalions could hold a ring of redoubts to protect the entrenched embarkation point.

Some 6 miles north of Lisbon, a single 25-mile line of individual redoubts was sited on the high ground stretching from Ericeira on the Atlantic Coast, via Mafra, the hills of Montachique and the Pass of Bucelas to the Tagus. Between 6 and 10 miles further north, a handful of redoubts covering the main routes to Lisbon at Torres Vedras, Sobral and Alhandra were to be built and, between the two Lines, some intermediate defences such as those on the high ground of Ajuda were designed to aid the army's withdrawal to the main Line. With the works progressing apace and the French not beginning their invasion until September, the forward redoubts were thickened up into an additional or 'First Line'. The original or 'Second Line' was still the main and strongest of the two Lines.

The conventional star design of São Julião (No. 97) and a plan of the Oleiros Redoubt (No. 23).

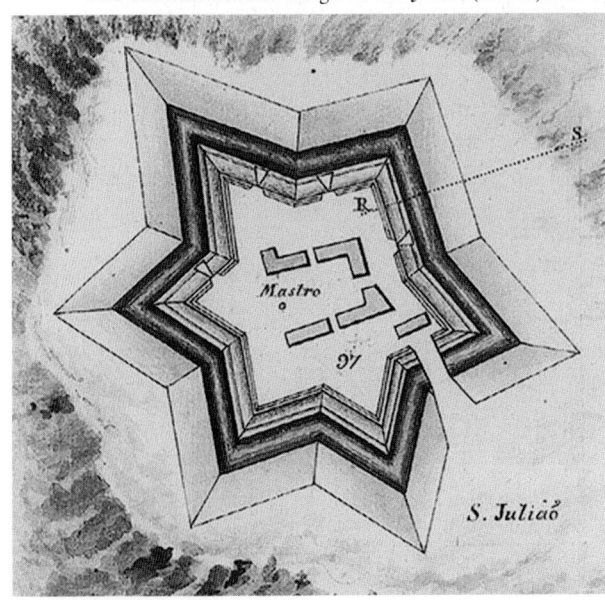

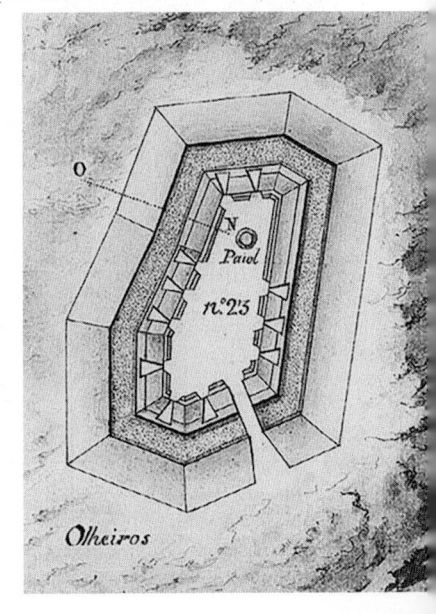

Jones's map of the Lines of Torres Vedras.

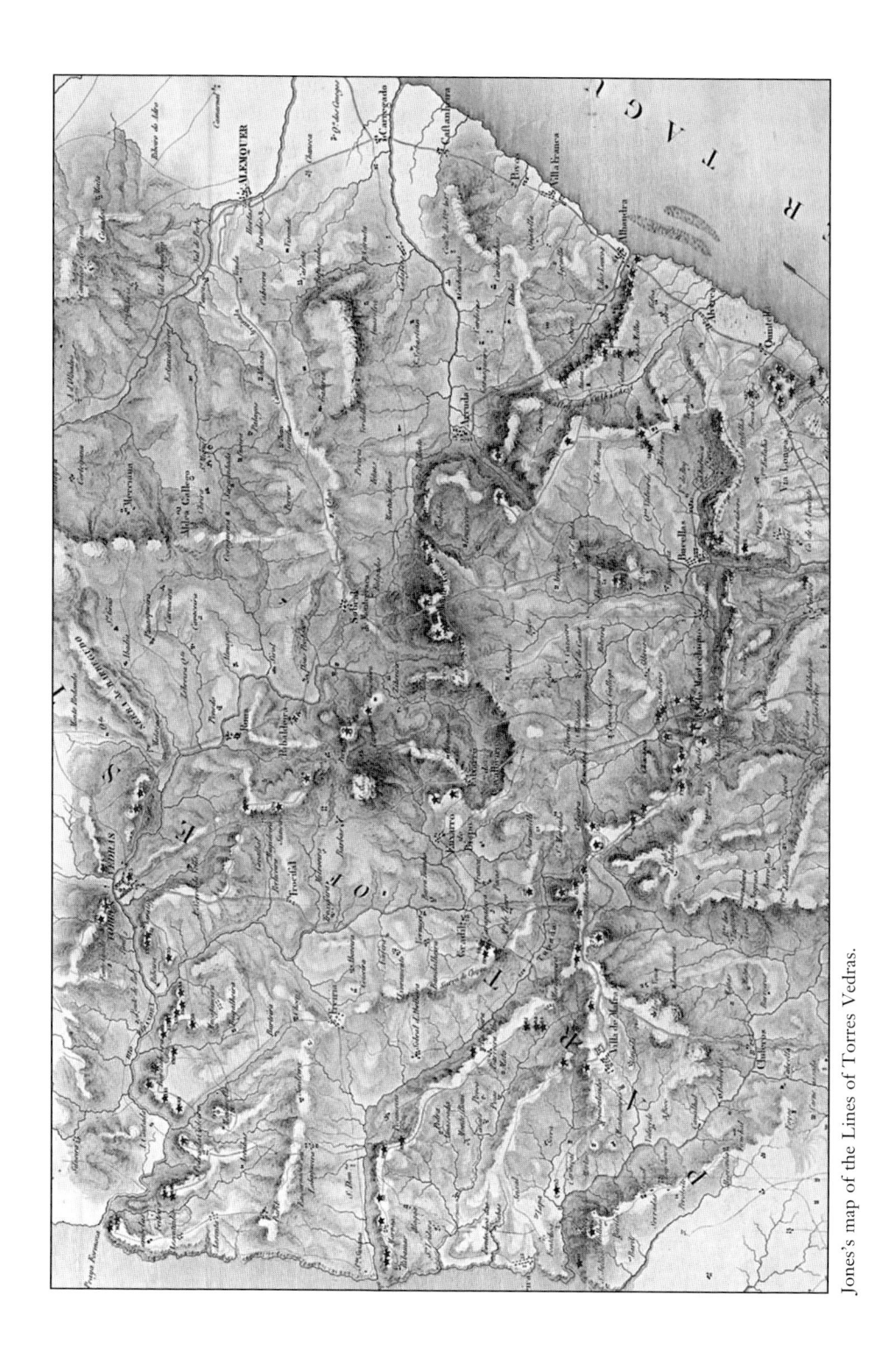

The works divided into eight districts were each under the command of a Royal Engineer officer, who oversaw the construction of each of the redoubts. As the project developed, they moved away from the traditional star design to layouts that used the ground to best tactical advantage. The work was carried out by Portuguese labourers paid by the British government without the latter's knowledge, thanks to Wellington's operational security measures. The impact of this expenditure on an already cash-starved army forced the commissaries to issue promissory notes for goods purchased, which the Portuguese were increasingly reluctant to accept, and similarly drove the army into months of arrears of pay.

Captain Jones described the defensive concept of the Lines:

> The redoubts, generally speaking, were merely securities for artillery in those situations where a fire of that nature was demanded by some specific object, such as to interdict the free use of a road, delay the repair of a bridge, or sweep along the entry of a pass; and in no instance were the guns considered as defensive weapons of the works in which they were placed, except at the position on the height of Calhandrix, where three redoubts in line were made to cross their fire with each other, and mutually support a fourth redoubt in advance. All the other redoubts were perfectly independent of each other and were made of a strength of profile to resist an assault and placed on points where artillery could with great difficulty be brought to cannonade them.

Most of the redoubts were relatively small, and mainly garrisoned by 200–400 Portuguese militia or embodied *ordenanza*.[5] In autumn 1810, the ramparts were nearly all in a 'field state'; that is to say constructed with wooden palisading, revetments and gun platforms with sandbagged walls. Many of these collapsed during the seasonal rains, requiring constant labour to keep them effective as defences. Replacing wooden embrasures and gun platforms with increasing amounts of stone – as can be seen today – took place the following year.

In October 1810 the 126 redoubts of the three Lines mounted some 427 guns of various origin, ranging from 6-pounders through to 24-pounders, often in mixed-calibre batteries, mostly crewed by Portuguese gunners.[6]

One of the features of the Lines of Torres Vedras was the use of a telegraph system, which in good trial conditions allowed messages to be passed the 29 miles from one coast to the other in as little as seven minutes. Within fifteen minutes of a French move, information could be passed around the lines and would have played a key part in setting the army marching to the threatened point. Portugal had a telegraph system and the army a mobile extension, which Wellington had been using extensively during 1810, and not unnaturally he specified one for the Lines. He, however, did not adopt the Portuguese system but wrote to Admiral Berkley on the establishment of signal stations:

> There are, however, two or three points in which I think you could [assist me] … One is to give us some of Popham's telegraph vocabularies …

Stone revetments and gun platforms, Olheiros Redoubt (No. 23), a part of the Torres Vedras group.

A recreation of the Royal Navy's telegraph system in one of the preserved redoubts.

32   *Masséna at Bay*

I should be very much obliged to you if you could [provide seamen] for each of these stations. I cannot spare officers to go down and learn how to use a telegraph; and I am afraid of the mistakes and blunders which will result from using them without [instruction].

Having received a positive response, a few days later he wrote: 'The establishment at each station ought to consist of the person to be in charge of the signals, and one or two men to assist him ... These officers and men should be paid and treated in every respect as parties from the fleet acting on shore.'[7]

In September the Royal Navy signallers were removed as a result of a dispute over payment for their rations and hastily replaced by Portuguese signallers and signal masts. In the event, the inter-service dispute was resolved and the two systems operated alongside each other.

The telegraph system established in the Lines of Torres Vedras.

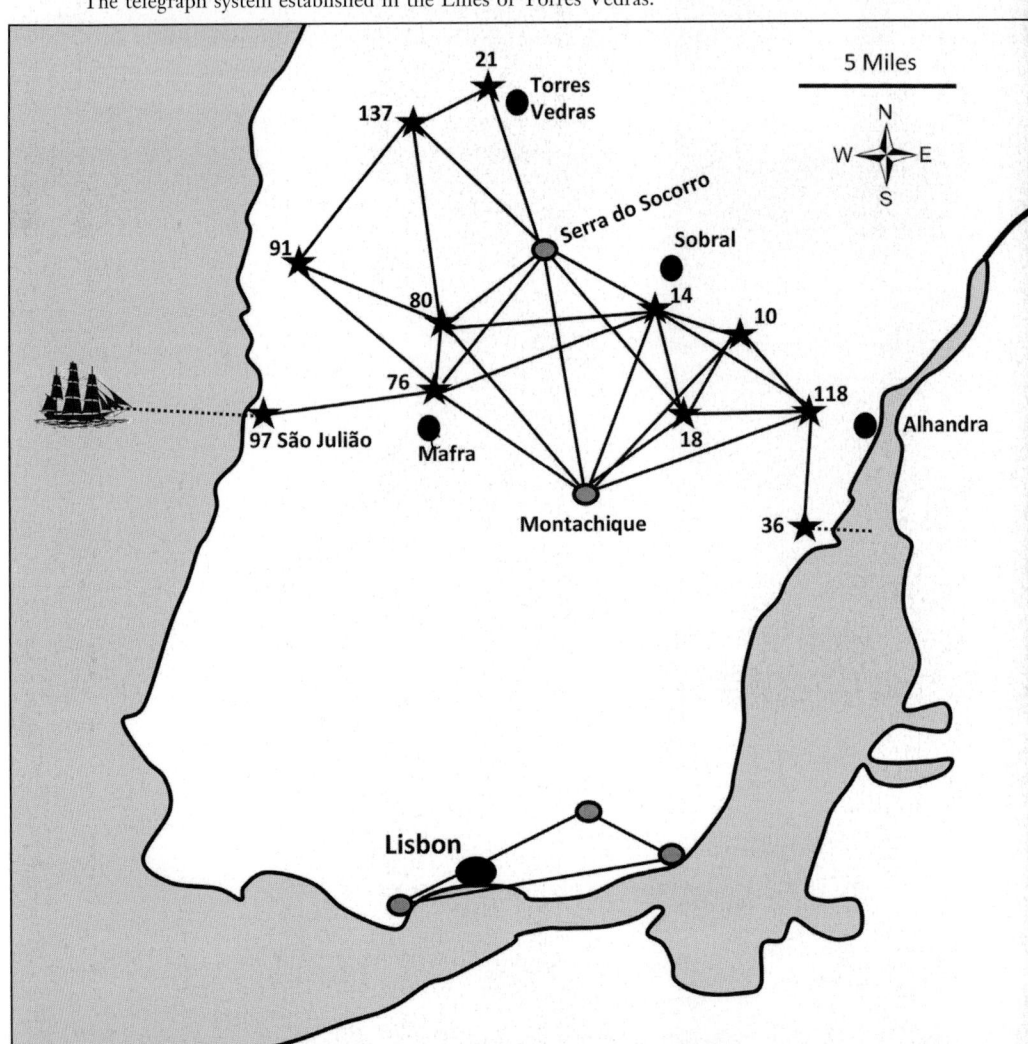

The signal stations, less those at Sierra do Socorro (adjacent to Wellington's HQ) and Montachique in the Second Line, were within redoubts.

Behind the first line of redoubts Wellington deployed his divisions. Most were concentrated in the centre, with Picton's 3rd Division as corps of observation on the Atlantic Coast and Hill's 2nd Division covering the Tagus flank.

To enable the allies to concentrate at any given point faster than the French could mass their divisions, improvements were made to lateral communications with the construction of military roads behind the redoubts of the First Line.

A key part of Wellington's defensive strategy was control of the sea and the ability to resupply from the United Kingdom. An added bonus was that the Lines

A stretch of the military road up to Redoubt No. 14 on Monte Agraço.

34 *Masséna at Bay*

of Torres Vedras were far from French magazines at Ciudad Rodrigo and Salamanca, with the intervening country impossible for the French except in increasingly large numbers. Wellington summarized the situation when he wrote '… if anyone wishes to know the history of this war, I will tell him it is our maritime superiority that gives me the power of maintaining my army while the enemy are unable to do so.'

Surprise and Dissent

The scales only started to fall from French eyes when cavalry patrols from General Junot's VIII Corps and Montbrun's cavalry reserve approached Sobral on 11 October on the Alenquer road. Sobral was not a part of the Lines but was held as an outpost and the French promptly drove in the British light dragoon's piquets. With low cloud obscuring the redoubts on the hilltops beyond the village, Montbrun only reported the presence of the cavalry and infantry, which were assumed to be the rearguard. Crucially, however, he only reported the presence of the hills rather than the plain stretching to Lisbon that was indicated on the Lopez map, which Masséna and his staff were using. On the same day, on the Tagus flank Colonel Pierre Soult's II Corps' cavalry encountered General Hill's 2nd Division's piquets at Vila Franca, which he drove out and then posted his own vedettes in the town, while his main body retired.

The Portuguese militia and *ordenanza* were occupying the redoubts of the First Line, which had originally been a handful of defences covering key approaches to the main defences. They were, however, still far from complete and there was a distinct gap in the chain of redoubts south-west of the Sobral area, where the Rio Sizandra turns south. Considerable work was still under way and the divisions as they arrived were soon at work labouring to improve the defences of the First Line, particularly in the Zibreira Gap.

Wellington wrote to Brigadier General Craufurd during the morning of 11 October and after enquiring about the comfort of the Light Division around Arruda, gave his appreciation of the likely enemy course of action:

> I do not think the enemy's plan is quite decided yet. He has still some troops at Alenquer, and there is a body of cavalry and infantry (I saw of the latter about 300 men) on this side of Alenquer. I mean, however, to hold the town of Sobral as long as I can. The peasants say that they [the French] were marching this morning upon Vila Franca, which is to attack our right, where Hill is. They can make no impression upon the right, positively; and they must therefore endeavour to turn Hill's position upon the Serra of Alhandra by its left. This is a tough job also, defended as the entrances of the valleys are by redoubts, and the villages by *abattis*, etc. However, that is what they must try.[8]

With the rain still falling, he went on to say that 'These roads are, however, not paved, and are, of course, now impracticable' and 'the only paved or at all practicable road … on this side of the river of Arruda passes through Sobral.'

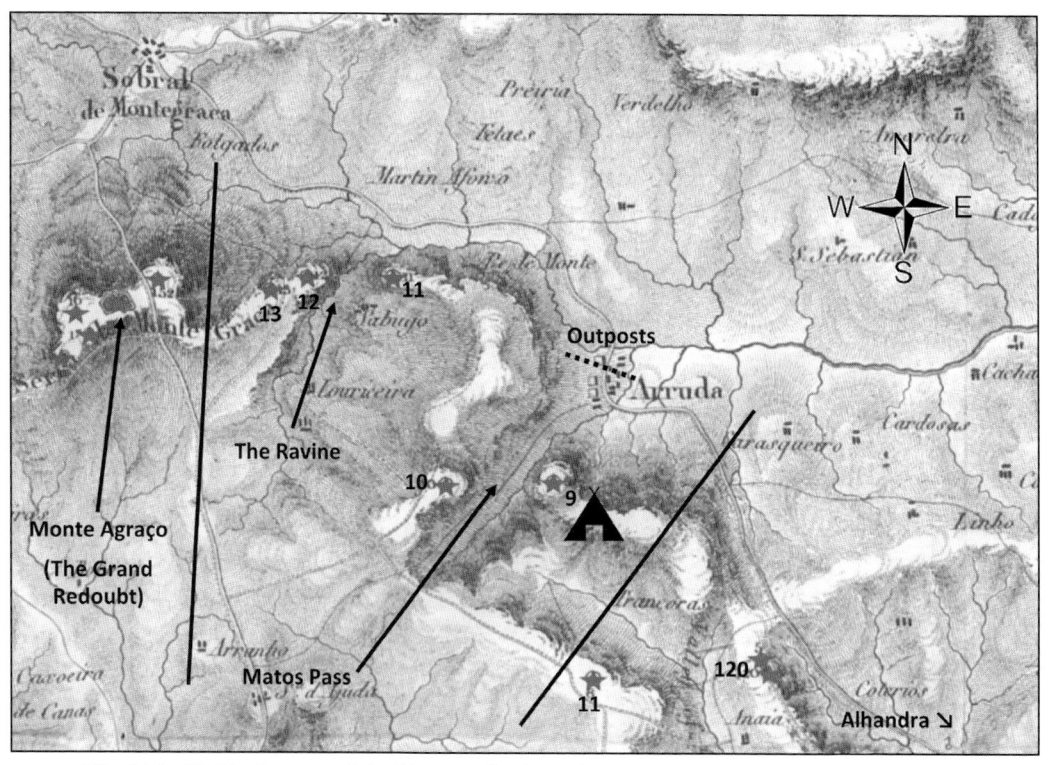

The Light Division's sector of the Lines south of Arruda.

What happened was that on 11 October Junot's VIII Corps advanced from Alenquer to conduct a reconnaissance in force. Major General D'Urban wrote in his journal that

> At about 4 o'clock in the afternoon the enemy reconnoitred in some force in front of Sobral, and by some mistake were unmolested, our Light Dragoons fell back upon the Infantry of the 1st Division with a rapidity which one would have wished let alone, and afterwards a Company of the 95th who were in the Town and the Vineyards about it abandoned it without a shot; 'tis difficult to account for all this which must be vexatious enough to the Commander-in-Chief, who aware of the importance of the heights in front of Sobral, must have wished them kept for the present.[9] Forty-second Regiment advance for the night. All the 1st Division alert.

Dragoons supported by infantry had advanced on Sobral, driving in the British cavalry outposts during the afternoon. The 71st (Highland) Light Infantry had that day joined the army in Sobral. A soldier of the 71st writing as 'Thomas' recalled that

> We had not been there three hours in the town, and were busy cooking, when the alarm sounded. There were nine British and three Portuguese regiments in [the area of] the town. We were all drawn up and remained under arms, expecting every moment to receive the enemy, whose skirmishers covered Windmill Hill. In about an hour the light companies of all the

regiments were ordered out, alongst with the 71st Colonel Cadogan called to us, at the foot of the hill, 'My lads, this is the first affair I have ever been in with you; show me what you can do, now or never.' We gave a hurrah and advanced up the hill, driving their advanced skirmishers before us, until about halfway up, when we commenced a heavy fire and were as hotly received. In the meantime, the remaining regiments evacuated the town. The enemy pressed so hard upon us we were forced to make the best of our way down the hill and were closely followed by the French, through the town, up Gallows Hill. We got behind a mud wall and kept our ground in spite of their utmost efforts. Here we lay upon our arms all night.[10] (See map p. 43.)

Meanwhile, Masséna's ADCs used the presence of the dragoons to carry out a reconnaissance of the defences in the area. Among them were Majors Marbot and Ligniville who rode west along the Sizandra valley. Their report to Masséna was that the lines could be carried:

> They were undoubtedly of imposing strength, but very far from what people were pleased to say ... Every officer of the least experience knows well that a position of this extent cannot present the same difficulties everywhere and must have its weak spots. We became aware of several such by seeing officers and even cavalry piquets ride up quite easily.
>
> When my comrade and I reported in this sense to Masséna, the old soldier's eyes sparkled with martial ardour, and he at once issued orders for his four lieutenants to hasten to his quarters and a stormy discussion took place.

The long shadow cast by the defeat at Buçaco, however, came into play, with senior commanders choosing to believe Pelet's report that 'the mountains on which we find the principal works of the enemy rise before Sobral as that of Buçaco ...' rather than Marbot's more optimistic assessment. He wrote:

> ... our heavy losses at Buçaco had chilled the ardour of Masséna's lieutenants, and bred ill-will between them and him; so that now all were trying to paralyse his operations, and representing every little hillock to be a new height of Buçaco, the capture of which would cost copious bloodshed.[11]

General Junot was in favour but Marshal Ney, supported by General Reynier, absolutely refused to carry out Masséna's orders. Consequently, there was to be no concerted attack on the Lines. Disquieting the Army of Portugal by dismissing Ney, the popular commander of VI Corps, as a result of his insubordination was at this point something that Masséna could not entertain.

Marbot concluded that without the experience of Buçaco, things could have been different: 'If that position had been turned, the enemy would have been taken in flank and have retired upon Lisbon, and our army, in full strength and ardour, would have attacked the lines on its arrival, and certainly have carried them.'

General Junot's VIII Corps' cavalry consisted of six regiments of dragoons, each of two squadrons.

With reports describing the chain of defences stretching from the Atlantic to the Tagus arriving one after the other at Masséna's headquarters at Alenquer, *Chef de Bataillon* Pelet recalled that

> At last we clearly discerned the English system of operations and the goal of their movements, which we had scorned until then. We had been ignorant of their plans, and it was impossible to guess them when we were given not only inexact but totally false information. We had been led along in the footsteps

Major Marbot.

of the English army to this inaccessible area where they could brave our efforts and ingenuity for a long time. The cruel ravages carried out by the enemy reinforced our ignorance, for it seemed they would not have abused a country they wanted to save.

Marbot criticized Napoleon's uncharacteristic lack of attention to intelligence for this belated revelation:

It is inconceivable how the Emperor, who had agents in every country, could have omitted to send some to Lisbon. At that time thousands of American, German, Swedish and English ships were daily bringing into the Tagus stores for Wellington's army; and it would have been perfectly easy to have introduced some spies among the numerous sailors and clerks employed on these vessels.

Wellington had kept the construction of the Lines on a strictly 'need-to-know' basis, from his army, including senior officers, and from the government at home. Reports in letters to families and politicians' tittle-tattle regularly made their way into the newspapers, which were one of Napoleon's chief sources of information. Consequently, without any indications to prompt the deployment of spies, the result was that the Emperor's subordinates in Portugal were surprised by the Lines.

Both Marbot and Pelet were also critical of General Junot and his senior commanders, who had occupied the area during 1807 and campaigned there in 1808, for not drawing attention to the defensive qualities of the hills north of Lisbon. Once again, however, with the British seemingly running for evacuation, there probably seemed little need for such detail. Pelet summed up the French attitude: '... the first announcement of the enormous English Lines did not make a very great impression on us.'

General Junot.

The Affair at Sobral

'In spite of this want of loyalty, Masséna dispatched the 8th Corps towards the enemy's centre.' [Marbot]

The result of the fighting around Sobral on the 11th was that the town had been left unoccupied by the 1st Division, but equally French patrols had not attempted to hold it. The following morning Sobral was reoccupied initially by a company of the 50th Foot. The 71st Light Infantry, also of Erskine's Brigade, and some 5th 60th Rifles companies were also deployed to the adjacent heights or 'Gallows Hill', which Wellington wanted held for its views of the approaches from the north. Thomas of the 71st Light Infantry gave an account of his day at Sobral:

> Next morning, by daybreak, there was not a Frenchman to be seen. As soon as the sun was fairly up we advanced into the town and began a search for provisions, which were now become very scarce; and to our great joy found a large store-house full of dry fish, flour, rice and sugar, besides bales of cloth. All now became bustle and mirth; fires were kindled, and every man became a cook. Scones were the order of the day. Neither flour nor sugar were wanting, and the water was plenty; so, I fell to make myself a flour scone. Mine was mixed and laid upon the fire, and I, hungry enough, watching it. Though neither neat nor comely, I was anticipating the moment when it would be eatable. Scarce was it warm ere the bugle sounded to arms. Then

When converted to light infantry the 71st had lost their highland uniform, but as a compromise were allowed to keep the tartan dicing on their 1805-pattern regimental caps or 'bonnets'.

was the joy that reigned a moment before it turned to execrations. I snatched my scone off the fire, raw as it was, put it into my haversack and formed. We remained under arms until dark and then took up our old quarters upon Gallows Hill, where I ate my raw scone, sweetly seasoned by hunger. In our advance to the town, we were much entertained by some of our men who had got over a wall the day before, when the enemy were in the rear, and now were put to get over.

On 12 October, with his army now settled behind the Lines, Wellington had a commanding view from the Grand Redoubt of the approaching French.[12] He had believed that after Alhandra on the coast road Sobral would be the focus of French activity, but he was justifiably convinced that the defences at Alhandra were strong enough to deter or hold an attack. Sobral, however, was a different matter. As noted by Captain Jones of the Royal Engineers, it was a potential battlefield: 'On the main road to Lisbon, [from Sobral] through Zibreira, where the works thrown up were fewer than on the other parts of the line, it being intended as a manoeuvring position for the main body of the army.'[13]

Consequently, Wellington prepared to redeploy four divisions on a 7,000-yard frontage in the Zibeira gap in the line of redoubts between those on Monte Agraço and the Portobello redoubts on the Sierra de Socorro. In the meantime, Major General Spencer's 1st Division stood ready to contest any advance on the Lines around Sobral, with Cole's 4th Division to the north-west.

In anticipation of a French attack on 12 or 13 October, Wellington sent Spencer a memorandum explaining a number of potential redeployments in the case of a French attack:

> Col. Hawker should receive orders to patrol well forward towards Alenquer, so as to ascertain whether there is any force of the enemy in Alenquer, and of what strength.
>
> If the enemy should move from Alenquer upon Sobral de Monte Agraço in superior strength, I should wish the following arrangements to be made.
>
> Gen. Sir B. Spencer's [1st] division to move to Zibreira, and Cantone in that village and Gozundeira. Headquarters to Patameira. Major Gen. Cole [4th Division] and Major Gen. Campbell [6th Division[14]] to retire when necessary from Dois Portos and Ribaldeira, and occupy the heights immediately behind those villages, extending their line across the high road from Ribaldeira to Enxara dos Cavaleiros.
>
> Gen. Pack's brigade is in that case to occupy for the present the redoubts on the heights above Sobral de Monte Agraço, with his light infantry in the redoubts on the points of the rocks above the road leading to Arruda, marked Nos. 11, 12 and 13. The largest number shoulde in No. 11, Nos. 12 and 13 require each about one third of No. 11.[15] (See map p. 44.)

In addition, the 5th Division and a temporary Portuguese division were in reserve. Of Pack's brigade, his Caçadore battalion and the line light companies

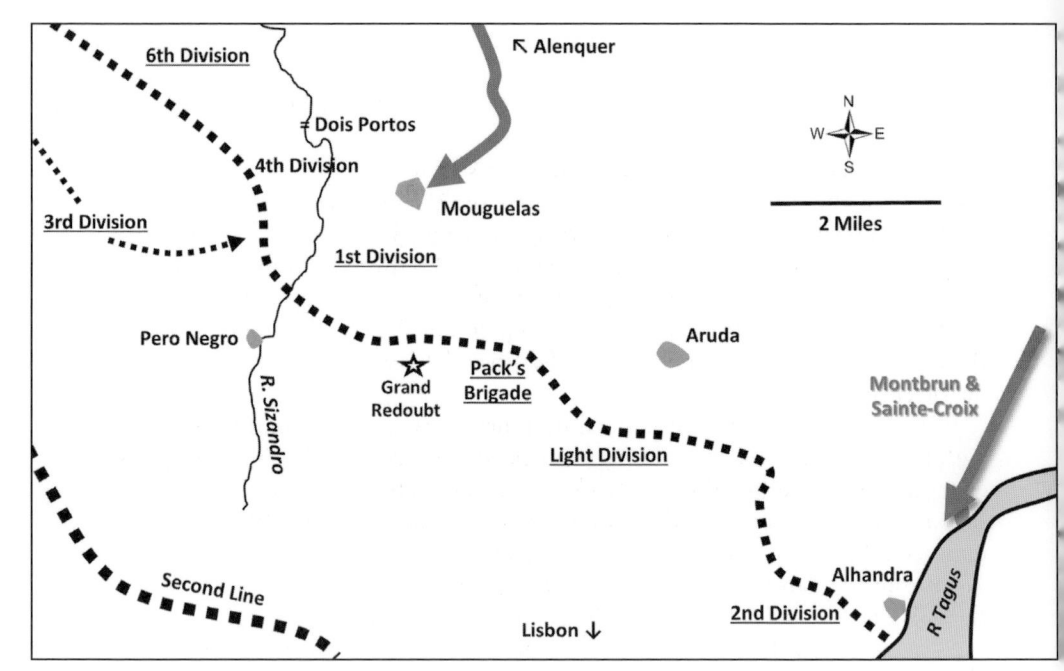

Wellington's plans for redeployments behind the central area of the Lines.

A silhouette of Major General Brent Spencer, commander of the 1st Division.

reinforced the redoubts listed above, while his centre companies were concentrated in the Grand Redoubt and the others on Monte Agraço.

On 12 October, with Clausel's division arriving, Junot's aim was, however, only to drive in the British outposts in that area as his divisions were in no state to mount a full-scale attack. The Corps' undernourished and exhausted infantry was strung out on the roads back beyond Alenquer and their artillery was still more than a day's march from their parent divisions, labouring along roads that had dissolved into deep mud.

When General Junot, as explained by Jones, 'pushed his piquets into contact with those of the allies, in adjusting their posts, a sharp skirmish took place, and everything denoted a meditated attack'. However, after some skirmishing in continual rain, it appeared that there would be no serious action that day, but Junot increased the tempo of Clausel's attacks on the Sobral area, forcing the battalions of Erskine and Low's brigades to retire beyond a ravine some 300 yards south of the village. Both sides barricaded the road a musket shot apart.

Meanwhile, on the other French axis of advance along the Tagus road from Santarém, General Montbrun's cavalry advanced south, but as General of Brigade Sainte-Croix at the head of three of his dragoon regiments left Vila Franca, allied gunboats anchored in the Tagus opened fire and the general was killed. Sainte-Croix was a bold and enterprising officer and his loss was a significant blow to the French cause, as he was supportive of Masséna and was well-regarded and influential. He could have been able to persuade the other reluctant commanders to follow his example and deliver Masséna's assault on the Lines.

On 13 October, with his corps still not fully assembled and seeing the 30,000 allied troops deployed in the Zibreira Gap, Junot contented himself with advancing west from Sobral towards the Sizandro into more open rolling country. Here, Solignac's division, which had arrived the previous evening, faced the outpost of Cole's 4th Division. The piquets were provided by the 7th Fusiliers and the black-coated Brunswick Oels, which were soon under pressure from a French brigade. Cole reinforced his skirmish line with a Portuguese brigade, which prompted Junot in turn to commit a second brigade to action. After several hours of skirmishing and being under orders not to get heavily committed and suffer unnecessary losses, the 4th Division withdrew steadily west towards the Sizandro, ceding a mile of ground.

That evening the French artillery finally caught up with VIII Corps and reached Sobral. According to artilleryman Captain Noël, he was 'ordered overnight to position a battery of four guns to cover the attack that was to take place the next day. This I did, concealing the guns under great barrels.'[16]

Belatedly on 14 October, Marshal Masséna and his staff rode forward to Sobral to see the Lines for themselves and, in criticism of the failure of intelligence to warn him of Wellington's defences, on seeing the hills, he famously expostulated: 'What devilry! Wellington didn't make these mountains!'

By the time the marshal reached Sobral, Ménard's division was already in action against the 71st Light Infantry's barricade across the road and musket-

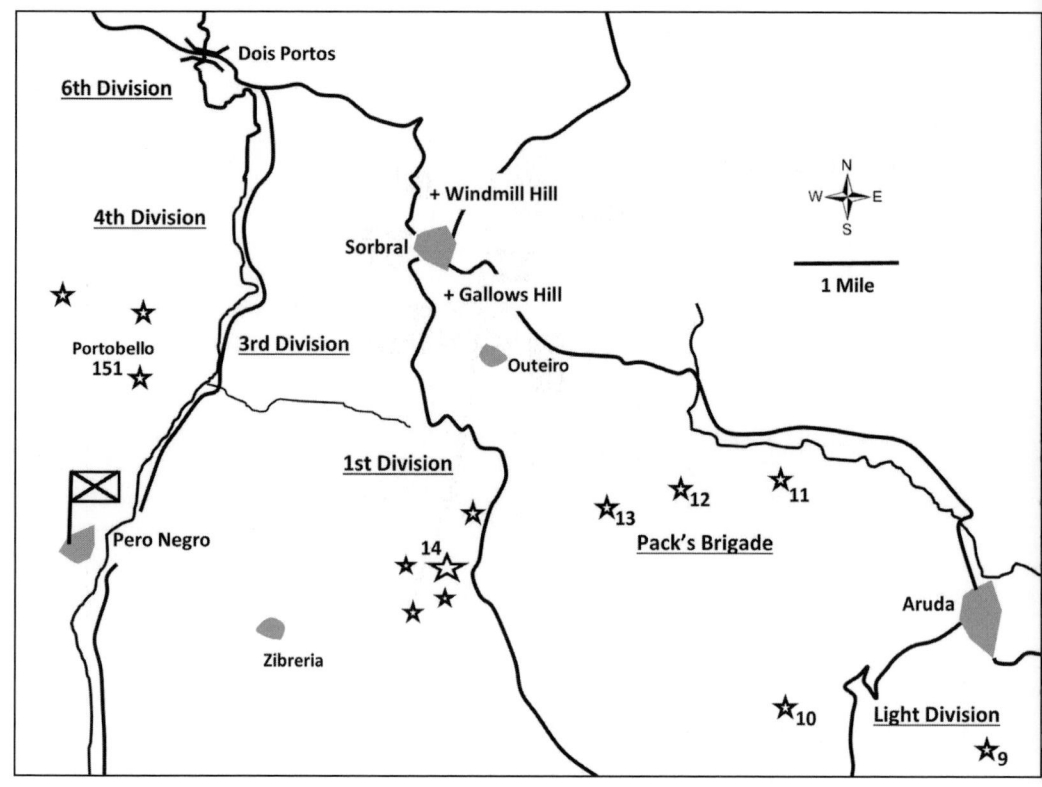

The affair at Sobral: 13 and 14 October 1810.

lined mud walls on the flanking slopes of Gallows Hill. The action began with a short bombardment by Noël's guns, after which the grenadier and voltigeur companies of the 4th Battalion 19th Regiment of the Line spearheaded the division's attack along the narrow crest of the ridge between Sobral and Gallows Hill. With only a short distance to cover, the French were quickly over the 71st's wall and into the firing line. Colonel Cadogan sent the battalion's supports forward to join the fight. Thomas of the 71st wrote a vivid account of the action:

> Next morning the French advanced to a mud wall about forty yards in front of the one we lay behind ... During the night we received orders to cover the bugle and tartans of our bonnets with black crape, which had been served out to us during the day, and to put on our greatcoats. Next morning the French, seeing us thus, thought we had retired and left Portuguese to guard the heights. With dreadful shouts, they leaped over that wall before which they had stood, when guarded by the British. We were scarce able to withstand their fury. To retreat was impossible; all behind being ploughed land, rendered deep by the rain. There was not a moment to hesitate. To it we fell, pell-mell, French and British mixed together. It was a trial of strength in single combat; every man had his opponent, many had two. I got one up to the wall, on the point of my bayonet. He was unhurt. I would have spared him, but he would not spare himself. He cursed and defied me, nor ceased to attack my life, until he fell, pierced by my bayonet. His breath died away, in a

The Lines of Torres Vedras 45

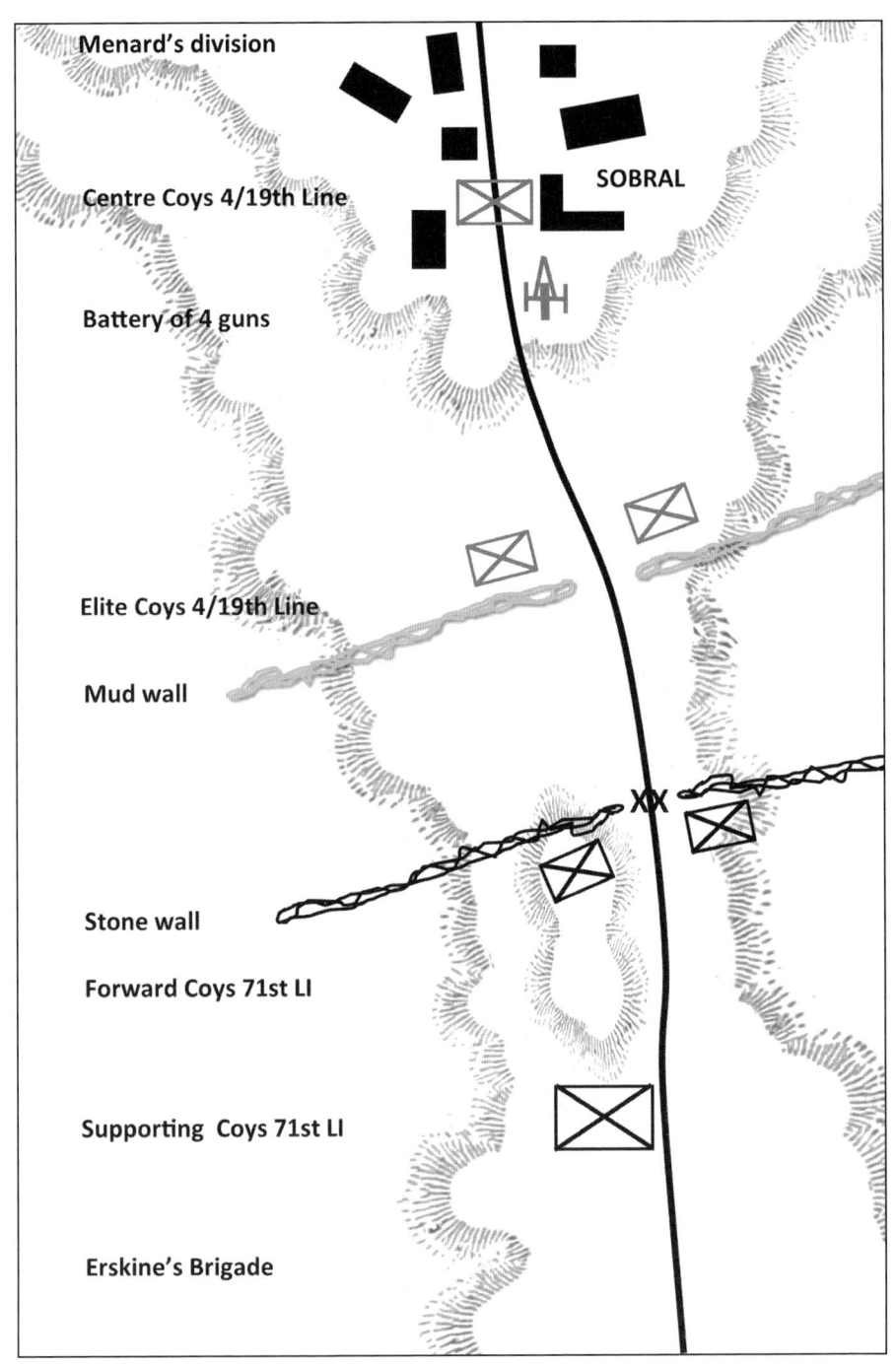

Menard's division

SOBRAL

Centre Coys 4/19th Line

Battery of 4 guns

Elite Coys 4/19th Line

Mud wall

Stone wall

Forward Coys 71st LI

Supporting Coys 71st LI

Erskine's Brigade

The 71st Light Infantry's action at Sobral, 14 October 1810.

curse and menace. This was the work of a moment; I was compelled to this extremity. I was again attacked, but my antagonist fell, pierced by a random shot. We soon forced them to retire over the wall, cursing their mistake. At this moment I stood gasping for breath, not a shoe on my feet; my bonnet had fallen to the ground. Unmindful of my situation, I followed the enemy over the wall. We pursued them about a mile and then fell back to the scene of our struggle. It was covered with dead and wounded, bonnets and shoes trampled and stuck in the mud. I recovered a pair of shoes; whether they had been mine or not I cannot tell; they were good.

They threw Ménard's men back and pursued through Sobral, but with the rest of Clausel's division coming forward, as Thomas recalled, the 71st withdrew back to their barricade. Even though the veteran the 1st Battalion 71st had been recently converted to light infantry, their performance for a newly-arrived battalion during 12–14 October was impressive.

With just 12,000 men against more than 30,000 allied soldiers arrayed before him and having seen the vigorous response to the advance on Windmill Hill, Junot would not attack out of Sobral or anywhere else that day; Masséna did not press the point. Colonel Delagrave, Junot's senior ADC, noted that 'The Prince seeing the enemy was better prepared and stronger than believed, put an end to the combat, and on either side the troops took up once more their original positions.'[17]

Marshal Masséna then 'with a crowd of officers on horseback, dragoons with led horses, and all the *cortège* of a general-in-chief' rode east to a knoll near Arruda and the Light Division's positions. According to Captain Jones, he

> ... made in person a very close reconnaissance of the right of the lines, and on the 16th, having remained an unusual time with a numerous staff examining the entry of the valley of Calhandrix, a shot was fired at the party

The view back towards the Lines from the *miradouro* [viewpoint] on Gallows Hill just south of Sobral on the N115.

A grenadier (right) and a *voltigeur*, the elite companies of a French infantry battalion.

An officer of the 95th Rifles.

from No. 120, which striking a wall whereon the Marshal was resting his telescope, he acknowledged the warning by taking off his hat, and moving on. This reconnaissance served to convince the French commander of the inadequacy of his means to attack an army so posted and supported.

With the French failing to accept his offer of battle, Wellington withdrew the 71st and the rest of Erskine's brigade to the rear in the area of Zibreira in order to tempt Masséna to attack but, as D'Urban noted in his journal, 'Each individual division has besides more than sufficient troops to occupy the space allotted to it, and the overplus will form a reserve to each respectively.'

Masséna and his commanders were only too aware of the British dispositions and numbers and would not gratify Wellington with an attack. On 16 October in a note to Ney, the marshal showed that any ardour for the fray he had had clearly evaporated, possibly confirmed by receipt of information on the presence of the second main line of defences. The marshal wrote:

> The enemy is dug-in to the teeth. He has three lines of works that successively cover Lisbon. If we took the first line of redoubts, he would retire to the second and we would not have achieved much; only we would have moved away from the resources of the country we are occupying to find ourselves in devastated places ... orders are given for the entrenchment of all the positions we occupy, so I think it is not the moment to attack the enemy, a failure would destroy all our hopes and would upset this state of affairs.

A British view of the French failure to test the Lines was advanced by Lieutenant Kincaid of the 95th Rifles who commented that 'the Prince of Essling ought to have tried his luck against them, as he could only be beaten by fighting as he afterwards was without it!'[18]

Instead of attacking, Masséna initially intended a close blockade of the Lines sustained by a temporary boost to his supply situation from food found in houses south of Coimbra. This was the result of Wellington's denial policy not being properly implemented due to the hasty withdrawal, but much of the food had not been systematically gathered by the foragers and a lot was wasted. Both armies settled down opposite each other, going into cantonments as the rain continued to fall.

Life in the Lines

Life for most of the British soldiers encamped behind the First Line for five weeks in the autumn of 1810 was far from comfortable or restful. Lieutenant William Grattan of the 88th Connaught Rangers, with Picton's 3rd Division, described the early-morning routine of standing to arms and how he and his soldiers were

> waiting for the signal to proceed to our alarm-post, a duty which the army performed every morning two hours before day. This was by no means a pleasant task; scrambling up a hill of mud, and standing shivering for a

Wellington's headquarters at Pero Negro.

couple of hours in the dark and wet was exceedingly uncomfortable; but I don't remember to have heard one single murmur; we all saw the necessity of such a line of conduct, and we obeyed it with cheerfulness.[19]

Wellington himself rode daily from his headquarters at Pero Negro to Monte Agraço before dawn in order to be ready for daylight to reveal a French advance. He spent most days in observation, only returning to his headquarters at dusk.

Initially, the line was, as indicated by Wellington's response to the French advance on Sobral, far from continuous and while the enemy were at close quarters his troops were labouring on additional defences. The 71st Light Infantry found themselves drawn back into the 1st Division's line in the Zibreira Gap. Thomas of the 71st described the routine:

On our arrival behind the lines, our brigade, consisting of the 50th, 71st and 92nd, commanded by Major General Sir William Erskine, was quartered in a small village called Zibreira. Our first care was to place outposts and sentinels between the batteries, about 20 yards distant from each other. We communicated with the Foot Guards on our right and the Brunswick infantry on our left. Those off-duty were employed throwing up batteries and breastworks or breaking up the roads, it being a place that no army could pass, save upon the highway. The day after we fell into the lines, the French placed sentinels in front of us, without any dispute. There was a small valley and stream of water between us.

On the Light Division's front around Arruda, which was just forward of the Lines, there was plenty of French activity in the form of skirmishes as both sides came to a practical understanding of who held which piece of ground. In the town matters were settled with the Light Division holding most of the buildings and the French occupying buildings on the northern outskirts. Wellington, in a letter to Brigadier General Craufurd, drew his attention to a weak area on the division's front: 'I need say nothing to you about the defence of the Pass of Matos. I think it would be desirable, however, that you should occupy with the 52nd or 43rd the high ground which continues from the right of the right-hand redoubt, looking from Matos to Arruda.'

Private Garrety of the 43rd Light Infantry described some of the labouring and construction work undertaken to secure the division's part of Sector 2:

> ... in a short time, the division, with prodigious labour, secured the position, in a manner which was spoken of with admiration.
>
> Across the ravine on the left, a loose stone wall, 16 feet thick and 40 feet high, was raised: and across the great valley of Arruda [Pass of Matos], a double line of abatis was drawn; not composed, as is usual, of the limbs of trees, but of full-grown oaks and chestnuts, dug up with all their roots and branches, dragged by main force for several hundred yards, and then reset and crossed, so that no human strength could break through. Breastworks at convenient distances, to defend this line of trees, were then cast up; and along the summit of the mountain [for the 43rd or 52nd], for the space of nearly 3 miles, including the salient points, other stone walls, 6 feet high and 4 in thickness, with banquettes, were built, so that a good defence might have been made against the attacks of 20,000 men.[20]

Major Marbot later justified his assertion that the Lines could have been breached by quoting General Picton's statement that 'If the enemy had attacked in the first ten days of our occupation they would have succeeded.' The respective numbers of troops alone dictated otherwise, and Pelet concluded that 'an attack would have cost us half the army'.

When the Lines were first occupied, the tents that had been promised by the Portuguese commissariat failed to arrive and the troops lived in the battalions' bivouac turf huts, but a lack of decent thatch meant that in the continuing autumn rains they leaked badly so officers and men were rarely dry. Eventually small Portuguese tents arrived, but these were later replaced by larger British bell tents and then for the officers of the Light Division it was a question of furnishing them. Lieutenant Charles Booth wrote:

> The pretty little town of Arruda was beautifully situated, and a favourite retreat of the rich merchants of Lisbon – their *quintas* being splendidly furnished and made as luxurious as possible. It was altogether a little paradise; but how soon was the scene changed! It was plundered, burnt and utterly destroyed; all the valuable furniture of the houses thrown into the

The British bell tent with a stout central pole and facility for hanging uniforms and accoutrements or supporting weapons.

picket fires, to the disgrace of our army; for unfortunately we did not permit the enemy to get possession of it, even for a moment to have shared the stigma.

Lieutenant Kincaid of the 95th lived in a mucked-out cowshed near Redoubt No. 9, which overlooked the Pass of Matos. 'We certainly lived in clover while we remained there; everything we saw was our own, seeing no one there who had a more legitimate claim', and continued writing that

> It was customary to put us under cover in the town during the day, but we were always moved back to our bivouac, on the heights, during the night; and it was rather amusing to observe the different notions of individual comfort, in the selection of furniture, which officers transferred from their *town house* to their *no house* on the heights. A sofa, or a mattress, one would have thought most likely to be put in requisition; but it was not unusual to see a full-length looking-glass preferred to either.

With the Royal Navy bringing supplies into Lisbon and a very short line of communication, the allied armies were well fed and recovered both fitness and weight. Lieutenant Vandeleur of the 71st Light Infantry in a letter home contrasts the fortunes of the armies:

> I have spoken to French officers who are prisoners; it was from them I heard the state of the army; the poor fellows say they are starved. Our soldiers have 1 pound and a half of good brown bread and a pound of beef each day, besides an allowance of either bacon or ham and wood to burn.

After weeks of campaigning, clothing was another issue. Craufurd reported to Wellington on 19 October that 'the Light Division was more miserably clad than any but the lowest description of beggars.' Clothing issues were duly made, and officers had access to tailors in Lisbon, if they had the money. Lieutenant Grattan recalled that '... those gentlemen who had or fancied they had, a taste for leading fashion, had now a fine opportunity to bring their talents to bear.' Fortunately for the fashion-conscious, Wellington was supremely unconcerned about officers' or even soldiers' uniformity:[21]

> Our fatigues for the time at an end, we occupied ourselves in such pursuits as each of us fancied. We had no unnecessary drilling, nor were we tormented with that greatest of all bores to an officer at any time, but particularly on service, uniformity of dress. The consequence was that every duty was performed with cheerfulness.

A subaltern officer of the 88th Connaught Rangers.

As was often the case when opposing piquets were at close quarters, an understanding developed between the soldiers. Vandeleur reported that 'The French and English piquets are so near that they speak to each other, and even give time to the enemy. They are not allowed to fire; no more are we, nor allowed to engage unless attacked.'

Officers, with their posts further back, were less likely to indulge in live-and-let-live, but most were always interested in 'foraging' opportunities. Lieutenant Simmons of the 95th Rifles was one such:

> On piquet [we saw] two French soldiers enter a house in our front. Hopwood and myself with three men crawled from our post into an avenue of trees, which covered us from the immediate view of the French vedette... and surprised the two Frenchmen, who were filling some canteens with wine, but sprang to their arms. One of them snapped his firelock, but it did not go off. They were instantly taken from them. A moment after, one soldier offered me some brandy he had in a calabash slung across his shoulders. I gave both a large goblet of wine, sent a soldier to get all the canteens he could muster from the piquet and return, we keeping a good lookout. We filled sixty, then destroyed the hogshead, took our prisoners to the piquet, and sent an escort with them to the General.

To the surprise of many, after five weeks the French were still before the Lines, but there was mounting evidence that they were in an increasingly parlous state.

The French were not the only ones suffering. Some 300,000 Portuguese civilians had been displaced by the denial policy and were behind the Lines, with the Portuguese Regency (and Britain) unable to feed or shelter them. Over winter 40,000 civilians died of disease, exposure and malnutrition. Portugal paid a very heavy price for its freedom.

Chapter Three

Winter at Santarém

Wellington's hope and the army's expectation that Masséna would launch an all-out attack were dashed when the French settled down in front of the Lines, sending their cavalry to the rear. It was hoped that Mortier's V and Drouet's IX Corps[1] would march to the aid of the Army of Portugal but neither marched to join Masséna, and worse, the army was virtually isolated with no effective line of communication back to Spain. ADCs with dispatches were captured and reports failed to reach Salamanca from the middle of September through to the middle of November. Masséna was truly isolated deep in a country that he had sought to quickly occupy.

An artilleryman with Clausel's division, Captain Noël, described life for a French soldier before the Lines:

> When we arrived, there were still some supplies to be had in the countryside. These were quickly exhausted and, in order to live, recourse was had to marauding. Each corps, each branch, organised itself in its own way. Detachments, at first sent out into the immediate neighbourhood, were forced to go further and further away. These parties, commanded by officers of various ranks, split up as they fanned out.
>
> The result was that the men, separated from their leaders, gave themselves up to every sort of pillage and even to the practice of cruelty on the miserable peasants who had thought that their wretched poverty would protect them from such violence. This was done, not so much to force the peasants to reveal hordes of grain, or the hiding place of cattle, as to compel them to hand over money.
>
> I organised my marauding service so perfectly that, as soon as a hoard was found, a train of wagons brought back supplies of corn, wheat and forage to the houses in Sobral that we occupied; provided, that is, none of it had been lost or stolen.[2]

It was, of course, not enough to find the grain: it had to be ground and made into bread, but as a part of the denial policy, mills had been disabled. With a field forge as a part of his battery's equipment Captain Noël was able to replace all the metal parts and his harness repairer replaced the windmill's sails with mattress cloth. In a citizen army millers and bakers were found among his gunners. The artillerymen, however, were not to benefit from their mill for long, as it was ordered to be handed over to the infantry. Captain Noël continued:

> Wretchedness became so widespread that discipline suffered to the point where even the most basic military duties were neglected.

An officer of French line foot artillery.

One day, accompanying General Clausel on a tour of inspection, we came upon a bivouac that had been established to protect Sobral and support the advanced positions. All the detachment's weapons had been stacked and not a single man, not even a sentinel, was on guard. The general ordered me to have the weapons removed and taken to the [artillery] park ... Hunger had driven all of them, officers and men, to go out pillaging although they were only a couple of paces away from the enemy's advanced posts.[3]

Meanwhile, the allies supplied by sea and with a short line of communication back to Lisbon, rarely lacked food, fuel, forage and clothing. Thomas of the 71st Light Infantry recalled:

The advanced piquet of the French lay in a windmill; ours, consisting of one captain, two subalterns and 400 men, in a small village. There was only a distance of about 150 yards between us. We learned, from the deserters, that the French were much in want of provisions. To provoke them our sentinels, at times, would fix a biscuit to the point of their bayonets and present [arms] to them. One day the French had a bullock, in endeavouring to kill which the butcher missed his blow and the animal ran off right into our lines. The French looked so foolish. We hurrahed at them, secured the bullock, brought him in front, killed him in style. They looked on but dared not approach to seize him. Shortly after, an officer and four men came with a flag of truce and supplicated in the most humble manner for the half of the bullock, which they got.[4]

The French Withdrawal to Santarém

After five weeks before the Lines, Masséna was faced with an impasse. The Army of Portugal was starving, particularly VIII Corps, whose soldiers were nearest the lines and were wracked with hunger and riven with disease. The hoped-for supplies and reinforcements from Spain had not arrived and as the weather deteriorated there was little prospect of the balance of forces swinging sufficiently in French favour to make an assault on the Lines practicable. On 10 November, Masséna finally decided to withdraw. He had already started to send more of the cavalry, the reserve artillery and hospitals to Santarém and began thinning out rearward elements of the army. They were ordered to retire some 30 miles beyond the Rio Mayor where the rich country around Santarém had not been stripped bare of food and forage. Santarém additionally offered Masséna a number of courses of action for a future offensive or retirement.

After a night when the glow of well-stoked French bivouac fires illuminated the sky to the north, above a fortuitous autumn ground fog, to the British piquets standing to arms at dawn, all seemed normal. Lieutenant Kincaid was with the Light Division's outposts in Arruda and it wasn't until the fog cleared that they realized that the enemy had gone:

He abandoned his position, opposite to us, on the night of the 14th of November, leaving some stuffed-straw gentlemen occupying their usual

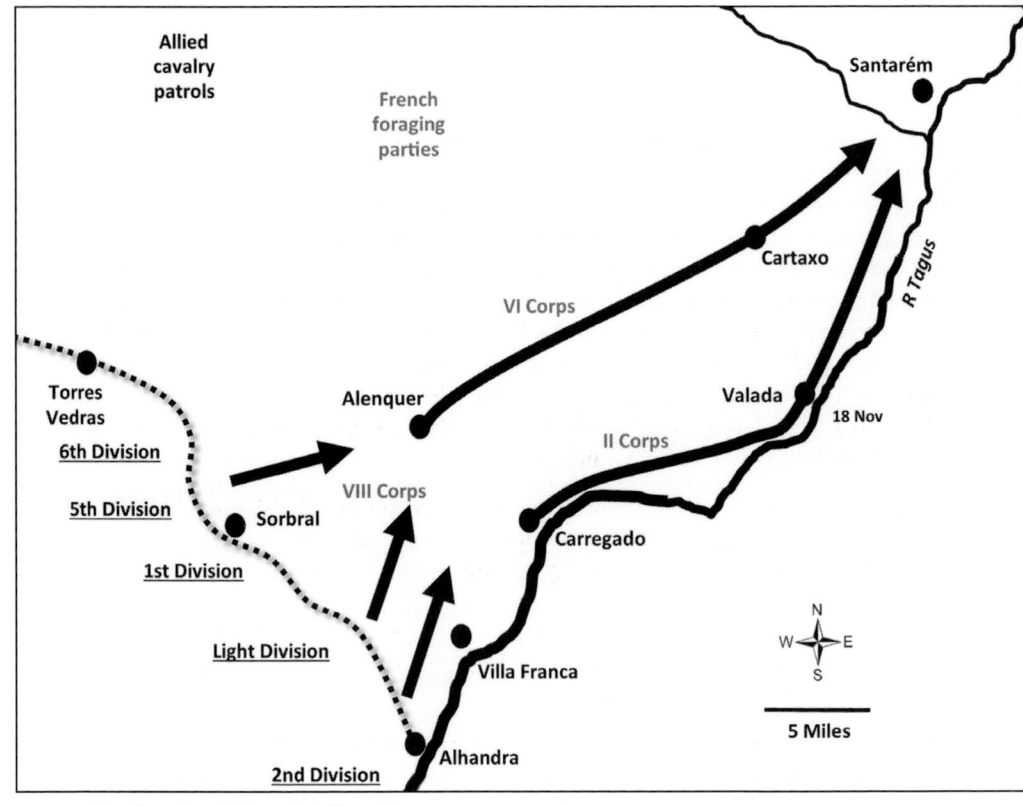

The French withdrawal to Santarém.

posts. Some of them were cavalry, some infantry, and they seemed such respectable representatives of their spectral predecessors, that, in the haze of the following morning, we thought that they had been joined by some well-fed ones from the rear; and it was late in the day before we discovered the mistake and advanced in pursuit.

When word arrived of the French departure at Wellington's headquarters at Pero Negro, 'the Peer' was shaving and calmly replied: 'Ay, I thought they would be off.' He rode to his accustomed observation post on Monte Agraço, where he wrote to Spencer, Hill and Craufurd giving them instructions:

> *To Brigadier General R. Craufurd.*
> On the Hill in front of Sobral, 15th Nov, 1810.
> My Dear General,   20m. past 10 A.M.
> You will have observed that the enemy have retired from the ground they occupied with their right, about Sobral, and I think it most probable that they will have retired their whole army towards Santarém.
>
> Sir B. Spencer's division is now feeling its way on towards Alenquer, and a patrol of our cavalry is just gone to the wood in front of [Redoubt] No. 11.
>
> If you should find that the enemy have retired their left, as well as their right, I beg you to cross the river at Arruda, and feel your way on towards Alenquer, by the direct road leading from Arruda.[5]

With the French having stolen a march on him, Wellington had contemplated attacking them, but eventually ordered that Masséna's rearguard was to be followed rather than pursued. He was keen to give battle if a favourable opportunity presented itself, but he was cautious, wondering if this was a ruse to draw him out of the Lines. Consequently, on the afternoon of 15 November, Wellington ordered the 1st, 2nd and Light divisions to follow the French in what was explicitly not to be a pursuit.[6] The Peer[7] was content to regain contact with the French and determine what Masséna intended, while other forces (Trant, Wilson and Beresford) were to 'operate upon the flanks and rear of the enemy'.

At 1530 hours that afternoon Wellington wrote again outlining his plan and expanding his instructions to Craufurd:

> I request you to communicate with the officer in command of General Hill's outposts [to his right], who will, I hope, be this night at Carregado. In the morning I wish you to feel your way cautiously to Vila Nova, and thence on the road to Santarém.
>
> I shall move General Spencer's division in the morning to Alenquer, and General Hill's corps I shall close up on the high road along the Tagus. I shall be up here very early in the morning.

In response Spencer's division entered the ruins of Sobral during the afternoon, while Hill's command marched on the river road via Vila Franca to Carregado. The Light Division led in the centre advancing towards Alenquer, without catching up with the enemy's rearguard. The town, as was the case with virtually every place encountered during the French withdrawal, presented a shocking state of devastation, having been comprehensively sacked. On the 16th Anson's and Slade's cavalry and Pack's Portuguese brigades joined the advance, most of the cavalry having marched up from cantonments in Mafra or from patrol bases forward of the lines in walled towns like Óbidos. The rest of Wellington's divisions remained in the Lines for another two days until it was apparent that the French withdrawal was not a trap and Masséna's intent was clear.

Brigadier General Craufurd's light infantrymen followed the French to Vila Nova. Ensign William Hay of the 52nd Light Infantry described the march:

> ... one morning, we found the enemy had disappeared from our front. On we went after them, and for some days ploughed our way through ponds of mud – for they did not deserve the name of roads – continuing to advance as long as the French army retreated, which was for about five days.[8]

Reaching Vila Nova, enemy engineers were found attempting to demolish a bridge, but they failed when the 95th Rifles overwhelmed the enemy's rearguard and chased off the engineers, taking a goodly proportion of the day's 400 prisoners. Lieutenant Simmons of the 95th Rifles, in his first march since recovering from wounds received on the Côa back in August, recorded in his diary the state of the French encountered en route: 'We took a number of stragglers this day who had been suffering sadly from starvation and disease. The

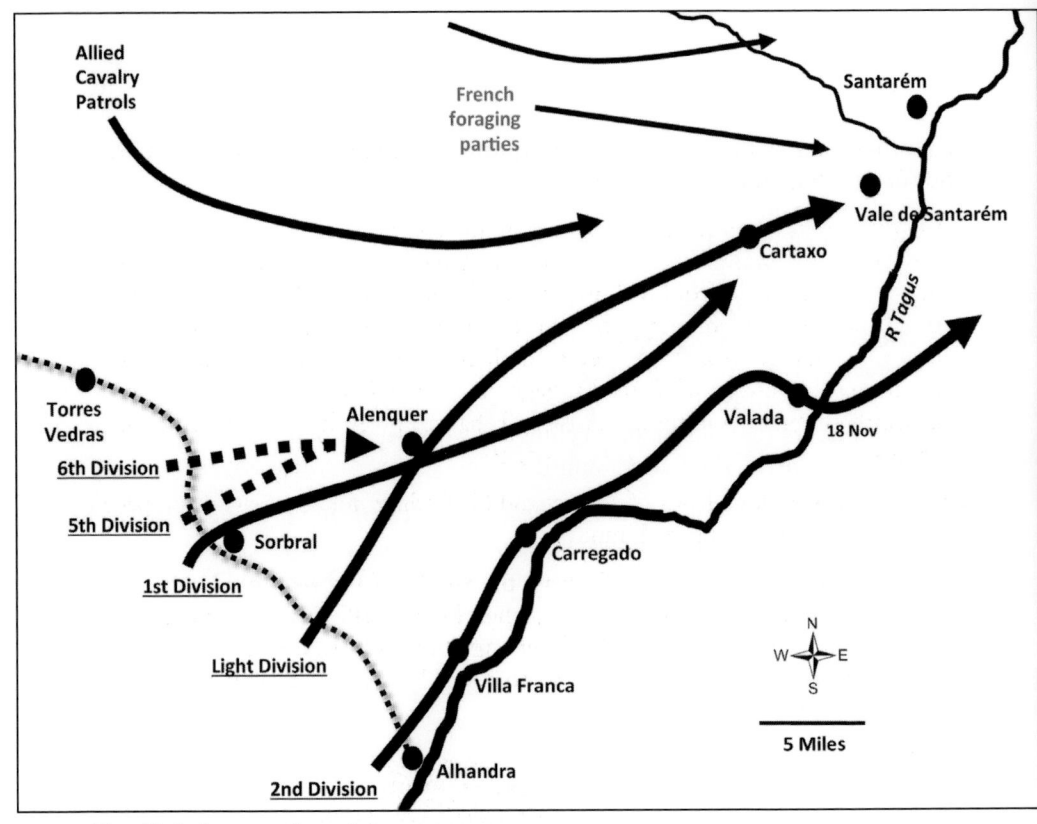

The allied advance to Santarém.

road was found strewn with rags and pieces of Frenchmen's appointments and caps, and occasionally a dead horse, mule or jackass to enliven the scene.'[9]

Brigadier Craufurd, who had the previous year issued particularly strict standing orders on the conduct of marches, was intensely annoyed by the execution of this advance in heavy rain. He saw his men repeatedly avoided going straight through the puddles and flooded ruts as his standing orders required.[10] He addressed his six battalion commanders in terms that justified his nickname of 'Black Bob':[11]

> If I ever have occasion to observe any man of the Brigade pick his road on the march and go round a pool of water instead of marching through it I am fully determined to bring the officer commanding the Company to which that man belongs to a Court Martial. Should the Court acquit the officer it shall not deter me from repeating the same ceremony on any other officer again and again. Every halting day, if necessary, I will bring an officer to a Court Martial who shall presume to allow the men of his Company to go out of the way of a pool of water. I will insist on every soldier marching through water and I will flog any man attempting to avoid it.

On 17 November, Craufurd nearly fell into a well-laid trap near El Valle 2 miles short of the Rio Mayor,[12] when Brigadier Fane reported that his cavalry patrols had caught up with the enemy's rearguard. Lieutenant Tomkinson of the 16th Light Dragoons recalled that

> On the main Lisbon road to Santarém on the banks of the Tagus, the enemy were followed by the Light Division, and General Slade's brigade. On the division's coming in front of Cartaxo [*sic* El Valle], General Crawford found three regiments of infantry with two of cavalry formed up in front of the bridge, or rather with the bridge to their rear, over the river to Santarém, covering the retreat of their baggage. He waited a short time for our [Anson's Brigade] coming up on his left, having given his directions to the troops.

Craufurd with six squadrons of cavalry and his leading infantry brigade prepared to attack what, according to Simmons:

> General Craufurd fancied … [it was] the whole of the rearguard and had made his dispositions to attack them, when Lord Wellington arrived on the ground and stopped the attack, observing, 'Are you aware, General, that the whole of Junot's corps is close to the advanced body you now see,

Brigadier General Robert Craufurd.

amounting to, at least, 23,000 men, a large portion of which is cavalry?' The attack was, of course, abandoned.

During 18 November the French rearguard fell back the last 2 miles and crossed the Rio Mayor via the Ponte Seca[13] near Santarém. They were now in a strong position with the broad flood plain of the Tagus on the French left and the all but impassable swamp of the Rio Mayor to their front, covered by pre-prepared entrenchments and batteries, all protected by an abatis of thousands of felled olive trees.

Later that day the leading squadron of the 14th Light Dragoons reached the river south of Santarém. Here they were joined by riflemen commanded by Lieutenant Simmons who remembered that with a strong force of enemy cavalry nearby the dragoons 'were highly pleased to see me arrive with some Riflemen and take up the post of honour from them, as the company I belonged to was sent on piquet, with orders to remain at the bridge'. The Rifles who had led the advance that day were relieved at nightfall by a company of the 52nd Light Infantry, whose turn it was to provide the piquets for the Light Division's 2nd Brigade. They were responsible for covering the 800-yard-long causeway and bridge across the river and its increasingly flooded valley.

That evening with only the Light Division and Slade's cavalry brigade forward, Wellington wrote to General Hill, whose division, followed by Fane's Portuguese cavalry, were being ferried across the Tagus at Valda by Admiral Berkley's gunboats: 'The enemy are still too strong for us this day at Santarém, and I have delayed the attack upon them till to-morrow morning, in order to have the assistance of the 1st Division. If they stay, we shall then attack them.'

With the rain still falling, on the evening of 18 November Craufurd was not convinced that the French rearguard would remain in place. To ensure that the French were not slipping away under cover of the rain and darkness, he embarked on a personal reconnaissance of the causeway, accompanied by Sergeant McCurry and two soldiers from the piquet. When he and the patrol were out on the causeway approaching the bridge, they were challenged by a French sentinel who fired a musket shot to warn his piquet. Simmons wrote 'The General ordered his men to fire and retire' but so alarmed were the enemy piquet, they 'imagined that the British army was passing the bridge', stood to arms and opened a heavy fire at what was an 'imaginary enemy'. Having provoked the French into revealing that they were still holding their positions in strength, Craufurd withdrew to his own lines, and 'was sadly annoyed at being deceived in his conjectures and having caused such an uproar, with a great chance of foolishly throwing away his life'.

The following day, 19 November, Wellington, still believing that he was only facing a rearguard rather than the whole of Reynier's II Corps, ordered an attack on Santarém by the Light and 1st divisions. The Light Division was to attack via the marshes of the Tagus plain, while the 1st Division was to assault the causeways, fixing the enemy, while a brigade further north turned what was supposed to be the French flank via the bridges at Ponte Celeiro and Ponte Azambujeira.

Winter at Santarém 63

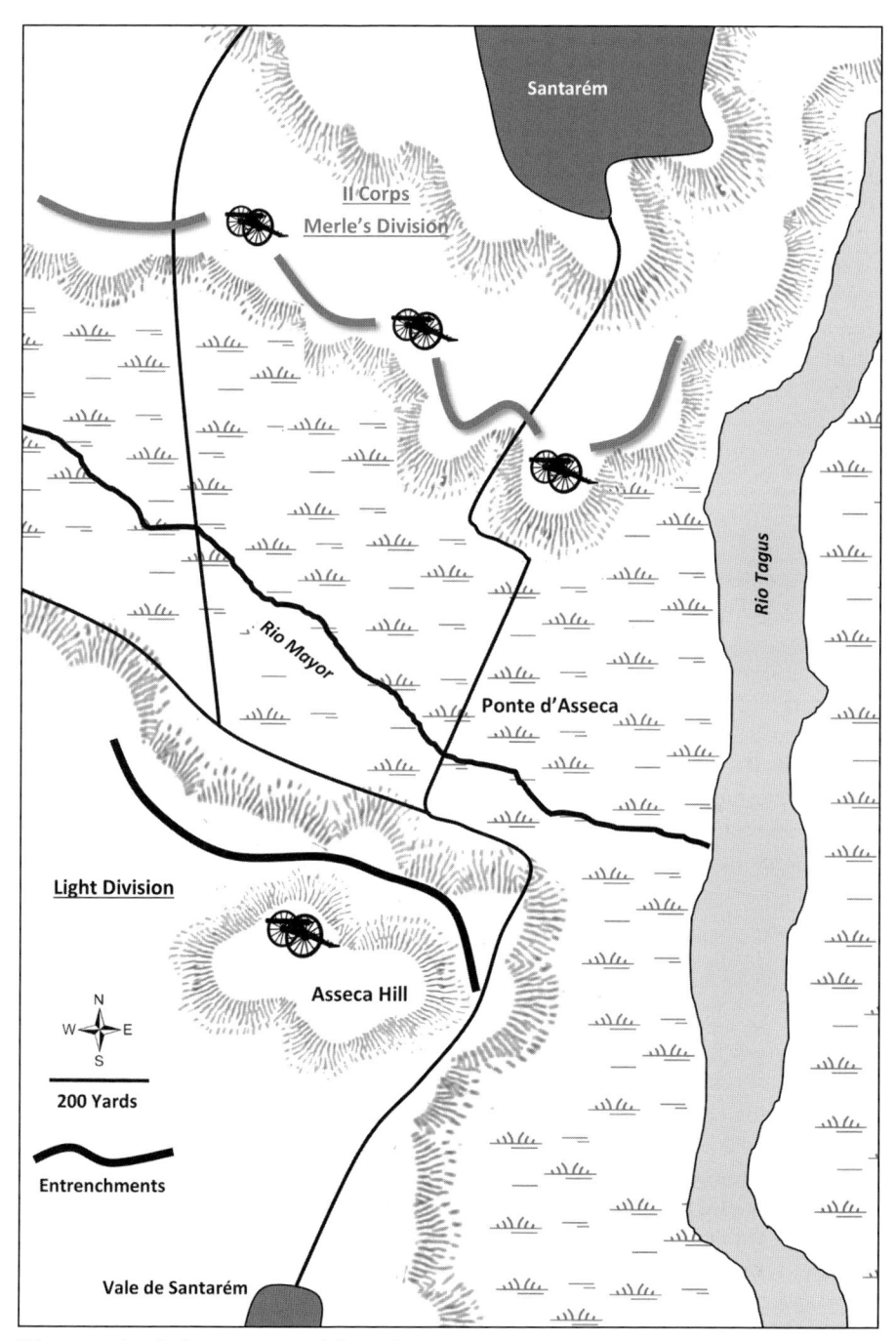

The respective deployments around Santarém.

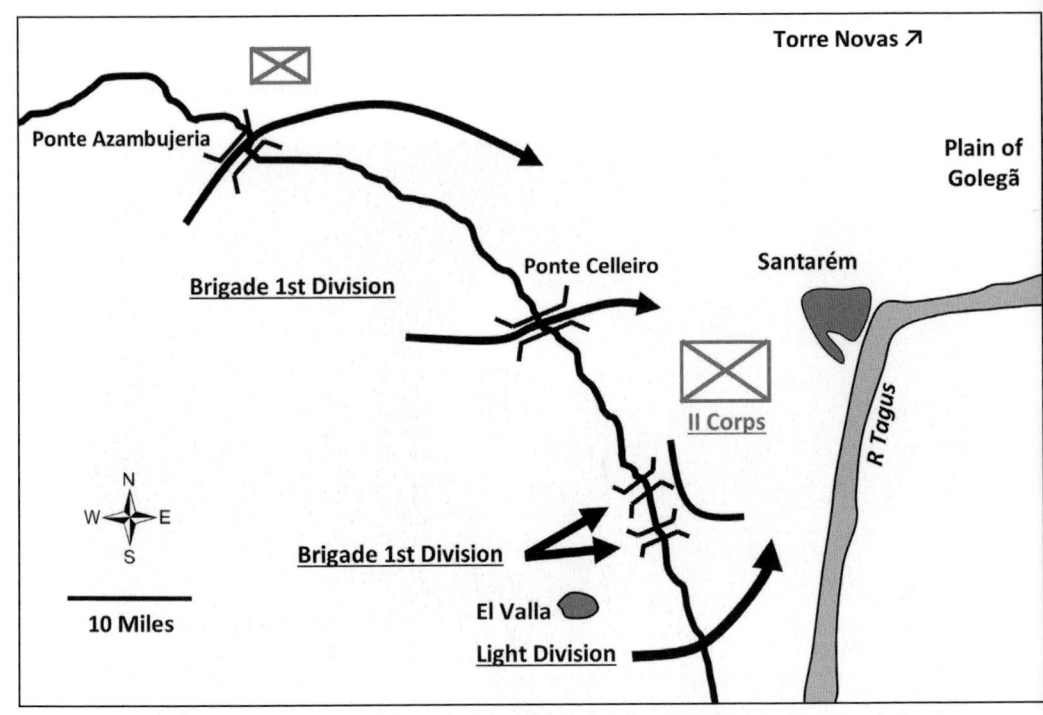

Wellington's plan for the attack on Reynier's II Corps before Santarém.

Lieutenant Tomkinson of the 16th Light Dragoons explained the plan to draw enemy reserves away to the north:

> The orders sent to General Anson were to make with his brigade and General Pack's brigade of Portuguese infantry, which was on its march to join us, a sharp demonstration on the Rio Mayor road, at the same time that the infantry attacked the bridge on the main road. A gun was to be the signal for the troops to move.

The action began with the Light Division's advance into the marsh, but fortuitously the Portuguese artillery, which was to support Pack's brigade, was late arriving having had to labour forward through the mud of the Lisbon road. This gave time and daylight for Wellington to examine the French position and spot works that had appeared overnight and Reynier's poorly-concealed soldiers. According to Simmons the advance into the marsh resulted in 'skirmishing for some hours, and in such rain … firearms were rendered useless'. Lieutenant Tomkinson continued:

> We waited until 2 p.m., when an officer from the Heavy Brigade was sent to say the attack on the right was all ready, and that we should move on immediately. General Pack was ready to cross the river; but since morning so much rain had fallen that even the bridge was impassable by which we had crossed in the morning. The 1st Division was to have attacked the main causeway, which had been barricaded, so that only one man could have got over at a time. The hills opposite were lined by troops and artillery, and the

Brigadier General Sir George Anson.

division formed up, ready to move on. The gun was fired, and before the troops could move off their ground, all was cancelled.

Wellington called off the attack. Later he wrote to General Hill, explaining:

> I did not attack Santarém this morning, as the artillery intended for the left missed its way; and I am rather glad that I did not make the attack, as the enemy have there undoubtedly a very strong post, which we must endeavour to turn; or, if they have not retired across the Zêzere, or towards the Alva, they must be too strong for us here. I believe, however, I shall attack them to-morrow.

By the morning of the 20th, however, it was apparent to Wellington that the French intended to remain at Santarém, as three rows of abatis and further entrenched positions had been established on the hillside that climbed up to the town. In his strong position it was Masséna's turn to have his hopes for an injudicious attack by the enemy dashed by sober counsel.

Wellington, having realized that his assumptions were wrong, built a picture of the poor state of the Army of Portugal from deserters, captured messages and intelligence from Spain. Such was their condition, he returned to his policy of letting starvation do its work rather than waste lives and expend resources in fighting. As for Masséna, if the allies did not oblige him by attacking, he still had the hope and expectation of reinforcement by Drouet's IX Corps rather than a winter withdrawal through the mountains back to Spain.[14]

Outposts and Winter Quarters

Over the succeeding days there were clashes between cavalry patrols and vedettes, but as the two sides established their territories, the amount of activity subsided and with Masséna showing every sign of remaining in Santarém Wellington put the army into cantonments in towns and villages as far back as Torres Vedras. The army was, however, in a position to block any sudden advance and the Lines remained fully occupied by the Portuguese militia. Private Joseph of the 94th (Scotch Brigade) recalled the 3rd Division's cantonment: 'From Torres Vedras, we removed to Alcoentre, a small village some miles in the rear of the Rio Mayor; and we were kept pretty busy while in it, strengthening our position, making batteries, breast-works, abatis, etc.'

During the previous winter General Craufurd's Light Division had provided the army's outposts and again found itself in that role on the Rio Mayor before

A sketch of the French view across the Ponte d'Asseca causeway to the Light Division's positions on the Asseca hill at the far end of the causeway.

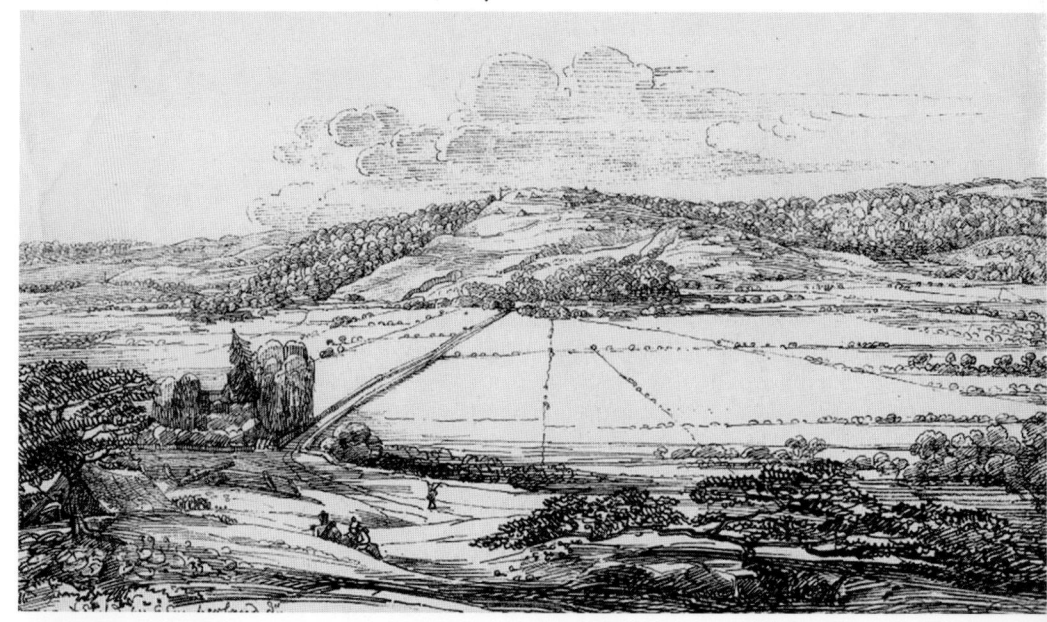

Santarém, while further north cavalry patrols were deployed as before to limit the scope of French foraging parties. The division's British and Portuguese battalions took turns to provide the piquets on the river line.

With the increasingly boggy Tagus flood plain to their right, the causeway over the flooded Rio Mayor valley was strongly held by the Light Division in entrenchments on hills overlooking them. Simmons recalled that '300 men being always on piquet at the head of the bridges [causeway], and several more on inlying picket', which were posted 'in roofless hovels near at hand'. Captain Leach stated that 'on the bridge we constructed an abatis; and to render our post on the causeway more secure, we made covert ways and traverses.' He concluded that 'since Masséna fell back behind the Rio Mayor, the rains, which never ceased falling, soon found their way through tents, so that we were seldom dry.'

Turns for battalions to leave the dubious shelter of the small town of Valle and take over the piquets in the entrenchments and at Ponte Celeiro and Azambujeira came around every five days or so.

During the period spent on the Rio Mayor, General Craufurd had Pack's Portuguese brigade and Arentschildt's cavalry brigade (16th Light Dragoons and 1st Hussars KGL) under command.[15] The cavalry provided vedettes and patrols further north along the river line to the town of Rio Mayor and beyond.

Ensign Hay described the uncomfortable conditions that the Light Division found themselves in when they

> ... went into what are called cantonments. This one being a sort of large farmyard surrounded by a low wall. A few houses which had been cleared

With the causeways being the sole practicable avenue of attack, they were covered by Captain Ross's Light 6-pound cannon.

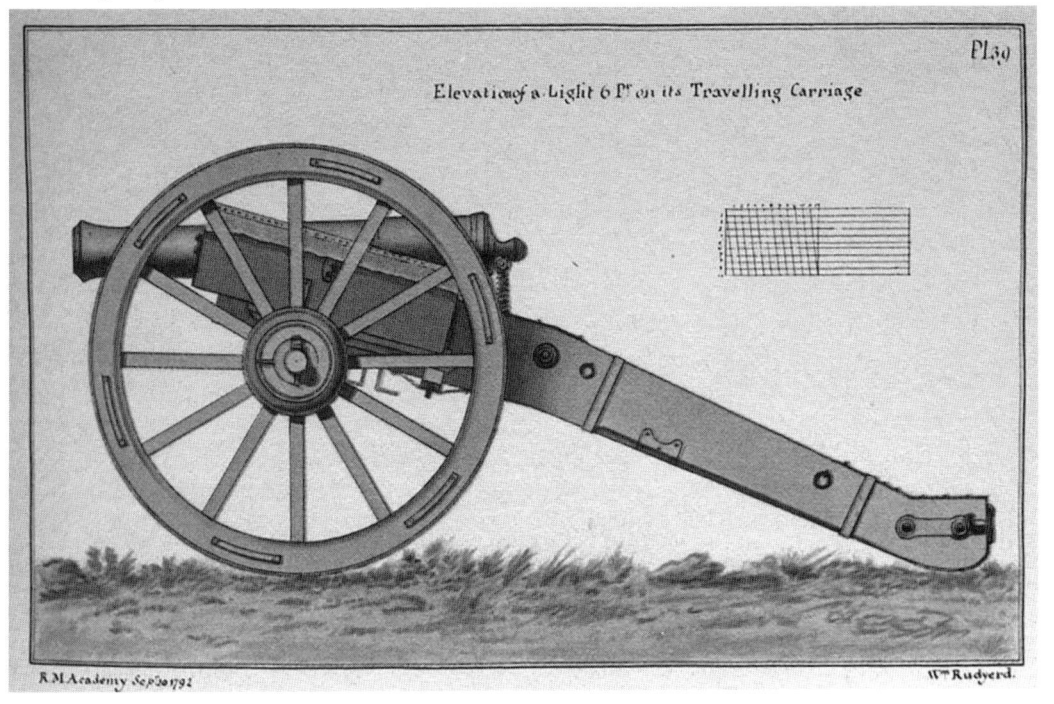

Ensign William Hay. After a year of active service with the 52nd Light Infantry, he purchased a lieutenancy in the 12th Light Dragoons. He is pictured wearing the 1812 uniform.

of all furniture – even doors and windows taken from their frames – were allotted to the officers, the men being in a field in front. My bed was half an old window-shutter, but on which I enjoyed most sound sleep, though my only covering was a camlet boat-cloak; my clothes were never off my back, or my shoes off my feet any night during that winter.

There was a long bridge and causeway over the river leading to Santarém, at one end of which our piquets were posted; at the other, the French had theirs; sentinels being about 50 yards apart in the middle of the bridge. Our quarters, in the houses I spoke of, were about 2 miles from this bridge and of course all hands on the outposts had to be pretty much on the alert. The regimental bugles sounded to turn out every morning an hour before daybreak, and we stood under arms until an hour after sunrise. After the duty was over, we amused ourselves riding, walking, or in the best way we could.

The Light Division was the smallest division in the army and, even with Pack's Portuguese, needed reinforcement due to the length of front they had to cover and the necessity of reducing the time spent exposed on piquet to a minimum. To this end nine companies of German light infantry, the Brunswick Oels, were temporarily attached to the division:[16]

> It was while we were here an event happened which I did not at all relish; it was the first actual bloodshed I had witnessed. Attached to the Light Division was a regiment of foreigners [the Oels] – French, Germans and others, some of whom had volunteered their services to us hoping that the chances of war would enable them to get back to their own country.
>
> One night, after we had retired to rest, we were called up by the alarm sounding 'To Arms'; several shots were fired toward the front. It turned out, however, to be fourteen of those unfortunate men making an attempt to desert to the enemy. Some were shot by the piquet, and five were taken prisoners. These were tried by court-martial and condemned to be shot. The division was drawn up for the purpose, and the sentence carried into execution on four of them; the fifth, a mere child, was pardoned, after having had his eyes bandaged, etc. The whole spectacle I did not forget for some time.

While the Light Division's battalions took their turns providing the piquets there was no such relief for their artillery, Captain Ross and A Troop, Royal Horse Artillery on Asseca Hill overlooking the causeway.[17] He complained that

> ... my troop has been so hardly worked and unfairly worked since here ... I have the mortification of seeing my troop in the highest health and condition, and the very reverse ... At the present we are stuck as artillery of position on heights looking towards Santarém, where we are certainly more for show than use, and where both men and horses have suffered extremely from the weather, which for some time was severe.[18]

Commissary Schaumann, however, records that soldiers of the French Hanoverian Legion also deserted in significant numbers to their fellow countrymen of the 1st KGL Hussars. Many of these deserters along with prisoners were rounded up 15 miles west near the town of Rio Mayor.

Meanwhile, to improve his options, Masséna ordered his chief engineer, General Eblé, to bridge the by now unfordable Rio Tagus, which would, when resources allowed, enable him to blockade Lisbon, at least from the south bank. Without a bridging train and with every kind of material lacking, building a bridge across the great river proved impossible. Only a few boats or barges were

In the foreground a green-jacketed, rifle-armed light infantry soldier of the Brunswick Oels.

found intact and demolition of buildings for timber rendered only poor-quality wood.[19]

In the area of Rio Mayor, Masséna was far from militarily inactive over the winter. Schaumann recorded an incident that demonstrates this when a large body of French cavalry approached the town while Schaumann was having breakfast. The regiment's trumpets sounded to arms and when he reached the alarm post Schaumann could see 'our sentries circling round in an anxious manner':[20]

> ... and then we saw them fix their carbines and make a dash to the rear. In a moment the French appeared in strong columns, and halting on the heights, examined our position through telescopes. They seemed to pay particular

attention to a formidable battery which we had mounted beyond the town in front of a church – though only as a ruse in order to deceive them; for being short of guns, we had erected dummies out of old camp kettles. If, however, the old kettles could have done the duty of a gun and swept the high road of Rio Mayor, the enemy might certainly have entered that town, though they could never have left it again! Our *jägers* [skirmishers] took post at the entrances of the town and all round it. Brave old Schwalbach stationed himself with his foremost outposts, and coldly explained to the fellows how close they were to allow the French to come before they aimed and mowed them down. The squadron was posted at the rear of the village and of the battery.

The enemy now deployed with about 3,000 to 4,000 infantry and a few squadrons of cavalry, and as they feared our battery, advanced cautiously and slowly in complete order of battle against our kettles. The *jägers* opened fire, and then, being outflanked, immediately withdrew behind the battery, which so much impressed the enemy that they continued to keep out of range. At last, seeing that the battery did not fire, the French *tirailleurs*, taking courage, stormed the kettles and took them. This little attack made a pretty picture. The *Caçadores* with the 6th English Dragoons withdraw to Caldas, while we retired along the road to Lisbon into a thick wood, which extends

Deputy Assistant Commissary August Schaumann attached to the 1st Hussars KGL.

behind the heights of the Rio Mayor. Hardly had we reached this cover and halted, and sent the skirmishers forward, than on the heights just above our heads we noticed a French general and his staff, accompanied by a cavalry escort, examining our position with a telescope. One of our skirmishers, a hussar named Dröse, climbed up the side of the hill under cover of the trees, and stealing forward, rested his carbine on the branch of a tree, aimed and fired, and at the same moment the general fell from his horse and was surrounded by his staff and carried away.[21]

The French occupied and searched Rio Mayor for food but retired the next day and the Hussars reoccupied the town. General Junot's excursion had the 3rd Division 'ordered under arms'. According to Private Joseph Donaldson, the 94th were

to defend our position [at Alcoentre], in the event of the French pushing forward. During that day, and the succeeding night, the baggage of the troops in front [mainly cavalry], along with the inhabitants of the surrounding country, filled the road leading through our village. It was a melancholy sight.

In the event Junot's regiments only advanced a short distance beyond Rio Mayor.

While life in the outposts was uncomfortable and demanding for the Light Division, for the rest of the army in winter quarters the main issue was boredom. With little prospect of action during the three months of winter, a stream of officers, including Brigadier General Craufurd, requested permission to go home on leave on various pretexts. These included medical, but the numbers were so great that Wellington had to insist that even senior officers appear before a medical board before being granted leave on medical grounds.

Craufurd was one of those who was granted leave, and command of his division devolved on Major General Sir William Erskine, who had been pressing Horse Guards for an active command. When Wellington was informed that Erskine was joining the army, he complained that he 'generally understood him to be a madman'. Horse Guards replied that 'No doubt he is sometimes a little mad, but in his lucid intervals he is an uncommonly clever fellow; and I trust he will have no fit during the campaign, though he looked a little wild as he embarked.'[22]

On the French side of the Rio Mayor life was increasingly difficult, but the French were able to remain spread out over the country north of Santarém for more than three months. Wellington had been cautioned by the Portuguese Regency that the population would not fully carry out the agreed denial policy and would attempt to hide food and valuables, but a French army used to living off the land was more than equal to finding even the most carefully hidden cache of Portuguese grain. The foragers often extracted the necessary information by torture and Masséna was forced to issue orders to limit the excesses of his troops.

When there were no civilians, French soldiers scoured the rich grain country around Santarém and during the winter, steam rising from the ground indicated a cache of hidden grain, while measuring buildings to find bricked-up doorways revealed valuables. Outside musket ramrods were used to probe for buried

Winter at Santarém 73

A hussar of the King's German Legion.

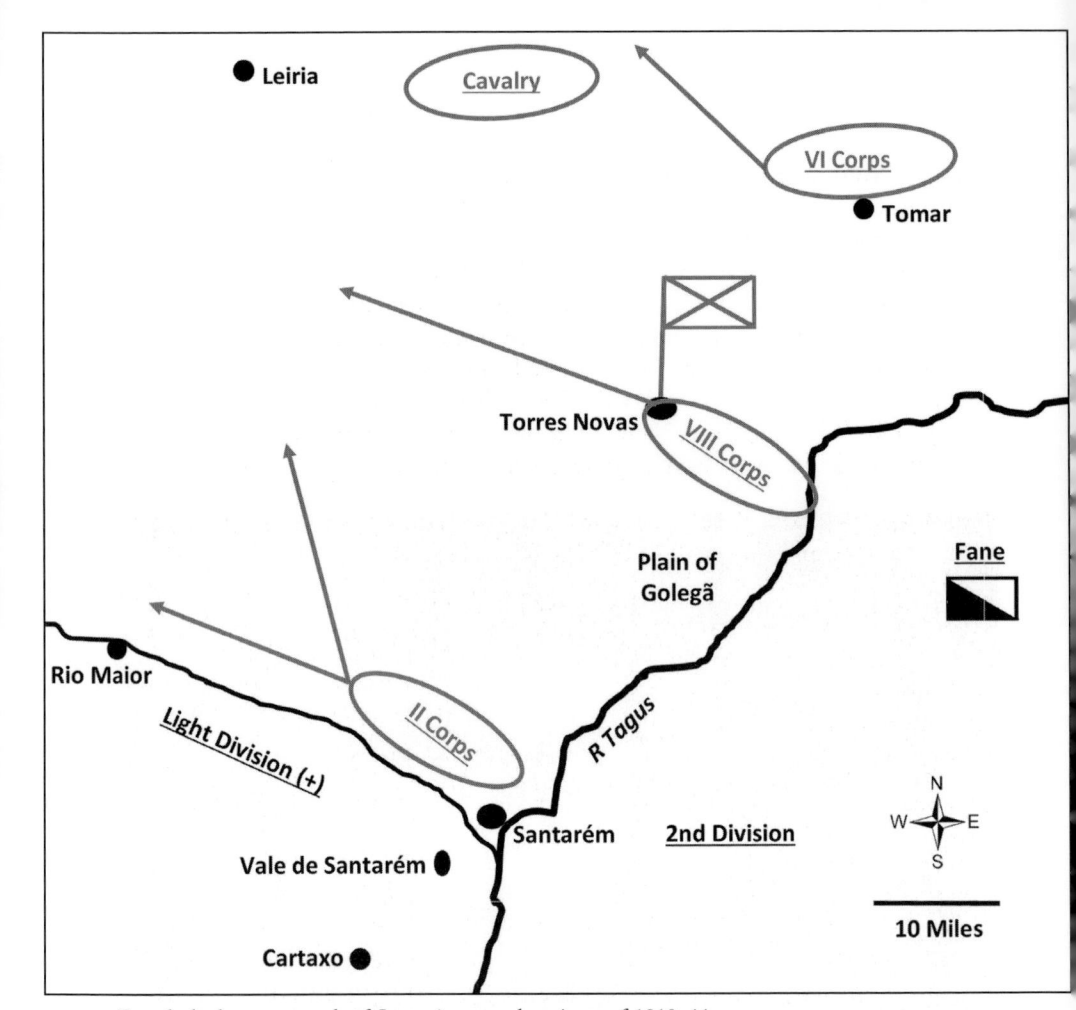

French deployment north of Santarém over the winter of 1810–11.

boxes. Using such methods, foraging prevented starvation but supplies became increasingly short and discipline slipped. Pelet mentions absentees

> ... who established themselves in houses where they could find plenty of food. Living quietly in their new domains, they would send someone to the camp from time to time to assure themselves there had not been any movement ... This type of provisioning occasioned considerable waste but whatever its disadvantages and dangers, it was becoming impossible to do otherwise.

Marbot provides an altogether more roguish and colourful picture of one of these bands:

> A French sergeant, wearied of the misery in which the army was living, resolved to decamp and live in comfort. To this end he persuaded about a hundred of the worst characters in the army, and going with them to the rear, took up his quarters in a vast convent deserted by the monks, but still

full of furniture and provisions. He increased his store largely by carrying off everything in the neighbourhood that suited him; well-furnished spits and stewpans were always at the fire, and each man helped himself as he would; and the leader received the expressive if contemptuous name of 'Marshal Stockpot'. The scoundrel had also carried off numbers of women; and being joined before long by the scum of the three armies, attracted by the prospect of unrestrained debauchery, he formed a band of some 300 English, French and Portuguese deserters, who lived as a happy family in one unbroken orgy. This brigandage had been going on for some months, when one day, a foraging detachment having gone off in pursuit of a flock as far as the

General Reynier, the commander of II Corps which held the Line of the Rio Mayor from November 1810 through to March 1811.

convent which sheltered the so-called Marshal Stockpot, our soldiers were much surprised to see him coming to meet them at the head of his bandits, with orders to respect his grounds and restore the flock which they had just taken there. On the refusal of our officers to comply with this demand, he ordered his men to fire on the detachment.

The greater part of the French deserters did not venture to fire on their compatriots and former comrades, but the English and Portuguese obeyed, and our people had several men killed or wounded. Not being in sufficient numbers to resist, they were compelled to retreat, accompanied by all the French deserters, who came back with them to offer their submission. Masséna pardoned them on condition that they should march at the head of the three battalions who were told off to attack the convent. That den having been carried after a brief resistance, Masséna had Marshal Stockpot shot, as well as the few French who had remained with him. A good many English and Portuguese shared their fate; the rest were sent off to Wellington, whose delivery of justice was prompt.[23]

The Retreat to Spain

Despite his promise to Masséna, Napoleon insisted on attempting to control events in Portugal from Paris and with exchanges of messages taking up to six weeks to arrive – if at all – the Emperor had little idea of the Army of Portugal's true situation. Consequently, at the beginning of November Marshal Masséna sent General Foy to Paris to explain exactly what was happening and the condition of the army. Delivering his dispatches to Napoleon on 21 November, Foy in turn received the Emperor's assessment of the situation:

> Massena must take Abrantes – Elvas would be of no good to us. The only way to get Wellington to make a forward move will be to force him to try to raise the siege of Abrantes. As long as Masséna stays in position opposite Lisbon, nothing is lost; he is still a terror to the English and keeps the offensive. If he retreats, I fear great disaster for him. But why did he not take up some regular plan of operations? The very day after he reconnoitred the Lisbon lines, it was clear that he would never attack them. I will send immediate orders for the V Corps [Mortier] to invade the Alentejo.
>
> Will they be obeyed? At that distance only by those who choose to carry out my directions. I tremble lest Masséna may call Drouet down to him, and then get his communications cut again. By communications I mean sure points, at two or three marches' distance, properly garrisoned and provisioned, where convoys can rest and be safe. An army without open communications loses heart and gets demoralised ... All the hope of the English is in that army of Wellington's! If we could destroy it, it would be a terrible blow to them.[24]

Napoleon sent a repetition of previous orders to General Drouet to assemble his corps at Almeida in order to cover the Army of Portugal's rear, establish a line of communication to Masséna and reinforce him. However, most tellingly, rather than sending Soult's army from Andalucía to pose a significant threat, he was only ordered to send a corps of 10,000 men into the Tagus valley, while Mortier was to demonstrate on the borders of Spanish Estremadura and the Alentejo.

The escort that had taken General Foy to Spain was to return to the army, under the command of General Gardanne, with those soldiers at Ciudad Rodrigo that had recovered from sickness or wounds, escorting a convoy of ammunition and other stores. The force, supposedly numbering 6,000 men, set out 1,000 short and was further attenuated by desertion and the need to garrison a line of communication until it became very weak. Ultimately, with poor intelligence about Masséna's movements, Gardanne turned the column back.

Drouet's IX Corps assembled at Almeida, chasing away a Portuguese blockading force, and advanced into the Mondego valley where, just 6,000 strong, the corps established communication with the Army of Portugal and reached

Foy was promoted to General of Division, partly for his clear briefing to Napoleon and partly to foster an air of success in Paris.

Leiria.[25] From here patrols probed west to the sea and in doing so, cut the allies off from northern Portugal. This was accompanied by probes such as that against Rio Mayor during which General Junot was wounded.

Meanwhile, Marshal Soult was entering the Tagus valley, necessitating the deployment of Marshal Beresford with the 2nd and the Portuguese divisions, supported by cavalry and eighteen guns, south to keep them in check. Ultimately, Soult's ability to support Masséna in a timely manner was thwarted by the necessity in the aftermath of the Battle of Barrosa of returning to secure Andalucía. Consequently, by the time he had laid siege to Badajoz and he was able to return to Portugal, the Army of Portugal was in retreat. If Soult had been ten days earlier, the outcome of Masséna's campaign could have been very different.

During January and February both Wellington and Masséna had plans, but both were thwarted. Wellington had wanted to go over to the offensive, but his expected reinforcements were delayed[26] and Masséna needed to force a crossing of the Tagus to effect a juncture with Soult whose operations he was only vaguely aware of, but he lacked the means. By March, with the Army of Portugal isolated and with barely enough food left for a withdrawal, Masséna faced an untenable situation. His subordinates demanded a withdrawal to Spain and as far as he knew there was no prospect of reinforcement or likelihood of resupply; consequently, he had to act.

On the night of 5/6 March, after several days of sending ahead his sick, the army's baggage and artillery, covered by deception and manoeuvres, Masséna quit his positions at Santarém in what Napier described as being 'in a manner befitting a great commander'. Marbot wrote that

> The Army moved in several columns on Pombal, Marshal Ney with the 6th Corps forming the rearguard, and valiantly defending his ground foot by

French line infantry pioneers were distinguished by the bearskin and the crossed axe badge.

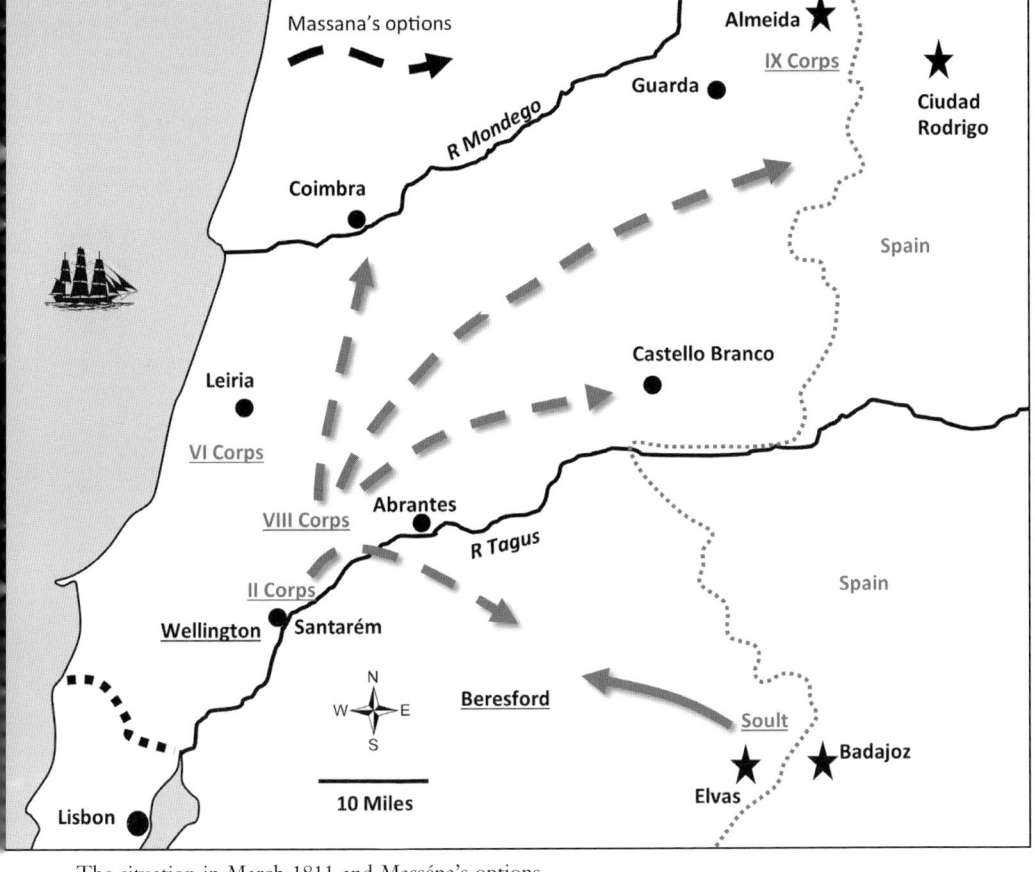

The situation in March 1811 and Masséna's options.

foot. As for Masséna, roused at length from his torpor, he gained between the 5th and 6th of March three days on the enemy, and completely organised his retreat – one of the most difficult operations of war. Contrary to his usual custom, also, he was so cheerful as to surprise us all.

Of his four options, Masséna chose the only entirely practicable solution, which was to head north and cross the Rio Mondego, but this was risky, requiring him to march his army across the front of the allies. To achieve this, VI Corps and cavalry were deployed at Leiria, where they could have been threatening to march on the Lines of Torres Vedras. This was effective and fixed Wellington in position for fear of exposing the Lines to capture, as he was not entirely sure of the purpose of Masséna's wider movements for several days.

The uniform of a Portuguese line infantry officer. British officers in service with the Portuguese Army also wore this uniform.

Chapter Four

Withdrawal to the Rio Mondego

While Marshal Ney adopted a threatening posture at Leiria, Generals Junot and Reynier started to fall back to the north at 0200 hours on the night of 5/6 March 1811, destroying all they could not move for want of horses and mules. General Eblé had the pontoons his men had been building for months at Punhete burned and the bridges were broken behind the withdrawing divisions.

A clear signal that the French were about to move had been given by deserters on 4 March. Lieutenant Simmons, serving in Captain Beckwith's company[1] of the 2nd 95th, recorded in his diary: 'Returned to my corps, as the reports that the enemy's moving off gain ground daily.' Some days later he wrote:

> March 6th – The *juiz de fora* [justice of the peace] of Santarém sent a peasant to give information that the enemy had retired through the place at two o'clock this morning and were in full retreat. The Light Division followed the enemy at daybreak and entered Santarém, where we remained about an hour. How different this town now appeared; when I last was in it all was gaiety and happiness ... but now the houses are torn and dilapidated, and the few miserable inhabitants, moving skeletons ... and many streets quite impassable with filth and rubbish, with an occasional man, mule or donkey rotting and corrupting and filling the air with pestilential vapours.

With the Light Division confirming that the French had gone, again leaving dummies and mock cannon, Wellington promptly moved his headquarters from Cartaxo to Santarém but it took some days for reports of French movements from his correspondents and exploring officers to produce a picture of exactly what Marshal Masséna was doing. In the meantime, however, the Light Division followed the enemy and would provide the army's advanced guard for the following month. Simmons' diary gives a flavour of the first days of the division's pursuit of the French north to the valley of the lower Mondego.[2] 'March 7th – Followed the enemy's rearguard to Torres Novas and halted near La Marrosa [*sic*]. The Horse Artillery and Royal Dragoons came up with the French rearguard and harassed it. We passed several of the enemy's killed and wounded men upon the road as we advanced.'

Meanwhile, from their cantonments further to the rear, the rest of the army was under orders to march. Wellington wrote:

> My Dear Beresford,   Santarém, 6th March, 1811. 4 P.M.
> I am just now returned from Pernes. All is clear on this side of that river, over which the enemy have destroyed both bridges, that at Pernes, and that at

Lieutenant George Simmons of the 2nd 95th Rifles.

> Ponte Velha. The Light Division is at the former, General Nightingall's brigade at the latter, and the 1st, 4th, and 6th divisions either are, or will be here this evening. Sir William Erskine is at Alcanede and will be at Torres Novas tomorrow. The 3rd Division is at Rio Mayor; but the 5th, and General Campbell's brigade, do not move till tomorrow.
>
> I shall have headquarters to-morrow at Torres Novas, with the 1st Division; the 4th and 6th will be on the right, either at, or well on towards Golegã.

Following an evening in the saddle, Wellington wrote to General Spencer (1st Division), with a note of caution:

> The enemy have quitted the Tagus and Zêzere, and have burnt their boats, and retired to Thomar and Chão de Maçãs. Their movement to this last place, and the report of the country that they are going to Coimbra, induce

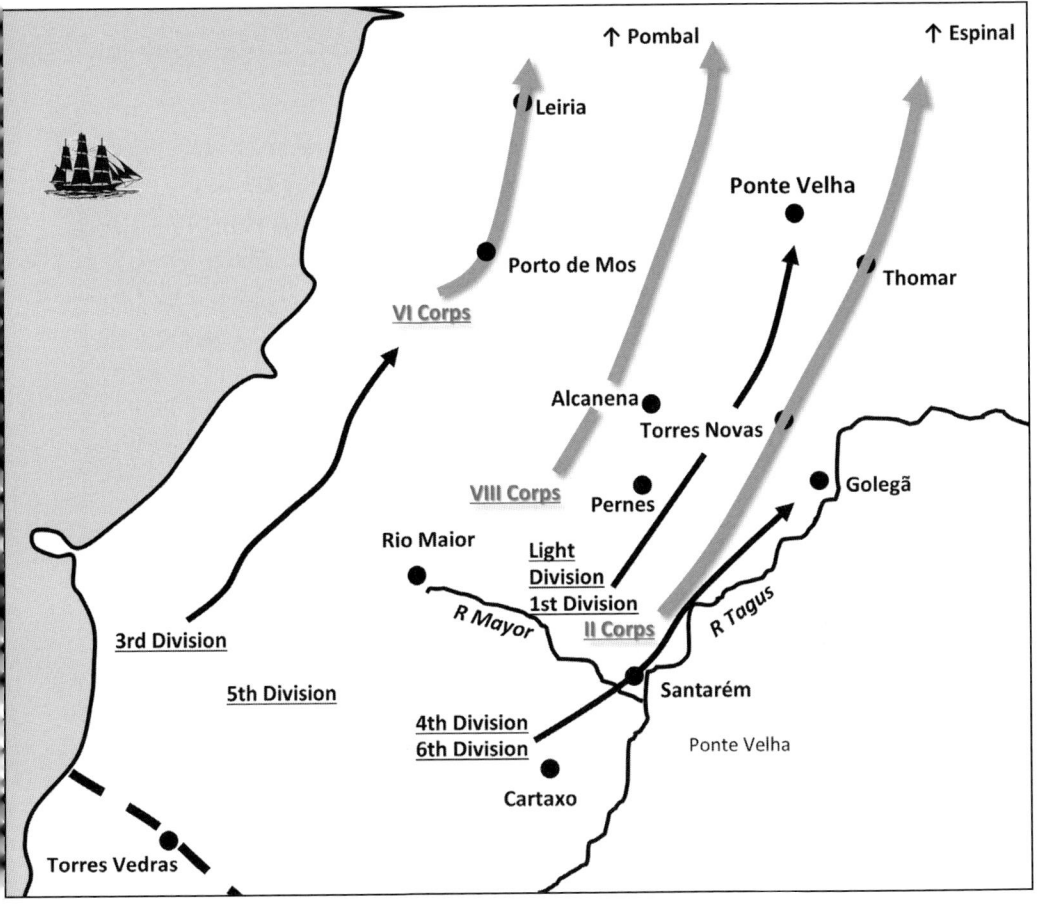

Initial stages of the withdrawal and pursuit.

me to defer moving the troops from Pernes and Alcanede till I shall have ascertained their designs more clearly than I have as yet. Some of our people were near them this day, but they showed no signs of a desire to turn upon us. They were reported to be in strength.

The Pursuit Begins

Virtually every British account of the advance from Santarém into areas that had been held by the retiring French army contain descriptions of wanton destruction of villages, houses and churches, along with gross brutality inflicted on Portuguese civilians. Private Donaldson's account is typical of the sights that confronted the 3rd Division in one village, Porto de Mós, on the road to Leiria and Pombal:

> When we entered the latter place there was a large convent fronting us, which, as well as many of the houses, had been set on fire by the French. I never before witnessed such destruction. The finest furniture had been broken up for firewood; the very floors torn up, beds cut in pieces, with their contents thrown about, intermixed with kitchen utensils, broken mirrors,

china, &c. &c. all in one heterogeneous mass of ruin, and not an inhabitant to be seen.

Later the same day, Donaldson was on duty with the battalion's commissariat as the 94th settled into their overnight billets in the devastated village:

> In searching for the cleanest place to set down the bags of biscuit, we found a door leading to some place apart from the chapel. As it was quite dark, I caught up a burning piece of wood to inspect the place but what was my horror, when I entered and found the half-consumed skeletons of human beings on every side; some lying, others kneeling, and more of them standing upright against the walls. The floor was covered with ashes, in many places still red. I stood fixed to the spot – the burning stick dropped from my hand. I informed some of my comrades of what we had seen, and we re-entered. Such an appalling sight was never witnessed. Of those who had sunk on the floor, nothing remained but the bones; while the others, who were in a kneeling or standing posture, were only partially consumed; and the agonised expression of their scorched and blackened features was awful beyond description.
>
> On going to the upper end of the apartment, I perceived a bag lying on the floor with something in it. I was almost afraid to open it, lest some new object of horror should present itself. I was not mistaken in my apprehension; for when the bag was examined, it was found to contain the dead body of an infant, which had been strangled; the cord used for that purpose still remained about its little neck.

The fact that such scenes made a lasting impression on soldiers inured to the sights and sounds of war speaks for itself. Having seen the depredations of the French for himself during the course of the 9th, in a report to Lord Liverpool Wellington wrote:

> On the same afternoon of the 9th, I was with the British advanced guard at Pombal, and saw in front of that town the collection of the enemy's troops ... It appeared to me then, that I must decide either to allow the enemy to retreat from Portugal unmolested, by the road he should prefer, and expose Coimbra and Upper Beira to be ravaged or force him east to Spain.

Action at Pombal: 10–11 March 1811

On 9 March the cavalry and the Light Division caught up with the French rearguard south of Pombal. Simmons recorded in his diary:

> March 9th – Advanced early this morning, and after marching five hours, came up with the enemy's rearguard at the junction of the road from Leiria and Lisbon to Coimbra. A large body of cavalry showed itself, and infantry in force was halted in rear. An advanced squadron of the 11th French Horse Grenadiers[3] were charged by the 1st German Hussars in pretty style, and

A representation of a British infantryman of the period.

twelve of them taken. The French had taken two hussars two days before, and it was believed had coolly sabred them. The Germans were so incensed at the report that they were going to put some of these men to death ... About forty straggling soldiers fell into our hands on this day's advance, and the road was often covered with dead Frenchmen, gun-carriages, wagons and pieces of different military equipment.

Ney's VI and Junot's VIII corps had met up at Pombal and Venda da Cruz with a view to crossing the Mondego at Coimbra, but Wellington wrote to Spencer questioning 'Whether offering battle or whether waiting for an opportunity to cross the Mondego I cannot tell.' The following morning, 10 March, Colonel Arentschildt's light cavalry and Ross's RHA Troop closed up. An officer of the German Hussars wrote:

> ... our advanced guard, which had been reinforced by several corps of heavy cavalry as well as some [Light Division] infantry regiments, broke up for the purpose of attacking the enemy, who had posted himself securely at Pombal. The road being dry and good, our horse-troops and artillery set forward at

Captain Hew Ross, commander of A Troop, RHA.

a brisk trot, and the foot-soldiers in quick march. To facilitate the progress of the latter, their knapsacks were entrusted to the charge of the heavy dragoons. At this rate did we journey ... the very earth seemed to vibrate under the multitudinous tramp of the warriors. In the afternoon, we arrived at Pombal, where we found the enemy.[4]

At Venda Nova, some distance short of Pombal, the French rearguard consisting of Montbrun's dragoons were 'drawn up in battle array' for what was the first in a series of actions to cover the withdrawal over subsequent days. Lieutenant Tomkinson of the 16th Light Dragoons wrote in his diary that

We followed the enemy up to the Pombal plain, where they showed eight squadrons formed on the heath in front. The Hussars [KGL] advanced with one squadron in front and three in support, on which the enemy's [mounted] skirmishers retired, and the whole eight squadrons began to withdraw. We passed the defile in our front and came up in time to join the Hussars in their charge. We charged and broke one squadron of the enemy, drove that on to the second, and so on, till the whole eight were altogether in the greatest confusion, when we drove them on to their main support. We wounded several and took a few prisoners ... The French officers called on the men supporting to advance but not a man moved.

Wellington, who had again been in the saddle with the advance guard for most of the day, wrote:

MY DEAR SPENCER,   Perucha, 10th March, 1811.
The enemy still continue on their ground in front of Pombal, but not, I think, in the strength in which they were yesterday. They are still, however, very strong; and my own opinion is, that they will draw off the corps which they have there in the course of this night. If they do not, I propose to attack them there to-morrow. I think it most likely that they will go back as far as Condeixa, where they will collect their force with more ease than they can at Pombal.
   Believe me, etc.
   WELLINGTON.

Meanwhile the 3rd Division, 'after five days of toilsome marches over rocky almost impracticable mountains', joined on the 11th, with the 4th Division, in approaching Pombal. A general attack on the French had been on Wellington's mind, but with the remainder of the divisions which were due to have taken part in the action delayed by the bad roads, it was postponed until the following day. Wellington, however, noticed that there were now few French to be seen. Overnight Marshal Ney had withdrawn two of his divisions from a potentially difficult situation contrary to Masséna's explicit orders, leaving Pombal defended by little more than a battalion. His orders were to form a rearguard position at Pombal, while the engineers attempted to establish a bridge across the Mondego,

An impression of a French line infantry *voltigeur*.

as Colonel Trant's irregulars had blown two of the arches of the bridge at Coimbra.

Wellington tested the enemy's resolution by sending forward the Light Division and an advanced guard, namely Lieutenant Colonel Elder's 3rd Caçadores and two companies of the 95th Rifles under Captain Peter O'Hare. They were quickly deployed for action against some French *voltigeurs*, which were occupying the walled paddocks and gardens surrounding Pombal. Making a spirited dash across the bridge outside the town, they drove the defenders back and Simmons recalled that 'Although the enemy disputed the ground obstinately, which, from the nature of it, was very defensible, yet they were driven sharply into Pombal.' Here the light troops fought *voltigeurs* who had occupied houses. The Rifles' regimental history records that

> After a lively interchange of fire Sergeant Fleming of the Rifles with a few men rushed one of the houses held by the French and took some prisoners after which the Riflemen by degrees cleared the other houses; Lieutenant Hopwood was severely wounded in the thigh when engaged in this task.

The riflemen and the Caçadores fought their way through the town towards the castle where some French dragoons had taken refuge. Marshal Ney, who watched the fighting from the high ground beyond the town, saw his rearguard in difficulty and sent forward four battalions of the 6th Light Regiment and the 69th Line to restore the situation. Elder's and O'Hare's men were in the process of attacking an 'obstinate enemy in the castle' when the French counter-attack

The restored Pombal Castle stands on an eminence overlooking the town.

struck home and rescued the dragoons who were determinedly defending the castle. Following this success, the French cleared the village, barricaded the main street and torched adjacent houses, which delayed the main body of the Light Division, which General Erskine had belatedly ordered forward. By the time the division had forced their way through the village, the French battalions were marching up onto the high ground, speeded on their way by 'a few shots from Ross's guns which had, as usual, pushed on to the front'.

The riflemen captured some French officers' baggage in the village, which was indicative of the French intent to have made a stand at Pombal and inflicted substantial delay. The baggage included that of Colonel Pierre Soult, brother of the marshal; his baggage and that of other officers was promptly auctioned by the Rifles, men each receiving 6 dollars from the proceeds.

In his first engagement in command of the Light Division, the officers were critical of Erskine's handling of the division, saying that it had been ponderous and bungling and was earning the nickname 'Asknine'. 'Already we were missing Craufurd' was a comment in the diary of one of their absent commander's erstwhile critics.

The action at Pombal may have been relatively small, but its effects were out of all proportion to its size. It put additional pressure on Masséna, who wanted to cross the Rio Mondego in good order, by placing the allied army close on his heels. Eventually, he would be forced to recognize that it would be impossible to

Major General Sir William Erskine.

cross the river while fighting a close rearguard action, and would be forced to abandon his plan for a northward withdrawal in favour of heading east back to Spain, a daunting prospect across devastated country.

Combat at Redinha: 12 March 1811

On 12 March Ney fell back 8 miles towards the Mondego, with the Light Division and cavalry hot on his heels, skirmishing with the rearguard en route. Captain Jenkinson of Ross's troop recorded that the army was expecting a fight:

> The enemy, however, disappointed us, and profited from the obscurity of night to withdraw to a more commanding situation. We continued our pursuit, and after a march of three hours came up with him strongly posted, with a show of considerable force, and a disposition to stand fast.

At Venda da Cruz Major William Napier of the 43rd Light Infantry described the French position on

> a high tableland on which Ney had disposed 5,000 infantry, a few squadrons of cavalry, and some light guns. His centre was opposite the hollow road, his wings were covered by wooded heights, which he occupied with light troops; his right rested on the ravine of the [Rio] Soure [Rio Arunca]; his left on the [Rio] Redinha [Rio Anços], which circling round his rear fell into the Soure. Behind him the village of Redinha, situated in a hollow, covered a narrow bridge and a long and dangerous defile; and, beyond the stream, some very rugged heights, commanding a view of the position in front of the village, were occupied by a division of infantry, a regiment of cavalry, and a battery of heavy guns, all so skilfully disposed as to give the appearance of a very considerable force.[5]

The allies approached Ney's outposts at Venda da Cruz with Picton's 3rd Division on the right, Cole's 4th Division and Pack's Portuguese in the centre and the Light Division on the left flank. The 1st Division followed, while the 6th was marching on Coimbra to the west with the aim of turning the French flank.

By 1400 hours Wellington was ready to attack, believing that the whole of Ney's corps was deployed before him rather than a single division. His plan was for Cole and Pack to fix Mermet's division, while the 3rd and Light divisions enveloped the flanks of the French position via some steep and wooded ground. The 3rd Division, in Picton's words, made a 'march over a rocky mountain to turn their left flank'. Erskine sent forward the 52nd Light Infantry, a company of the 43rd and two of the 95th Rifles to clear the French outposts from the wooded slopes. Lieutenant Kincaid, as he makes clear, was up with the fighting:

> Be it known then, that I was one of a crowd of skirmishers who were enabling the French ones to carry the news of their own defeat through a thick wood, at an infantry canter, when I found myself all at once within a few yards of one of their regiments in line, which opened such a fire, that had

92 *Masséna at Bay*

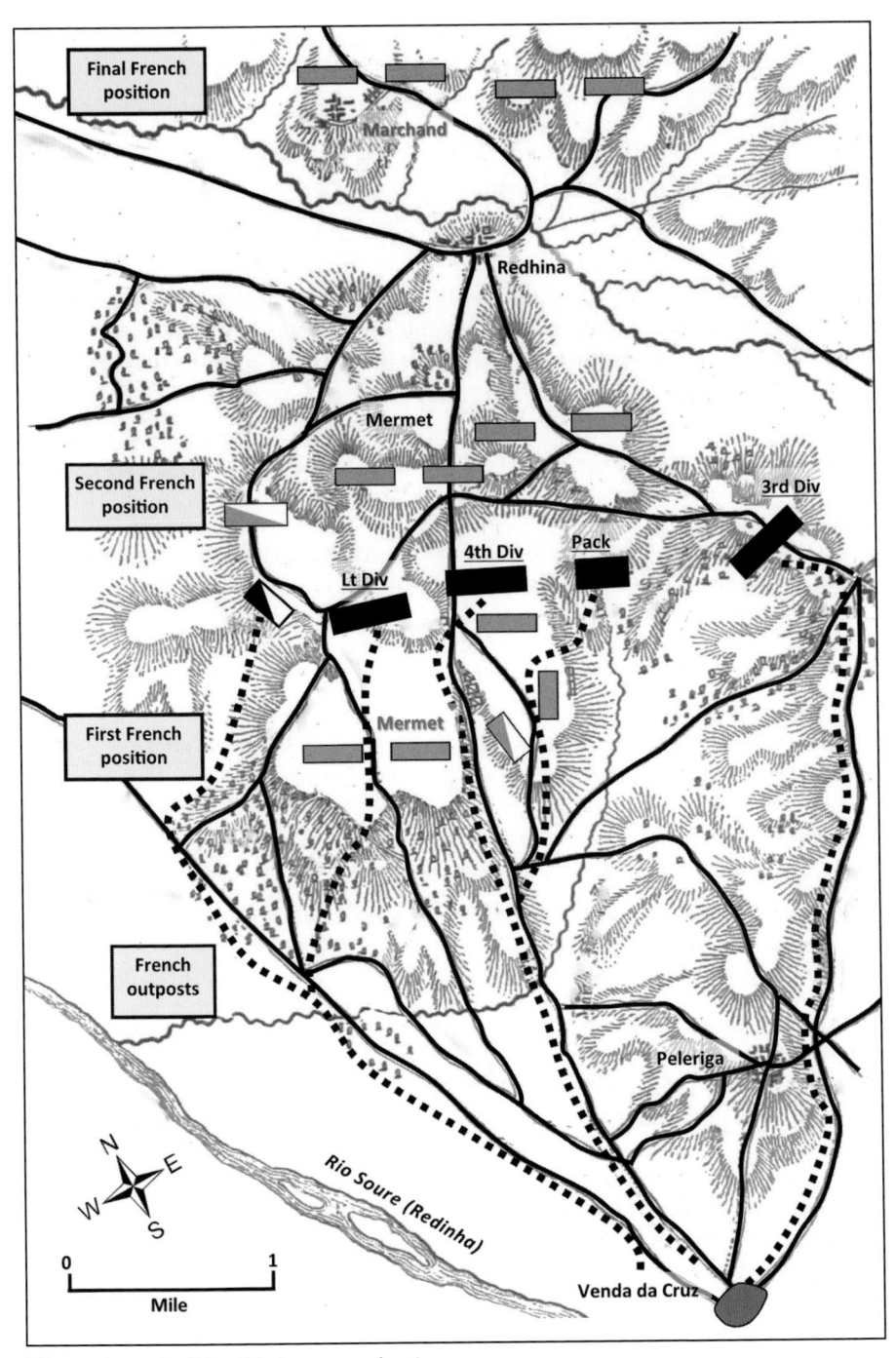

The combat at Redhina: Ney's rearguard action.

I not, rifleman-like, taken instant advantage of the cover of a good fir tree, my name would have unquestionably been transmitted to posterity by that night's gazette.

In a report to Lord Liverpool, Wellington wrote: 'Major General Sir William Erskine particularly mentioned the conduct of the 52nd Regiment, and Colonel Elder's Caçadores, in the attack of the wood; and I must add that I have never seen the French infantry driven from a wood in a more gallant style.'

Gallant, indeed. Within an hour the British skirmishers had driven back the opposing light troops and the Light Division emerged onto the plain and pushed forward with perhaps too much enthusiasm. Ney promptly launched a counterattack with the 3rd Hussars and 6th Dragoons. Major Napier recalled that

> the French battalions, supported by four guns, immediately opened a heavy rolling fire, and at the same moment, Colonel Ferrière, of the 3rd French Hussars, charged and took fourteen prisoners. This officer, during the whole campaign, never failed to break in upon the skirmishers in the most critical moments, sometimes with a squadron, sometimes with only a few men; he was always sure to be found in the right place, and was continually proving how much may be done, even in the most rugged mountains, by a small body of good cavalry.

With the check to the Light Division, Wellington explained that there was a delay:

> There was but one narrow bridge [at Venda da Cruz], and a ford close to it, over the Redhina river, over which our light troops passed ... but as the enemy commanded these with cannon, some time elapsed before we could pass over a sufficient body of troops and make a fresh disposition to attack the heights on which they had again taken post [Merle's first position].

In due course Erskine had five battalions deployed in line, supported by cavalry and Ross's troop of guns. Rifleman Costello was among those who appeared on the crest overlooking a plain:

> From its eminence, I remember to have seen one of the finest views of the two armies I ever witnessed. The Rifles were extended in the distance for perhaps 2 miles and were rapidly on the advance to the enemy's position. These were followed by our heavy columns, whose heads were just emerging from a wood about a quarter of a mile in our rear. Everything seemed conducted with the order and regularity of a field day. Meanwhile the rear columns of the French were slowly retiring, but in a few minutes the scene became exceedingly animated by our artillery opening their fire upon the retreating forces.
>
> This was the signal for us to set to work. We instantly moved down from our lofty station and were soon engaged skirmishing and endeavouring to out-flank and drive in their light troops, which, after a hard struggle, we at

The 3rd Hussars were distinctive in their grey uniforms with red braid and lace.

length accomplished, but not before many men had fallen on both sides. The enemy, however, although they slowly retired, continually turned, making temporary stands, whenever the ground seemed favourable.

The 'heavy columns' seen by Costello belonged to the 4th Division which was advancing in the centre and the 3rd Division on the right. General Picton described his division's march:

> ... at 5 o'clock in the morning, this division was again detached over goat paths and precipices, to make a demonstration on the rear of the enemy's left, and if possible to pass the river in their rear. After many hours' laborious marching over shelving rocks, and through difficult ravines, where we, with difficulty, crawled on one by one, we at length suddenly appeared considerably in their rear, which again made them decamp, and we succeeded passing the river at a ford and defile where twenty men might easily have stopped the whole division.

Charles Hamilton-Smith's depiction of riflemen of the 60th and 95th. Both regiments were in action at Redinha.

96   Masséna at Bay

Major Napier wrote of the ensuing action:

> Nevertheless, that marshal [Ney], observing that Lord Wellington, deceived as to his real numbers, was bringing the mass of the allied troops into line, far from retreating, even charged Picton's skirmishers, and continued to hold his ground with an astonishing confidence if we consider his position; for the 3rd Division was nearer to the village and bridge than his right, and there were already cavalry and guns enough on the plain to overwhelm him. In this posture both sides remained for about an hour, when three shots were fired from the British centre as a signal for a forward movement, and suddenly a most splendid spectacle of war was exhibited. The woods seemed alive with troops, and in a few moments 30,000 men, forming three gorgeous lines of battle, were stretched across the plain, bending on a gentle curve, and moving majestically onwards, while horsemen and guns, springing forward simultaneously from the centre and from the left wing, charged under a general volley from the French battalions: the latter were instantly hidden by the smoke, and when that cleared away no enemy was to be seen!

Ney had been able to remain in position for so long mainly because the 3rd Division had difficulty crossing the river and was, consequently, delayed in assembling in any significant strength on the heights. They had been counter-attacked by the 25th and 50th regiments of the line and brought to a temporary halt but the 4th Division was, however, coming into action. Private John Cooper of the 7th Royal Fusiliers was among them:

> Next day, the enemy being hardly pressed, made a stand near the village of Redinha. After skirmishing in a wood on our left, we debouched into the open plain, and prepared to attack. 'Form close column'; 'prime and load'; 'fix bayonets'; 'shoulder [arms]'; 'slope [arms]'; 'silence'; 'steady'; 'deploy into line'; 'forward'. We moved across the plain in three or four parallel lines towards the French batteries, which now opened upon us briskly. This was immediately followed by as heavy a fire of musketry as I ever heard in the Peninsula. The balls flew from both combatants like hail. But this duel did not last long: the enemy gave way, and carried off their artillery at a rattling pace, followed by loud English hurrahs, and our skirmishers.[6]

In his report to Lord Liverpool Wellington commented: 'The light infantry of General Picton's division, under Colonel Williams, and the 4th Caçadores, under Colonel de Regoa, were principally concerned in this operation.'[7] The ground across which they fought was broken by ravines, walls and woods, where light infantry were at their best.

Marshal Ney's aim was to delay the allied advance, and only once he saw that the Light and 3rd divisions were about to envelop his flanks did he order Mermet to withdraw. It was well-timed, if a little late. Napier continued:

> Ney, keenly watching the progress of this grand formation, had opposed Picton's foremost skirmishers with his left, and, at the same moment,

withdrew the rest of his people with such rapidity, that he gained the village ere the cavalry could touch him: the utmost efforts of Picton's skirmishers and of the horse artillery scarcely enabled them to gall the hindmost of the French with their fire.

One French howitzer, however, was hit by a British battery and dismounted and, in a display of physical bravery that matched his tactical handling of the rearguard, Ney led the saving of the gun. Lieutenant Kincaid was with the Rifles following the withdrawing French:

> ... a last and a desperate stand [was] made by their rearguard, for their own safety, immediately above the town, as their sole chance of escape depended upon their being able to hold the post until the only bridge across the river was clear of the other fugitives. But they could not hold it long enough; for, while we were undergoing a temporary sort of purgatory in their front, our comrades went working round their flanks, which quickly sent them flying, with us intermixed, at full cry, down the streets.
>
> When we reached the bridge, the scene became exceedingly interesting, for it was choked up by the fugitives who were, as usual, impeding each other's progress, and we did not find that the application of our swords to those nearest to us tended at all towards lessening their disorder, for it induced about 100 of them to rush into an adjoining house for shelter, but that was getting regularly out of the frying-pan into the fire, for the house

A French 6-pounder Gribeauval-system howitzer.

The Romanesque bridge across the river at Redhina.

happened to be really in flames, and too hot to hold them, so that the same 100 were quickly seen unkennelling again, half-cooked, into the very jaws of their consumers.

John Bull, however, is not a bloodthirsty person, so that those who could not better themselves had only to submit to a simple transfer of personal property to ensure his protection. We, consequently, made many prisoners at the bridge, and followed their army about a league beyond it, keeping up a flying fight until dark.

The 3rd and 4th divisions followed the Light Division, including Private Cooper of the 7th Fusiliers: 'We hurried through the burning village to overtake them; but they waded the river and made good use of their legs. Marshal Ney commanded the retreat, and did it well, so that few prisoners were taken.'

Donaldson of the 94th recorded that 'A portion of the [3rd] division crossed the river by swimming, headed by Major Lloyd; but the columns moved on towards the bridge ... Our troops having crossed the river drove them back upon the main body [Marchand's division].'

Wellington began to re-form the line to resume the advance, but Ney withdrew towards Condeixa, which was just 6 miles from Coimbra and the Mondego bridge. Even though the allies had only advanced some 10 miles during the 12th, they were now exerting too much pressure for Masséna to consider fighting to get across the river and conducting a rearguard action at the same time.

It is worth noting that French accounts all mention defensive success, heavy casualties to the enemy and only minor losses to themselves. Ney did repeatedly delay the allies and withdraw in reasonable order when he was manoeuvred or otherwise driven out of successive positions by Wellington. French losses of men and material, however, mounted during the retreat and of course Masséna was deflected from his chosen course of action north of the Mondego. Captain Noël's account of Redinha reads:

> The Anglo-Portuguese army, constantly reinforced by the arrival of new troops, had by the 12th, increased to 25,000 men [*sic* approx. 16,000 engaged]. With such a force, its general thought that he could attack the 6th Corps, which consisted of fewer than half that number. He attacked the front and attempted to outflank the 6th Corps on both sides. Ney halted his men before Redinha in a favourable position, kept one division in reserve and, using his infantry, cavalry and artillery with the skill and boldness he always displayed in the presence of the enemy, pushed the English back on all fronts, putting 1,800 [*sic* 206] of their men out of action. If he had not feared risking too much, he would have routed them completely.

Marshal Masséna was virtually alone among the French commanders in wanting to remain in Portugal. Ney and other generals firmly believed that they should return to the borders of Spain and the suspicion is that they didn't try too hard to make Masséna's plans work. For example, Montbrun was sent with his dragoons

The Rio Mondego and the bridge at Coimbra.

to locate fords that the staff had been told about, but after three days they could not find them and a skirmish with the Portuguese around the Coimbra bridge resulted in an unlikely success for Trant's *ordenanza*. Add to this Ney's unauthorized withdrawal from Pombal, and there is a convincing picture of continuing disloyalty and deliberate undermining of their commander's plan. Captain Noël summarized:

> If the rumours that were circulating were well-founded, it appeared that Marshal Ney's impatience to leave Portugal, together with the tendency to insubordination that he had shown throughout the campaign – and he had never concealed it – would be sufficient to foil the Prince of Essling's plan. By retreating precipitately, without having been attacked, from Condeixa, which he had been ordered to defend, Marshal Ney, so brave and determined during the retreat, had delivered up the road leading from Coimbra to the lower Mondego to the enemy, forcing the commander-in-chief to return up the valley formed by this river and its tributaries and subsequently continue his withdrawal into Spain. I report this rumour, although I do not usually pay much attention to army gossips, as it gained credibility from the fact that General Junot and the 2nd Division, together with General Montbrun, were suddenly recalled from the lower Mondego, where they were constructing a bridge over the river and where, after the 6th Corps retreated from Condeixa, they were in danger of being cut off.

Chapter Five

Pursuit to Spain

On 13 March, with the allies having fought at Redhina and advanced 10 miles towards Coimbra the previous day, Masséna, who had not entirely given up hope of crossing the Mondego, recast his plans. He now hoped to secure a crossing of the Mondego further east near Ponte da Mucela and thus be able to rest his army in a fertile part of northern Portugal until reinforced. He had contemplated standing and fighting at Condeixa, but patrols informed him of Wellington's manoeuvring, which on the previous day saw the 3rd Division taking to narrow tracks through the hills to turn his left flank, while the 6th Division was committed to a similar venture on his right. The Light and 4th divisions would again be in the centre. This pattern of the Light Division leading the advance and engaging the enemy while the 3rd Division executed a flanking march was used throughout Wellington's pursuit of Masséna. Lieutenant Grattan commented that the division's marches invariably saw the enemy retiring as they marched into sight: 'The Light Division, so celebrated even at this early period of the war, was ever in advance; it had almost all the fighting as well as the fag, while ours (the 3rd) had plenty of fag but scarcely any fighting. The army, however, soon afterwards styled us "The Fighting Division".'

Wellington explained the basis of his plan for the 13th, having seen Masséna's baggage moving off towards Ponte da Mucela:

> From this circumstance I concluded that Colonel Trant had not given up Coimbra, and that they [the French] had been so pressed in their retreat, that they had not been able to detach troops to force him from that place. I therefore marched the 3rd Division, under Major General Picton, through the mountains upon the enemy's left, towards the only road open for their retreat, which had the immediate effect of dislodging them from the strong position of Condeixa; and the enemy encamped last night at Casal Novo, in the mountains, about a league from Condeixa.[1]

The French had indeed moved off promptly towards Miranda do Corvo, in time to avoid being caught strung out in the defiles by Picton's flank march.

That evening Masséna halted at Fuente Cubierta, believing that Ney's rearguard was still between him and the allied advanced guards, but VI Corps had withdrawn further east some hours earlier and the message informing Masséna of this was delayed. Along with his staff, the marshal had with him, according to Marbot, 'only thirty grenadiers and twenty-five dragoons' and

> finding the place agreeable and the weather fine, he had ordered his dinner to be served in the open air. We were sitting quietly at table under the trees

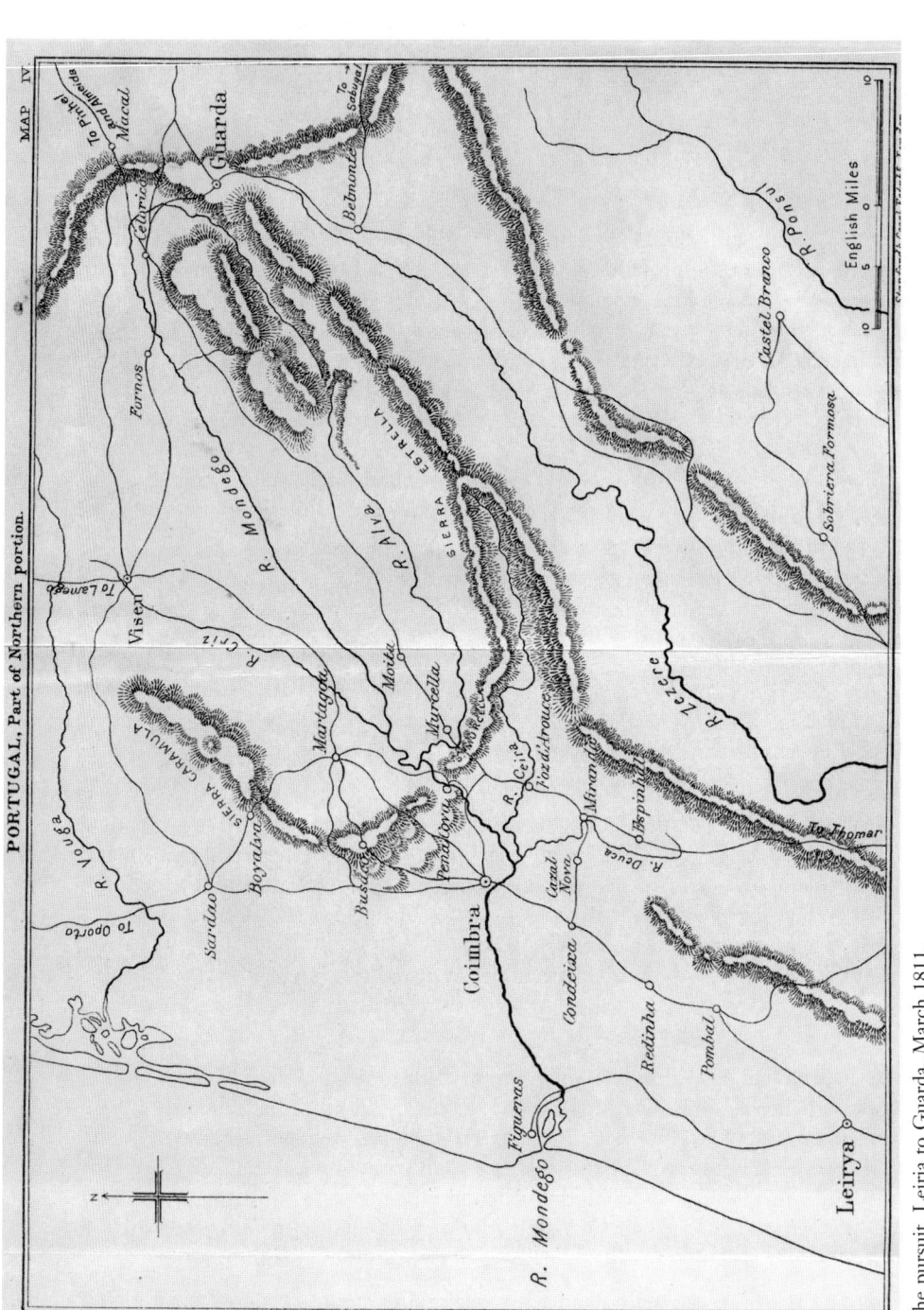

The pursuit, Leiria to Guarda, March 1811.

Marshal Ney, commander of VI Corps, and the rearguard during the retreat to Spain.

near the entrance of the village, when suddenly there appeared a detachment of fifty English hussars, less than 100 yards away.[2] The grenadiers surrounded Masséna, while the aides-de-camp and the dragoons mounted and rode towards the enemy. As they fled at once, we supposed they were some stragglers, seeking to re-join their army; but we soon saw an entire regiment, and perceived that the neighbouring hillsides were covered with English troops who had almost completely surrounded Fuente Cubierta.[3]

The Hussars had not realized how close they were to capturing the enemy's army commander. Nonetheless, Masséna had to cut his way out along with his staff and escort, with, according to Major Napier, the marshal removing the feathers from his hat to disguise his identity.[4] The resulting night's march for the headquarters was tortuous, being via a typically poor road and with brushes with the 3rd Division's outposts. The march is probably best remembered for Marbot's account of his brother, an English-speaker, bluffing their way past a cavalry regiment, and the misfortunes of Masséna's mistress:[5]

> During this toilsome march, Masséna was much occupied with the danger to which Mme. X – was exposed. Several times her horse fell over fragments of rock invisible in the darkness, but although cruelly bruised, the brave woman picked herself up. After several of these falls, however, she could neither remount her horse nor walk on foot and had to be carried by grenadiers. What would have happened to her if we had been attacked, I do not know. The marshal, imploring us all the time not to abandon her, said repeatedly: 'What a mistake I made in bringing a woman to the war!' However, we got out of the critical situation into which Ney had brought us.

Combat at Casal Novo: 14 March 1811

On 14 March the French halted in a strong position at Casal Novo in order to allow the artillery and baggage to get to the rear, through the town and difficult defiles towards Miranda do Corvo. The French were closely pursued by the

The pursuit to Spain, March 1811.

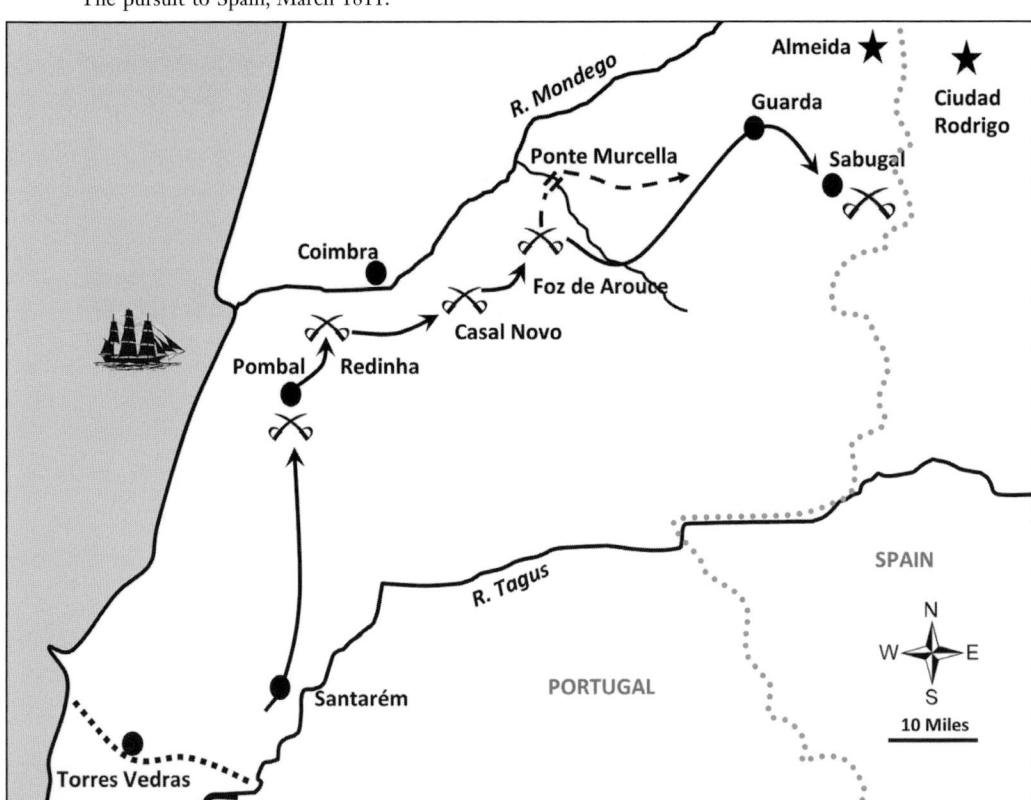

army's advanced guard provided by Major General Sir William Erskine's Light Division, with Arentschildt's cavalry and Pack's Portuguese under command. Their orders were to remain in contact with VI Corps. Picton's division was again advancing on the right flank.

Overnight the Light Division's piquets had been at close quarters with those of the enemy, separated only by a narrow valley bottom. Sounds of activity and movement during the night had been interpreted as the French artillery and baggage going to the rear; it was, however, a substantial body of VI Corps assembling in front of Casal Novo to cover the rest of the Army of Portugal's retreat to the east. Major George Napier recalled that Erskine

> ... came up and asked why we were not in march and following the enemy. Colonel Ross[6] said because the enemy were not gone but were within cannon shot of us at that very moment, for the captains of the pickets, [William] Napier, 43rd, and Dobbs,[7] 52nd, had patrolled up to their sentinels a short time before, and reported that the enemy was still in position. This did not satisfy Sir William Erskine, who kept blustering and swearing it was all nonsense and that the captains of the pickets knew nothing about the matter, and that there was not a man of them there.[8]

Major William Napier recorded that there was a morning fog:[9]

> The morning was so obscured that nothing could be descried at the distance of 100 feet ... nevertheless Erskine, with an astounding negligence, sent the 52nd forward in a simple column of sections, without a vanguard or other precaution, and even before the piquets had come in from their posts. As the road dipped suddenly, descending into a valley, the regiment was immediately lost in the mist, which was so thick that the troops, unconsciously passing the enemy's outposts, had like to have captured Ney himself, whose bivouac was close to the piquets. The riflemen followed in a few moments, and the rest of the division was about to plunge into the same gulf, when the rattling of musketry and the booming of round shot were heard, and the vapour slowly rising, discovered the 52nd on the slopes of the opposite mountain, engaged, without support, in the midst of the enemy's army.[10]

George Napier explained what had happened:

> Still the wise Sir William was sure it could be nothing but a single gun or two and a piquet of the enemy and desired Colonel Ross [52nd LI] to send my company [and Captain Jones's] to drive them in on the flank ... I pushed forward immediately and had just leapt with the men over a low wall into a narrow road and was almost instantly charged by a squadron of dragoons which was waiting for us behind some trees.
>
> However, by this time it was broad daylight and the mist nearly dispersed; so perceiving what it was, and seeing the French officer commanding the squadron at its head, I had just time to form up half a dozen files and, giving

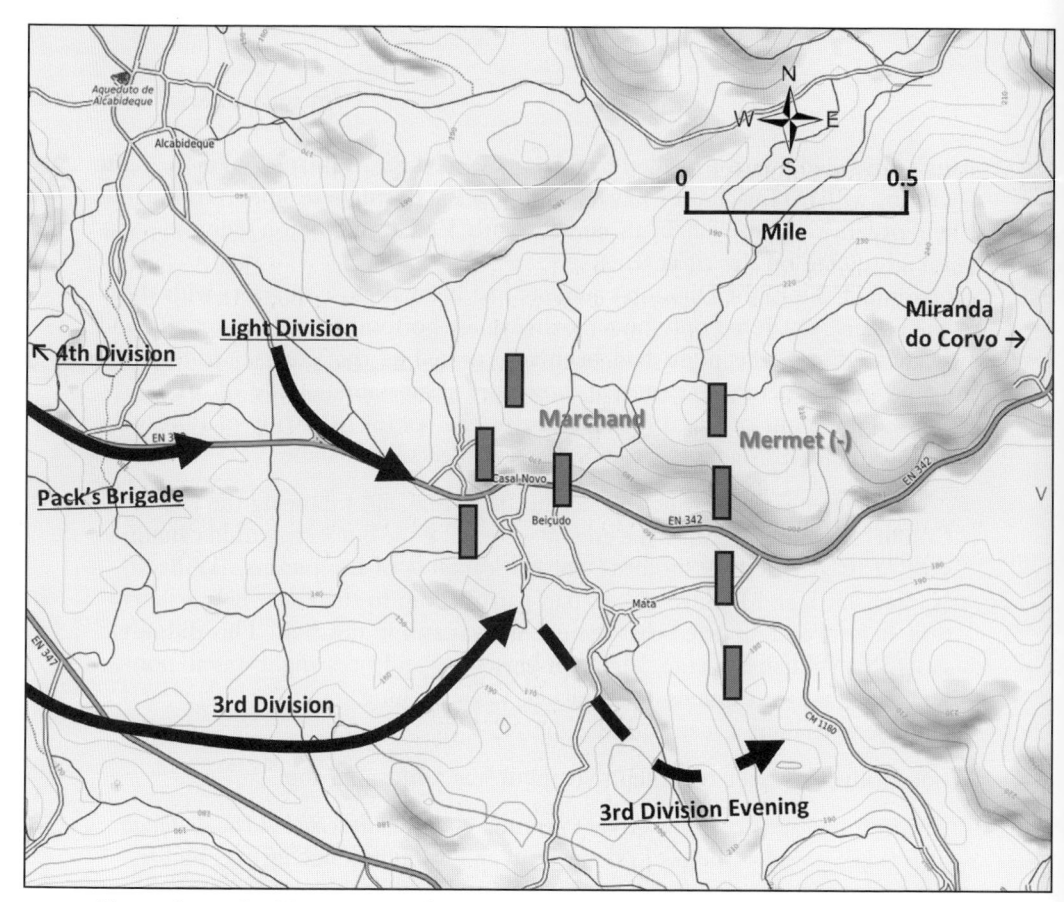

The combat at Casal Novo, 14 March 1811.

the gentlemen a volley, down came the officer and a few of his men and horses, upon which the rest galloped off and I instantly made my company leap over the opposite wall into a vineyard where I knew I was safe from their cavalry; and forming a line of skirmishers, I advanced towards a French brigade which was drawn up at some distance in my front. However, they sent forward a cloud of sharpshooters to oppose me, and in a few minutes the action became very sharp.

I continued advancing, but very slowly, for they were quadruple my strength; which my commanding officer, who was following with the regiment, perceiving, sent several other companies to my support, and ere long we were 400 strong, under Major Stewart, of the Rifle Corps. We then made a grand push, and drove the enemy from vineyard to vineyard, constantly advancing and keeping up a hot fire, the whole Light Division supporting us.

It was the left wing of the 1st 95th under Major Stewart that had also been sent forward to support the 52nd, but the French, occupying some stone walls, could not be driven back and Major Gilmour's right wing was deployed from support to join the fight. Rifleman Costello recalled: 'The country all about was greatly intercepted by old walls and afforded excellent facilities for skirmishing. In a few seconds some of our division was observed moving upon our right, and we were ordered instantly to extend, and at it we went.'[11]

In what was becoming a protracted fight, the fog finally cleared to confirm what the Light Division's officers had been claiming since dawn: that they were not dealing with just a rearguard but the whole of Ferey's brigade, with the rest of Marchand's eleven battalions drawn up on the ridge beyond. It was a dangerous situation with the division's five battalions either committed to battle in skirmish order or strung out along the road being engaged by Marchand's artillery. As with the combat on the Côa, it was the quality of the Light Division's officers and men that saved Erskine from presiding over a disaster.

At this point Wellington, who on hearing the boom of artillery had ridden forward, arrived and saw the 52nd and 95th isolated among the French and described them as 'appearing like a red pimple on the face of the country, black

General Jean Marchand, commander of Ney's 1st Division.

A cross-belt plate belonging to the 52nd Light Infantry found in the peninsula.

with the French masses!' A further reinforcement of six companies of the 43rd under Major William Napier was deployed to their aid. Meanwhile, the 3rd Division had advanced and 'relieved a potentially dangerous situation' created by Erskine's negligence, by starting to drive in the enemy's left flank.

Wellington, in a report to Lord Liverpool, outlined his plan:

> Accordingly, I moved the 4th Division, under Major General Cole, upon Penela, in order to secure the passage of the River Deixa [*sic*], and the communication with Espinhal, to which place Major General Nightingall had been in observation of the movements of the enemy's corps since the 10th; and the 3rd Division, under Major General Picton, moved immediately round the enemy's left; while the Light Division, and Brigadier General Pack's brigade, under Major General Sir W. Erskine, turned their right; and Major General Alexander Campbell, with the 6th Division, supported the light troops ... These troops were supported by the cavalry, and by the 1st and 5th divisions, and Colonel Ashworth's brigade in reserve.

By late morning there was a pause in the fighting as most of the sixty cartridges carried by the infantrymen had been expended, but in mid-afternoon the Light

Pursuit to Spain 109

Division was resupplied with ammunition and with Pack's Portuguese Brigade in the centre and the 3rd Division on the right, the attack was renewed. According to the 43rd's regimental history, when the battle resumed around Casal Novo, 'The fight was vigorously carried on amidst numerous stone enclosures' and the 'enemy's right partly turned'.

A British 1805-pattern cartridge pouch, block and tin. Loose ready-made cartridges were placed in the holes in the block at the top of the pouch for immediate use. Below left, cartridges – loose patched and unpatched rifle balls. Packs of ten cartridges were stored in the tin at the bottom of the pouch.

By now George Napier was commanding the assault, being the senior officer standing, Major Stewart of the 95th having been killed:

> As soon as I got my men supplied with fresh ammunition, I moved forward with all the companies under my command, my brother William being my second as he was next senior officer. We drove the enemy from hill to hill with great slaughter, and about three o'clock, while leading on my men to charge a strong body of French which was a few yards before me, and which I thought I might be able to take prisoners, I received a shot in my right wrist which completely shattered it and forced me to go to the rear, as I was also very much fatigued, having been incessantly engaged with the enemy from three o'clock in the morning to past three o'clock in the day.

After some three hours Ferey's infantry were driven out of the village and up to the heights beyond. Meanwhile, the 3rd Division was in action. Picton wrote: '... we [were] engaged in a continual series of skirmishes until near 5 o'clock in the evening. This day afforded a complete military lesson in this kind of warfare.'

Wellington summarized the effect of his deployment:

> These movements obliged the enemy to abandon all the positions which they successively took in the mountains, and the corps d'armée composing the rearguard were flung back upon the main body, at Miranda do Corvo, upon the river Deixa, with considerable loss of killed, wounded and prisoners.

VI Corps' stand at Casal Novo had bought time for Masséna to withdraw the rest of his army, and during the evening, Ney once again skilfully disengaged and withdrew Marchand's division 2 miles to a new position behind Mermet's division. When this was turned by a flanking march by the Light Division, the rearguard withdrew without a fight a further 4 miles east towards Miranda do Corvo. In somewhere over twelve hours of manoeuvring, Wellington had fought and marched across 14 miles of difficult ground. Lieutenant Kincaid wrote of that day:

> We drove them from one stronghold to another over a large tract of very difficult country, mountainous and rocky, and thickly intersected with stone walls and were involved in one continued hard skirmish from daylight until dark. This was the most harassing day's fighting that I ever experienced.[12]

For the Light Division, the combat at Casal Novo was the costliest day in the campaign to drive the Army of Portugal back to Spain, with the division suffering the majority of its 155 dead and wounded. George Napier's company of the 52nd was one of those most closely engaged throughout the day, and he commented:

> To show that it was pretty hot work I need only mention that I went into action with sixty-six soldiers, three sergeants, and three subalterns, and I lost one officer, one sergeant, and ten or twelve soldiers killed; myself, two sergeants, and about fifteen or sixteen wounded, so that of my original number nearly half were killed and wounded.

A pair of soldier's rough-side-out leather shoes. Ankle boots were first issued in 1812.

One other result of the day's fighting was that Erskine finally lost Wellington's remaining confidence, having early on in the day committed his division without proper reconnaissance or listening to the commanders of the piquets.

The week's march from Santarém had taken its toll on the allied army. Ensign Hay of the 52nd recorded that

> I was getting used to horrid sights but was terribly shocked at seeing the number of dead and dying, as we marched past, lying on the roadside. Our own men knocked up, and those of the enemy – poor fellows – alike unable to go further. My own kit, which was very limited, was in a sad plight! My stockings were worn out and I replaced them by strips of blanket laid in my shoes which were well worn by constant marching.
>
> We were moving all day and arrived with little and frequently nothing to eat, on some hillside where the French had taken up their position for the night. An hour before daybreak we were at it again.

Combat at Foz de Arouce, 15 March 1811

After the surprise in the fog the previous day there was a late start to the march on 15 March. General Picton recorded that

> The enemy again profited of the night, and of a very thick fog on the morning of the 15th, to withdraw to a strong position, covered by the river Ceira, leaving a very strong rearguard to cover the bridge of France de Raine [Foz de Arouce] and the approaches on the main road. We did not march

112 *Masséna at Bay*

until near eleven o'clock owing to the obscurity of the morning, and it was near two o'clock before we ascertained the situation of the enemy's rearguard. It was full four before the necessary dispositions could be made for the attack, which was again allotted to the Light and 3rd divisions.

Another sight that all of the commentators in the 3rd and Light divisions mention is the French draft animals abandoned when the Army of Portugal needed to lighten its load in order to get over the mountains to the Spanish frontier rather than cross the Mondego. Lieutenant Grattan recalls the approach to Miranda do Corvo:

> As we approached the town, the road leading to it was covered with a number of horses, mules and asses. All maimed; but the most disgusting sight was about fifty of these asses floundering in the mud, some with their throats half cut. Others were barbarously houghed, or otherwise injured... the poor brutes would have been of no use to us, or indeed anyone else, as I believe they were unable to have travelled another league; the meagre appearance of these creatures, with their backbones and hips protruding through their hides, and mangled and bleeding throats, produced a general feeling of disgust and commiseration.

Chef de Bataillon Pelet makes the point at length that the French soldiers and camp followers were not happy to lose their animals on the road to Foz de Arouce

The army commander's son, Captain Prosper Masséna, was one of the marshal's ADCs.

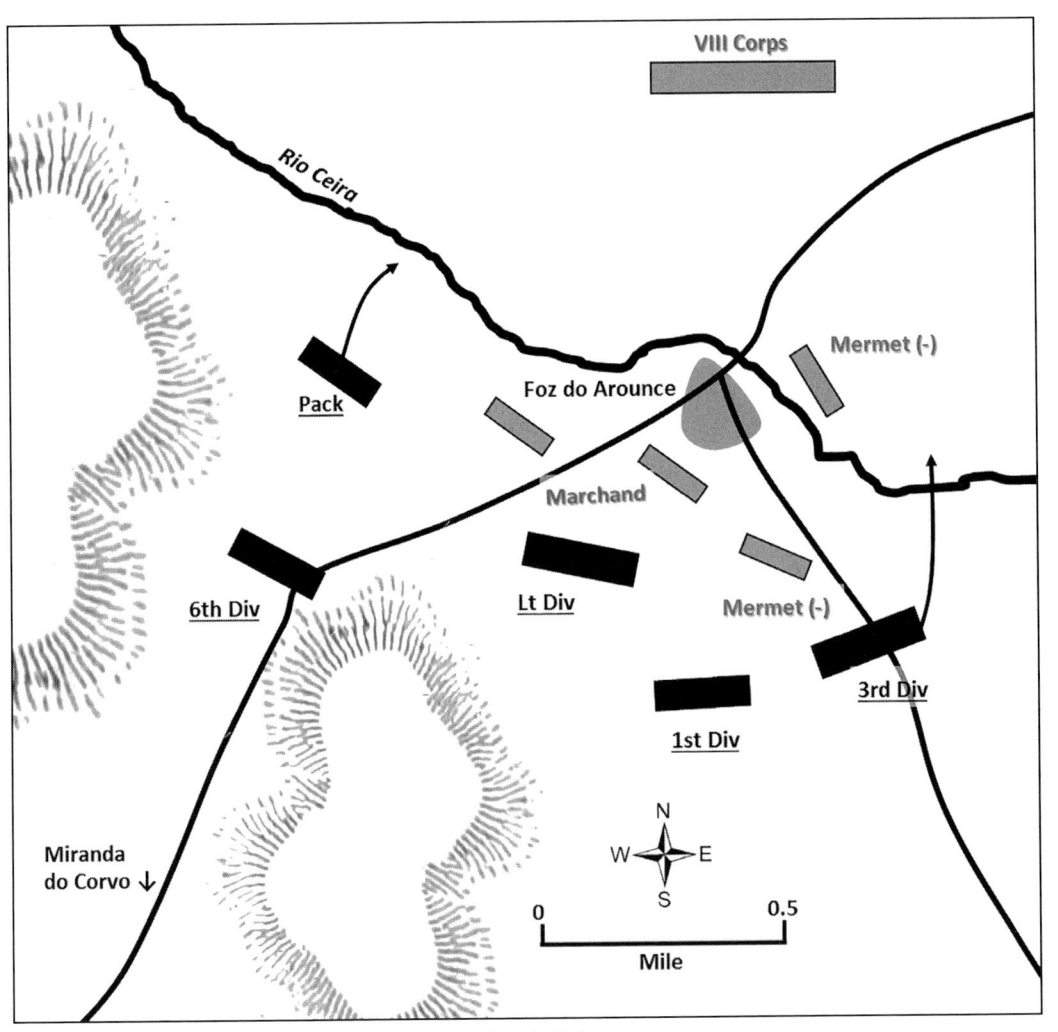

Outline of the combat of Foz de Arouce, 15 March 1811.

in what the army referred to as the 'Massacre of the innocents'. Some had avoided 'execution', but when they reached the bridge they were stopped:

> The men fled in all directions with their donkeys and threw themselves into the water to shield them from their murderers. Since the poor beasts were of a very small species in general, they could not cross the fords themselves as their drivers did; two soldiers would get together and carry them by the head and tail. The *cantinières* fought to defend their donkeys and several of them, their heads covered with feathers, gathered their silk or velvet dresses above their hips and carried their mounts across the river. On these donkeys were beautiful parrots, infants, monkeys and Japanese liquor services used as bottle cases.[13]

Ney had been ordered to cross the Rio Ceira and destroy the Foz de Arouce bridge, but instead, in what can only be described as an increasingly poisonous relationship between the Army of Portugal's marshals and generals, Ney had once again disobeyed orders. He left Marchand's division and half of Merle's west of the river as a strong rearguard. The Light Division, having followed a trail of VI Corps' hamstrung draft animals and abandoned vehicles of all types, reached the French outposts just short of Foz de Arouce where they had halted. The 52nd Light Infantry's historian wrote: 'The men had lighted fires, and were making preparations for bivouacking for the night, when the division was suddenly ordered to fall in, and instantly commenced a vigorous attack on Marshal Ney's corps.'

What had happened is that Wellington and his exploring officers had realized the vulnerability of Ney's faulty deployment forward of the Rio Ceira. One of Mermet's brigades was in the process of crossing to the right bank and deploying to cover a withdrawal of the rest of the division. With the river behind them in spate and with only a single damaged bridge for the French to retreat across, despite daylight fading, Wellington decided to attack Foz de Arouce.

Lieutenant Simmons was near his brigade commander, Colonel Beckwith, when Wellington rode up and made his decision. Simmons heard 'an order given by Lord Wellington himself to Colonel Beckwith: "Fall in your battalions and attack the enemy; drive in their skirmishers, and I will turn their flank with the 3rd and 1st Divisions".' The enemy was duly taken by surprise. Simmons continued: 'The whole Light Division were smartly engaged. The enemy opposed to the company I was with (Captain Beckwith's) were behind a low wall. The approach was through a pine wood, and the branches were rattling about our ears from the enemy's bullets.'

Lieutenant Kincaid witnessed some of the freshly-arrived reinforcements who, seeing that they had taken the enemy by surprise, pressed too far forward too quickly:

> About the middle of the action, I observed some inexperienced light troops rushing up a deep road-way to certain destruction, and ran to warn them of it, but I only arrived in time to partake the reward of their indiscretion, for I was instantly struck with a musket ball above the left ear, which deposited me, at full length, in the mud.

Unconscious, Kincaid was unable to witness the effect of this bold dash into the centre of the enemy position, already taken by surprise and with the 3rd Caçadores coming around the flank and into the village from the north and the 3rd Division approaching from the south closing in on the defenders, the French 25th Light Regiment. Simmons wrote in his diary that 'The French fought very hard, and, some finding resistance to be in vain, threw themselves upon our generosity, but the greater part rushed into the river, which was tumbling along in its course most furiously, and there soon found a watery grave.'

Outnumbered, the 25th Light Regiment gave way in confusion and fell back on the 39th Line, which was moving forward in support, but when their colonel was wounded, they promptly dissolved into panic. The soldiers of the two regiments rushed the 200 yards from the village to the bridge, which was jammed with vehicles and blocked by Ney's cavalry, which was in the process of being redeployed forward to help. As a result, the fleeing infantry attempted to ford the swollen Rio Ceira.[14]

Pelet accounts for the failure and its results:

> After a few moments of fine resistance as usual, alarm spread among our troops for some unknown reason. Some said that it was because Colonel Lamour had been killed in front of the 39th Line (he was only wounded and taken prisoner); others because the soldiers who were withdrawing the artillery were ordered to run. Perhaps it was because the soldiers felt that this was a bad disposition, since they were excellent judges of such matters and had been able to see all the defiles behind them. The fact was that the 25th *Léger*, a very brave regiment, was thrown back on the 39th Line and the latter on the 50th or 59th Line. Everything was extremely confused – all mixed up. The disorder was carried to the divisions of Marchand and Mermet. The cannon were abandoned in the village and everybody ran toward the bridge, which was crowded with troops. Instead of containing the

The combat of Foz de Arouce, 15 March 1811.

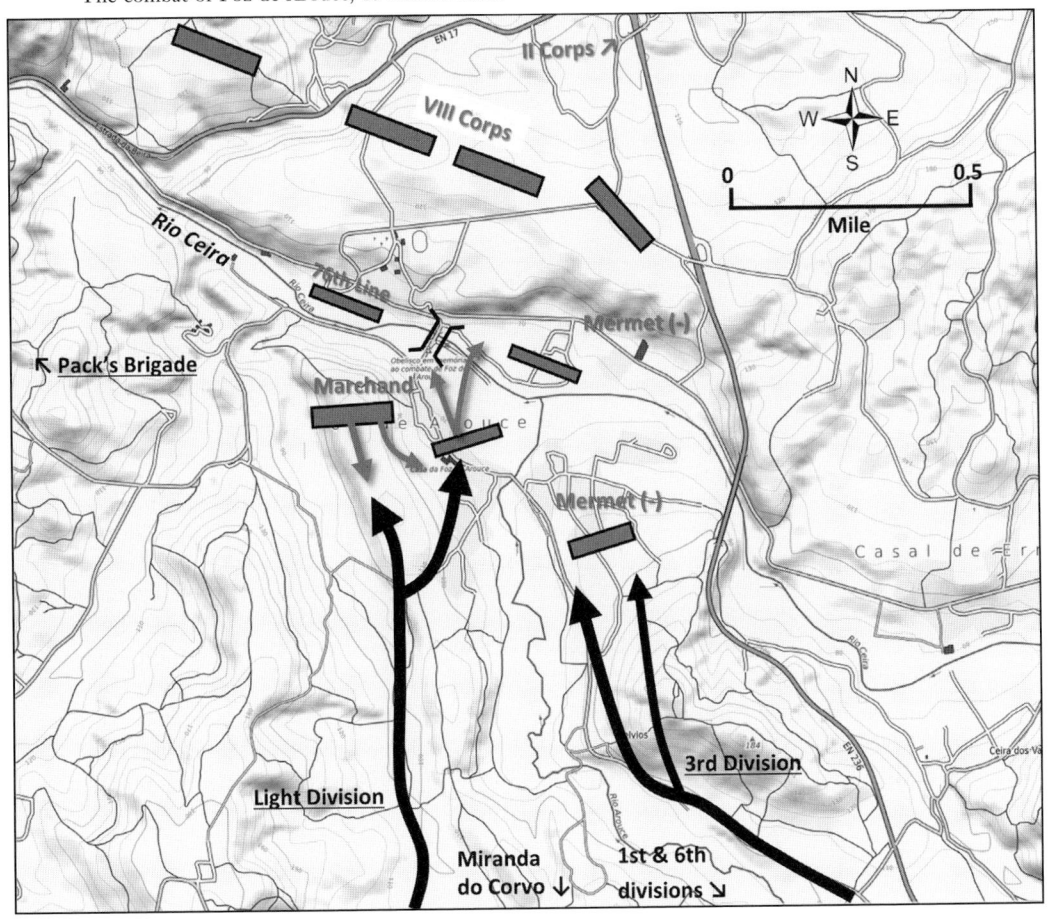

The bridge over the Rio Ceira at Foz de Arouce and the memorial to its liberation.

enemy or at least crossing by the ford, the light cavalry came through the middle of the infantry and trampled them.

Many French soldiers drowned as they struggled through the fast-flowing water which was already obstructed by caissons and waggons that had come to grief earlier. The eagle-bearer of the 39th was one of those who drowned, and the eagle was lost with him.[15]

While the French centre and left had collapsed, the regiments on the flank facing the Light Division remained steady, with Macune's brigade of Marchand's division (6th Light and 69th Line) still in position on the plateau immediately west of Foz de Arouce. Pelet again shed light on a confusing phase of the battle, including several incidences of fratricide, including one by Mermet's 76th Regiment:

> The 76th Line, which had crossed just before the attack, deployed itself on the right bank of the Ceira, firing against the plateau in the belief that they already saw the enemy there. The error was soon realised, but the embarrassment to the Marshal [Ney] was great. He always showed more strength of mind when the danger was greatest. Seeing the English advancing in force onto the heights through the pines and upon the village by the road, he directed a battalion of the 69th Line in tight column and a few companies of the 6th *Léger* to attack with bayonet. The other battalion was deploying with its left near Foz de Arouce. He had them execute a frontal change with the

The 1804-pattern French regimental eagle. These venerated symbols were personally presented by the Emperor.

right wing in front and then open ranks to fire point-blank on the English entering the village.

This sudden attack plus the fire of a dozen French guns from the right bank brought the Light Division and leading elements of the 3rd to a halt. Pelet adds more detail:

> Three companies of *voltigeurs* of the 39th Line, running ahead of our right, shooting and trumpeting continuously, continued their forward movement and found themselves behind the enemy columns. At length hideous shouts came from the bridge; perhaps the English believed that they were calls for an attack. All or some of these factors affected their columns; they were soon pushed back and started fleeing on their side while we fled on ours.

The now disorganized riflemen and Caçadores were forced out of the village and fell back on their supports provided by the 52nd. Lieutenant Grattan of the 88th Connaught Rangers summarized subsequent events thus: 'The village of Foz de Arouce was warmly contested, and more than once retaken.'

With both sides recoiling from the village, Ney's men were able to continue what Pelet described as a 'disorderly withdrawal', sped on its way by the grape-shot of both Ross's and Bull's troops, which had come up in support of their respective divisions. The French battalions started to re-form on the opposite bank, but it was now getting dark and, in the confusion, they again fired on one another; a fratricide that VIII Corps' artillery posted on the high ground to the rear joined. The bridge had been prepared for demolition and the French engineers promptly blew it, stranding some of their infantry on the wrong side.

With the French taken by surprise, believing that it had been too late in the day for further action, the British divisions found an unexpected and no doubt much appreciated bonus in Foz de Arouce:

> The attack had been sudden and unexpected, that they were obliged to leave their kettles boiling over their fires, to abandon their entire stock of provisions, among which was a supply of excellent biscuit; a great prize to our men, who, having outstripped the commissariat, had received no bread for four days.[16]

Rifleman Costello recalled that 'This afforded a happy regale to some of our unfortunate hungry stomachs; the more especially as the food thus come by was eaten with a sense of having been fairly earned.' Lieutenant Simmons, clearly relieved to be alive, recorded in his diary that

> We quartered ourselves in the French camp; they left us good fires. I roasted some pork which the French left, and had plenty of biscuit, took a glass of grog and a pipe, talked over the business of the day with my brother officers. Very happy to find I had a whole skin, which was more than I expected.

Picton summarized the action with a simple sentence: 'After a severe contest of about two hours, they were completely dispersed', and somewhat optimistically

Pursuit to Spain

Officier et Fusilier du 21me Regiment

French Line infantry.

added 'had not darkness unfortunately intervened, the whole of them must have been sacrificed.'

In the aftermath of the fighting, the rest of the army closed up onto the wooded hillsides above Foz de Arouce. Commissary Schaumann was with the German Hussars:

> Here we stood in order of battle until late in the evening when it grew dark and the rain came down in torrents. At last we were ordered to bivouac. As, however, you could not see your hand in front of your face, the infantry, artillery and baggage got badly mixed up, lost themselves in the wood, dashed into trees, the thick branches of which increased the darkness, and everywhere the cry arose: 'Have you seen this or that regiment?' As my baggage was still in the rear, I joined some men of our regiment, who with great pains at last succeeded in making a fire with branches from the pine trees; and in the end, whole trees were thrown into the flames.

Masséna's Retreat

After a week of solid marching, General Picton recorded that Wellington's army finally spent a day static before the river, having the enemy rearguard to their front and having outrun their supplies.[17] Picton explained:

> Our Army depended wholly for its subsistence on what we were able to transport from Lisbon on the backs of mules, which every day's march, indeed, every mile in advance rendered more difficult ... we were, in consequence, under the necessity of halting to wait for our resources, which could not possibly keep pace with the rapidity of our continual movements.

The army was not, however, entirely inactive, as Picton explains:

> On the 16th, the enemy, having blown up the bridge, made a great display of their force on the commanding hills behind the river, and the whole day was employed in reconnoitring and making the necessary dispositions, and at daybreak of the morning of the 17th, the 3rd Division was detached by a forced-march to possess itself of a passage over the river, and turn the enemy's left, whilst the other divisions of the army menaced their front.

While the allies awaited supplies and the building of a bridge, during the 16th the French stood in a strong position on the hills beyond the Rio Ceira but, as recalled by Captain Noël:

> During the night of the 16th/17th we ascended the Sierra Mucela and descended into the Alva valley [to Ponte da Mucela]. We crossed the bridge over this steeply-banked river boldly. The English had fortified the position and blown up the main arch of the bridge as a precaution in case our [invasion] route into Portugal took us by way of the left bank of the Mondego. Our sappers had soon rebuilt it. The Mucela bridge that we crossed was level

Major General Sir Thomas Picton. His flanking moves repeatedly saw Ney promptly resuming the retreat.

with the Alcoba on the right bank and, from the artillery park, we could clearly see the east side of the Buçaco mountain.[18]

It had been a withdrawal of 12 miles to the line of the Rio Alva which, judging by the French infantry's entrenching, Masséna hoped to hold.

Wellington, however, already knew it to be a very strong position for it was where he had intended to stand the previous September before Masséna diverted north of the Mondego to Buçaco. To avoid having to make a frontal attack that Picton confirms was 'impossible', on the 17th Wellington dispatched the 1st, 3rd and 5th divisions, plus the independent Portuguese brigades south-east to cross the Alva and turn Masséna's left flank. Meanwhile, the cavalry and the Light and

6th divisions were directed to head for Ponte da Mucela and its bridge over the Alva, which was as usual defended by Ney's rearguard.

The French spotted the allied movement upstream; having, however, only seen allied cavalry patrols at Ponte da Mucela, they assumed that it was the whole of the allied army heading from Foz de Arouce towards crossings higher up the Alva. This was a move that would cut off their line of retreat: the Celorico road to Spain.

Late on the 17th and into the 18th the allied divisions crossed the Rio Alva uncontested via a number of fords east of Pombeiro and the Light Division revealed itself at Ponte da Mucela to fix the attention of Ney's VI Corps. While the guns of the Light and 6th divisions made a noisy demonstration at Ponte de Mucela, the rest of the army north of the Alva crossed the Sierra de Guiteria to menace the French left. Picton wrote:

> On the 18th the 3rd Division was again detached to make a lateral movement and demonstration on the enemy's rear, which completely succeeded, as the

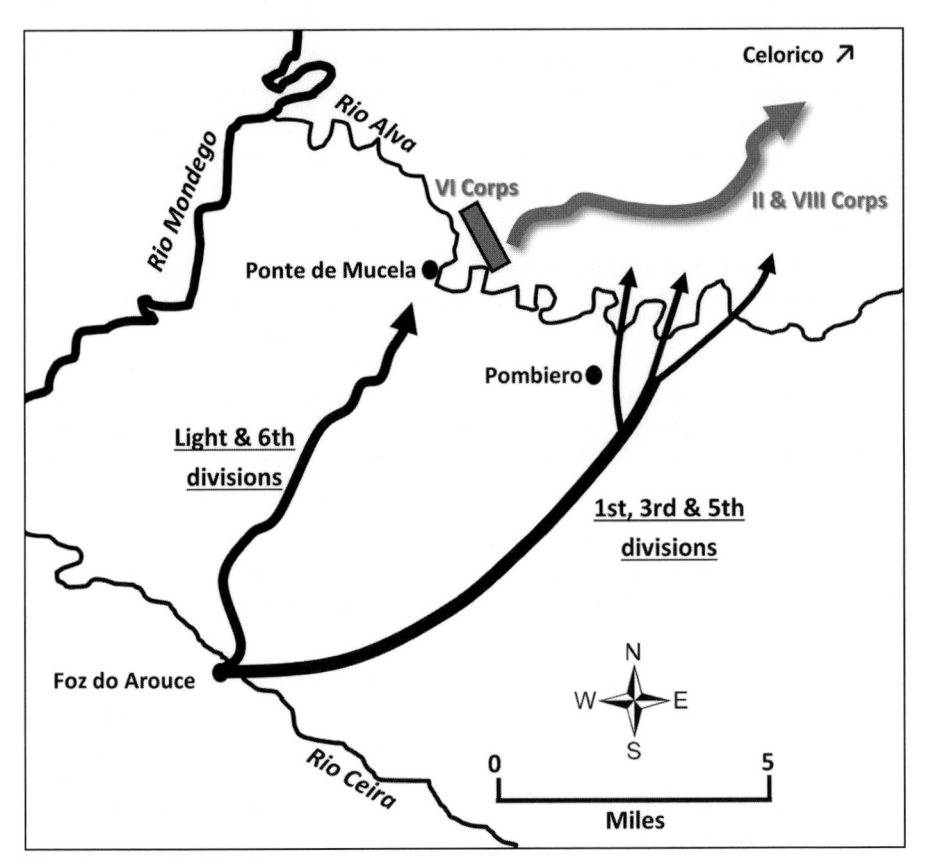

The advance to the Rio Alva.

enemy, on discovering it, immediately abandoned the position, and fell back with great precipitation, which left open the river to the [6th and Light] divisions which followed the main road.

Captain Noël was among those given orders to move immediately:

> We should have remained on the banks of the Alva but, at four in the afternoon of the 18th, we were ordered to leave at once for Galizes, where we arrived at one on the following morning. Almost immediately another order, to continue on our way, was received and we marched three leagues further; then all the artillery went on for yet another league, on the road to Celorico. At five in the evening we halted at last, having marched for twenty-five hours with exhausted horses harnessed to heavy vehicles!
>
> This sudden departure had been the result of a movement by the English threatening our left flank, which was, as always, ill guarded by the 2nd Corps who were, as usual, off marauding.

The speed with which the French were now retreating caused them considerable losses, not just among those who were unable to keep up with the march of their battalions. Not only were individuals taken prisoner on the road, but whole foraging parties as well. For example, on 20 March Captain Aly's squadron of the German Hussars which were on duty as the advance guard and 'under protection of fog made a most extensive capture consisting of one captain, three subalterns and 525 infantry, 1,200 sheep, twelve bullocks, and ten horses.'

Commissary Schaumann was with Arentschildt's light cavalry:

> We continued our pursuit, and found the plain covered with stragglers, dead Frenchmen, arms and baggage. Gradually they were compelled to abandon upon the high road all the silver, gold, valuables, silks and velvets, costly ecclesiastical vestments, monstrances and crucifixes, which they had plundered from the churches, convents and private houses; and as the Portuguese peasants cut the throats of all the Frenchmen they encountered, the Light Division became the heirs to all their abandoned treasure. The villages through which we marched were nothing but heaps of debris.[19]

On a typical day some 400 stragglers and men from isolated foraging parties were captured by the cavalry and the Light Division. Not all were, however, so lucky as to fall into allied hands. On one occasion Lieutenant Grattan of the 88th Connaught Rangers came upon

> two French soldiers of the 4th of the line – their appearance was frightful. They had been wounded by our advance, and their companions either being too much occupied in providing for their own safety to think of them, or, their situation being too hopeless to entertain an idea of their surviving, they were abandoned to the fury of the peasants, who invariably dodged on the flanks or in the rear of our troops. These poor wretches were surrounded by half a dozen Portuguese, who, after having plundered them, were taking that

An officer of the 16th Light Dragoons.

horrible vengeance too common during this contest. On the approach of our men they dispersed, but, as we passed on, we could perceive them returning like vultures that have been scared away from their prey for the moment, but who return to it again with redoubled voraciousness. Both the Frenchmen were alive and entreated us to put an end to their sufferings. I thought it would have been humane to do so, but Napoleon and Jaffa flashed across me, and I turned away from the spot.

Stories such as these are more easily understood when recalling the fate of numerous Portuguese at the hands of the French. Costello recounted one such incident during the French retreat:

The parents of one of our Caçadores had lived in this village, and immediately we entered, he rushed to the house where they resided. On reaching the doorway, the soldier hesitated a few seconds, but the door was open, and stretched across the threshold he beheld the mangled bodies of his father and mother, the blood still warm and reeking through the bayonet stabs, while an only sister lay breathing her last, and exhibiting dreadful proofs of the brutality with which she had been violated. The unhappy man staggered, frenzied with grief, and stared wildly around him.

During the retreat Wellington had to send a letter to Masséna via an ADC under a flag of truce

in order to remonstrate with him for the barbarous treatment of the poor inhabitants and also inform him that if this were not discontinued it would no longer be possible to protect numbers of French prisoners gathered together in the various depots against the fury of the populace.[20]

During this phase, as Picton pointed out again, 'allied resources could not possibly keep pace with the rapidity of our continual movements. The enemy, on the contrary, retreating through an untouched country, met with greater facilities in proportion as they fell back.' In this circumstance Wellington was forced to halt the 1st and 5th divisions and Pack's brigade for five days. All the remaining food that a single convoy had brought forward was issued to the Light, 3rd and 6th divisions, who along with the light cavalry would pursue the French.

Private Joseph Donaldson of the 94th was a hungry soldier serving in Picton's 3rd Division:

One day we had halted rather early; at this time we had been without rations for two days. Many a curse was poured on the head of the commissary, who was considered the responsible person.

'There comes the stores, at last,' cried one of the men. 'Where? Where?' said those around. Every eye was now directed to a hill at some distance, where a long train of mules were perceived successively rising over its summit and bending their way towards the division. The men were in transports of joy; a general cheer greeted their appearance. 'We will have full

Locally-hired bullock carts and brigades of mules were the backbone of Wellington's logistics.

rations to-day,' cried one, 'and rum too,' said another, 'for I can see casks on the mules.'

Another cheer succeeded this discovery; and we were dancing about overjoyed. 'Who goes for the rations? Get out blankets for the biscuit, and camp kettles for the rum.' There were soon enough of volunteers for this duty. The mules had by this time got into a sort of defile. Every eye was on the stretch, waiting for their re-appearance. As the first mule emerged from the place where they were hid, every face was dressed in smiles; but the next second produced an effect, similar to that which a criminal might feel, who had been informed of his reprieve on the scaffold, and the next moment told it was a mistake; for it turned out to be mules with ammunition for the division. Never did I witness such a withering effect on men, as this disappointment produced. We stood looking at each other for a minute, in all the agony of hope deferred: the next was opened by a torrent of execration on all concerned. Those who have never experienced extreme hunger can form no idea of our feelings.

For the divisions of the pursuing force the period to the end of the month is best characterized as one of repeated long, hungry and testing marches with only the cavalry occasionally making contact with the French rearguard. Lieutenant Simmons of the 95th concluded a letter home with the words 'We march in the morning, but the enemy seem to wish to be off and have no more to do with us.'

The Light Division's marches, regulated by General Craufurd's standing orders, were well-managed but Wellington complained 'all our troops, cavalry as well as infantry, are a little inclined to get out of order of battle.'[21] With newly-arrived battalions and moves from one division to another, Wellington took steps to improve performance. He wrote to Beresford on 20 March:

> Our divisions and their baggage make their marches (however short) so very ill, that I am obliged to halt the greatest part of the army again to-day. However, I have now begun a new system with them, which is, to state in the orders at what hour each is to start and is to arrive at each place. By degrees I shall bring them to some system.

Later that same day Wellington wrote to General Spencer whose 1st Division had provided an example of the problem:

> We certainly want a little practice in marching in large bodies, as at present no calculation can be made of the arrival of any troops at their station, much less of their baggage. The order for the march yesterday was sent by Reynett, who reported that he had delivered it at twenty minutes past eleven; the whole distance to be marched was not 5 miles, and yet the head of the column did not reach its ground till sunset. Seeing how late it was before the head had arrived at the turn of the road, I desired Murray to request you to halt any that had not crossed the river on this side of it. I conclude this order has miscarried, although it was sent from hence some time before sunset. In future I propose to order the period of departure and arrival of each division of the army, by which means I shall know exactly how all stands, and by degrees the troops will become more accustomed to march in large bodies on the same road.

During this phase of the retreat the British cavalry bore the brunt of the advance and attempted to keep in touch with the French. They consisted of two brigades: Lieutenant Colonel Frederick von Arentschildt's (16th Light Dragoons and 1st Hussars KGL[22]) and Major General John Slade's (1st Royal Dragoons and 14th Light Dragoons). They were supported by Ross's and Bull's Troops RHA. Patrols from the regiments' duty squadrons would fan out ahead of the supporting squadrons, confirming or identifying the route the enemy were taking and ensuring that there were no traps being laid for the main body of the brigade or the following infantry divisions.

The French advance guards reached Celorico on 21 March where they finally re-established communication with Almeida and Ciudad Rodrigo. Meanwhile, the British divisions, marching with negligible rations were rarely less than 15 miles behind them.

During the campaign to eject Masséna from Portugal dedicated provision was finally made for the transportation of the wounded. A German Hussar officer recalled in his memoirs:

> During the whole of this march every possible care and precaution was taken by the English authorities and Commander-in-Chief respecting accommodations for the sick and wounded. To each division was attached a certain

An officer of the 1st or Royal Dragoons wearing the pre-1812 uniform.

number of covered cars so contrived as to admit of about twelve men each, and, as they hung upon springs, the invalids were secured from jarring motion as well as from wet: upon these abominable roads, it is true, there was always some chance of an overthrow and, instead of two horses, which would have sufficed upon a decent highway, eight were absolutely necessary for every car.

Marshal Ney Dismissed

As the Army of Portugal neared the Spanish frontier, Masséna proposed swinging south into the Tagus valley, presumably believing it to be fertile and well-stocked instead of having been repeatedly denuded since the invasion of 1807. The corps' commanders were open and vociferous in their criticism; Marshal Ney, of course, was chief among the critics.

Ney had been lucky to escape dismissal before the invasion of Portugal the previous year and on several occasions since. His 'tendency to insubordination that he had shown throughout the campaign' had been expected by Masséna, who had warned Napoleon that this would be the case, but he was forced to tolerate him. It is widely believed that Ney, a popular commander, had only held on to his command because of a fear of the reaction of his corps, one that he had commanded since 1804.

At first Ney wrote to question the initial outline, and then when full orders arrived, he wrote again pointing out, quite correctly but in the strongest terms the fundamental faults in the plan: they lacked guns and ammunition; there was no food in the area; but, above all, the army needed rest. Then for the third time in three hours he again put pen to paper, this time announcing that on the following day he would be taking VI Corps back to Almeida. Faced with an insubordinate Ney verging on being mutinous, Masséna finally had to act. He relieved the younger marshal of his command and temporarily replaced him with General Loison.

Pelet was promptly dispatched to Paris to report Ney's dismissal to ensure that Masséna's side of the story reached the emperor first.

General of the division, Loison.

The Final Phase

In order to demonstrate that he was in command and that the 'spoilt child of victory' was not prepared to give up Portugal, Masséna stood by his orders and the army started to turn south from Guarda. These tentative moves, as had been predicted were in vain, when after five days of march it became obvious that Ney had been correct and starvation faced the army in the upper Tagus valley.

Meanwhile, the three allied divisions pursuing the Army of Portugal towards Guarda struggled on, receiving just one ration of bread in four days, while the 1st and 5th divisions awaited the arrival of convoys to feed and supply them before they could rejoin the advance. Wellington, with little information coming in from his exploring officers, was puzzled by Masséna's southerly movement but with a continuing French presence in the mountain town of Guarda he resolved to mount operations against them with the 3rd, 6th and Light divisions, but had to wait until 29 March when the 1st and 5th divisions would be moving up to within supporting distance. (A full transcript of Wellington's orders for 29 March which feature his enhanced march instructions is reproduced in Appendix II.)

Rather than the whole of the Army of Portugal in Guarda, it was two divisions of VI Corps providing the rearguard in what was now a general withdrawal of the

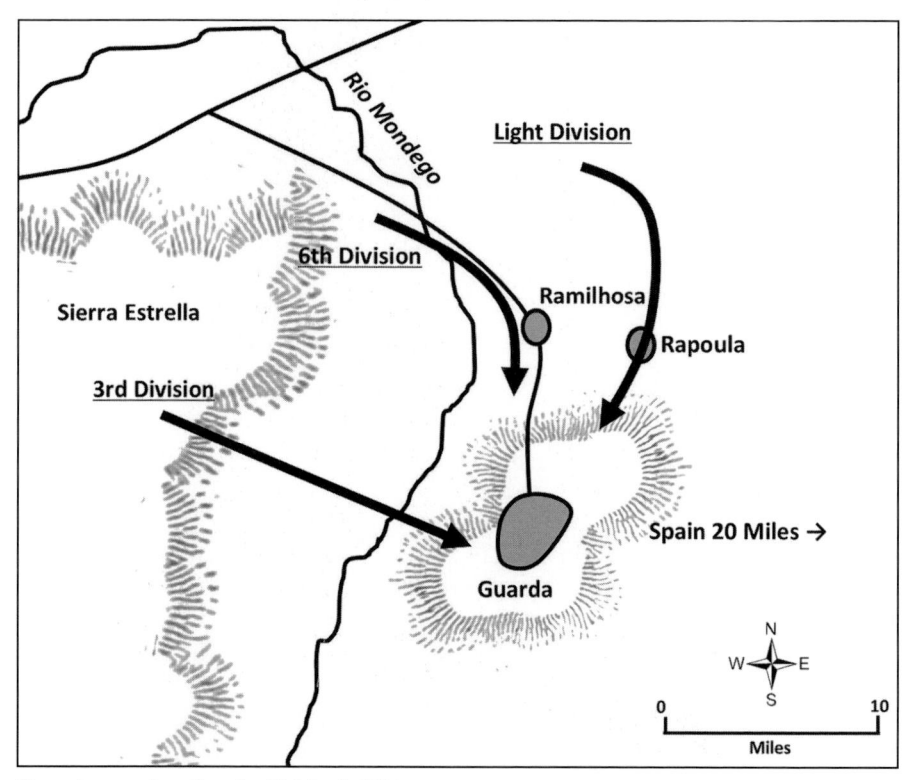

Operations against Guarda, 29 March 1811.

Portuguese line infantryman.

Army of Portugal to Spain. Picton's command was the first to approach the city at 0900 hours 'with three British and two Portuguese regiments'. He wrote that

> The 3rd Division passed the River Mondego at an unguarded ford before daylight, and, by a rapid march, fortunately got possession of the commanding ridge, on which the city of Guarda is situated, and suddenly appeared within 400 yards of Masséna's [sic Loison's VI Corps] headquarters, before he had any notice of its approach.
>
> He ought immediately to have attacked me but allowed me to remain within 400 yards of his main body for about two hours, before the other columns came up. But of course, their movements were alarming him, and decided him not to hazard an attack, the failure of which would have probably brought on the total discomfiture of his army.[23]
>
> The great general [sic, Loison] lost his head on the occasion, and ... he immediately withdrew, with precipitation, the bodies opposed to the other columns, and commenced his retreat, filing off about 20,000 within cannon shot of the Division. If the whole of our army had been up so as to take advantage of the favourable conjunction which presented itself, I have no doubt but we should have annihilated his whole corps. They marched off, followed by some squadrons of cavalry for a few miles, and retreated under cover of the night.

The Army of Portugal completed its retreat to Spain at speed, but in doing so it was dangerously dispersed thanks to the aborted southern movement. Fortunately for Masséna, Wellington's normally efficient intelligence service was not able to report the exposed position of VIII Corps in time to exploit the situation.

By the last day of March 1811, six months after they entered the country, the Army of Portugal was back across the Rio Côa holding just a sliver of Portuguese territory running some 25 miles between the Rio Côa and the Águeda-Azaba rivers. As recorded by Oman, 'the troops were reduced to the last extreme by exhaustion and hunger.' Masséna had been given an impossible task by Napoleon; he simply had insufficient men and resources to do the job. Coupled with dissent in his own army, the emperor attempting to control events from Paris and a chain of command in the peninsula that allowed other French commanders to put their own interests first, the final invasion of Portugal had been doomed to failure.

The extent of the French losses during the five-and-a-half-month campaign is exemplified by Captain Noël's note on the losses to the artillery of his corps:

> When we had crossed into Portugal on 15 September 1810, the artillery of the 8th Corps possessed 142 wagons, guns, caissons, etc. and 891 horses in the train. When we returned to Spain we had only 49 wagons and 182 horses, so our losses consisted of 93 wagons, destroyed or burned, and 709 horses of the train, but the enemy had neither captured nor killed a single wagon or horse.

Noël concluded: 'So, this was the end of this pitiful Portuguese expedition.'

Chapter Six

Combat of Sabugal, 3 April 1811

Wellington's pursuit of Masséna's Army of Portugal had been governed by the principle of why risk battle when destitution would do the job for him? He explained at the time:

> I have now an opportunity to inflict a severe loss on the enemy, but not without losing many of my own troops; I prefer therefore to harass them, and send them out of the country as a rabble – when from want of organisation, and from sickness, they will not be able to act for many months; and keep my own army entire, rather than to weaken myself by fighting them, and probably be so crippled as not to have the ascendant over the fresh troops on the frontiers.[1]

When the allied army reached the frontier area, Wellington had five divisions in hand, having sent Cole's 4th Division south to join Marshal Beresford during the pursuit to the Spanish frontier when the fortress city of Badajoz was threatened by Marshal Soult. The city, however, surrendered in what Wellington believed to be dubious circumstances, with the relieving force less than a week's march away. To make up for the loss of Cole's division, on the arrival of delayed British battalions during March 1811 the 7th Division was formed under Major General Houston, bringing the army in Beira's strength back to six divisions and a Portuguese brigade. The new division consisted of a single 'British' brigade, which incorporated the Brunswickers and a battalion of the Chasseurs Britanniques, alongside a Portuguese brigade. During the spring, drafts of belated replacements were arriving at the front, which included in the case of the Light Division an additional battalion, the 2nd 52nd Light Infantry.[2]

For the French, with supplies now coming up from Ciudad Rodrigo, the Army of Portugal held its ground beyond the relative safety of the upper Côa during 1–2 April, with Masséna seemingly unwilling to give up the last corner of Portugal that he held. The corps remained where they were, despite being deployed beyond immediate support of each other, and were consequently vulnerable to attack in detail. It had, however, been reported by the British cavalry that Reynier's II Corps, the southernmost of Masséna's troops, was isolated on the left of the army, some 10 miles' march from VIII Corps at Alfaiates and was vulnerable to attack and ultimately destruction.

During 1 and 2 April Wellington deployed his divisions from Guarda and Celorico to attack the French left flank. Now, thanks to allied reinforcement and

French attrition, numbers in the two armies were approaching parity. Consequently, Wellington could have attacked Drouet's small IX Corps in the Almeida area with some confidence and cut Masséna's main line of communication with his magazines at Ciudad Rodrigo. This was, however, a predictable course of action and the destruction of II Corps represented a bigger prize and the hills north of Sabugal provided cover for the assembly of the army for a surprise attack. An officer of the 16th Light Dragoons, Lieutenant Tomkinson, wrote in his diary:

> The whole of the army this day closed up to the hills near Sabugal on the left bank of the Côa. The enemy had only a small piquet on our side, which withdrew on our sending a patrol to drive it over. Our outposts were on the Côa; and if the enemy in the morning holds the position he had today, we shall attack. The brigade[s] bivouacked.[3]

The plan to turn the left flank of the Army of Portugal's position required careful sequencing from the south where Erskine's Light Division and the cavalry were to cross the river beyond the point where it swings from its north-south course to east-west. From this position they were to attack Reynier's II Corps in the flank and rear. This area being not far from the Côa's source, the river was not very wide and certainly not in a ravine as deep as it is near Almeida. In addition, there were numerous fords both north and south of Sabugal. The 3rd Division would cross the river, a mile south of Sabugal at the fords near the Sanctuary of Nossa Senhora da Graça[4] and advance on Reynier's flank. Only once these attacks had developed would the 5th Division cross the bridge and advance through Sabugal, while the 1st Division crossed by fords north of that town. Together with the cavalry they would cut II Corps' withdrawal route. Further north, the 6th Division was to menace Loison's VI Corps and fix it in place and still further in that direction Colonels Trant and Wilson were to cross the Côa with their Portuguese militias and threaten Almeida's lines of communication. This was intended to fix Drouet's attention on the obvious allied axis of advance. (See Appendix III for a transcript of Wellington's orders for the attack on Sabugal.)

Amid rain on the morning of the 3rd, Reynier was in the process of withdrawing II Corps to Alfaiates and had already sent his artillery on ahead via the appalling road to Souto. Meanwhile, the British piquets were reporting that their French counterparts were still on the river line, so the attack was on; but as dawn rose, so did a patchy fog that eddied up and down the river valley. As a result, Wellington's sequencing of the attack broke down from the start. At 0800 hours General Picton hesitated to act in the circumstances, sending a request for confirmation that the operation was to go ahead from Wellington who was positioned on a nearby hilltop south of Sabugal. Meanwhile, Erskine with the cavalry and the Light Division led by Colonel Drummond's 2nd Brigade had marched down into the valley directly to their supposed crossing-points. Consequently, Erskine's battalions were in a real danger of becoming isolated on the enemy's side of the Côa. In the event, however, whether through disorientation or a lack of reconnaissance, Colonel Sydney Beckwith's 1st Brigade halted

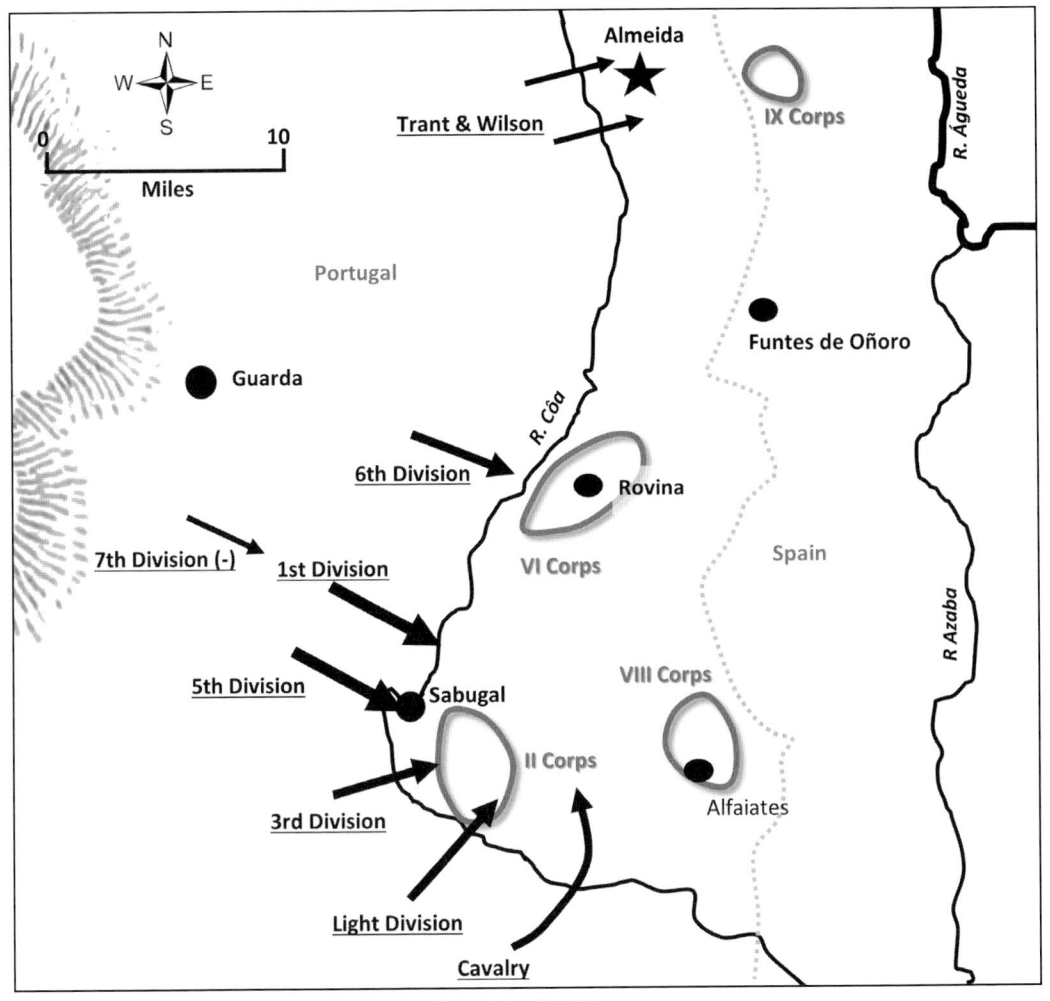

French deployment and Wellington's plans, 3 April 1811.

at a ford a mile short of where they should have crossed, having failed to march far enough around the bend of the Côa. Here Beckwith awaited orders to begin the crossing. Eventually, at around 1000 hours, Erskine, who had gone on with the cavalry, sent back one of his ADCs who, despite Beckwith's lack of orders, demanded to know why he was not attacking and, in his general's name, ordered him to cross the river.[5] The result was that rather than getting behind Reynier's corps as intended, the brigade, once across the river, was immediately tangling with the French outposts covering the flank of Merle's division, the bulk of which was up on the high ground.[6]

Beckwith's brigade consisted of the 43rd Light Infantry, 3rd Caçadores and a wing of the 1st 95th Rifles consisting of four companies. Lieutenant Simmons was with the riflemen leading the crossing of the Côa: 'It was deep and came up to my armpits. The officer commanding the French piquet ordered his men to fire a few shots and retire. On getting footing, we moved in skirmish order and followed in the track of the piquet.'

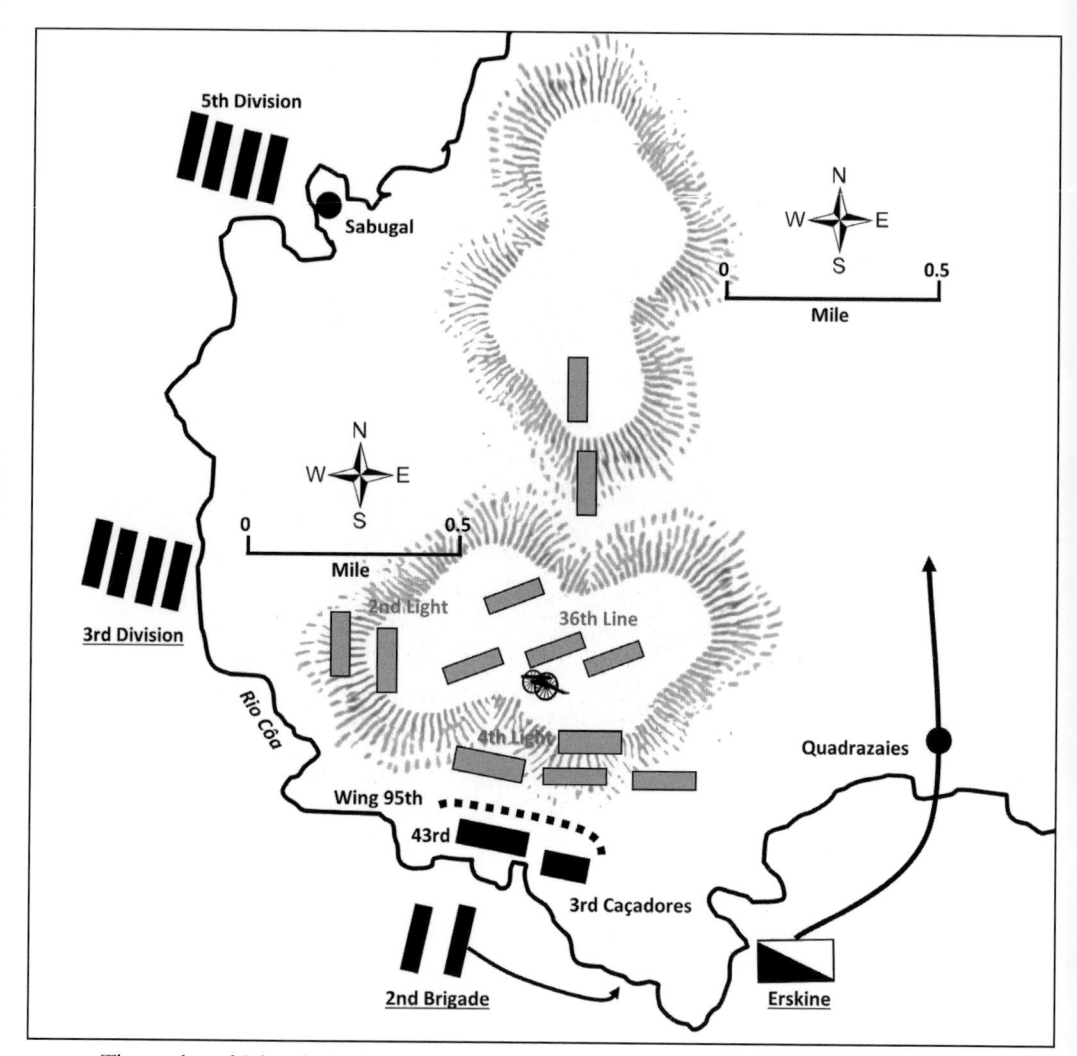

The combat of Sabugal: the first phase.

Further east, in contrast to Beckwith, the cavalry had gone too far along the river before crossing near the village of Quadrazais. Consequently, not only was the timing necessary for Wellington's sequencing slipping but Beckwith's brigade would be without the support of the cavalry.

Separated by some 3 miles from the cavalry, Major Gilmour's wing of the 1st 95th Rifles and three of Colonel Elder's 3rd rifle-armed Caçadores quickly drove the French piquets up the scrub-covered ridge with the 43rd Light Infantry filing along behind them. Assuming that they had correctly crossed behind the French position, they inclined to their left and thanks to scrub and fog, they were unaware of what lay ahead of them. With no sign of either friendly forces or the enemy, Beckwith rode further in an attempt to locate the 3rd Division, which should have been coming up alongside him.

Meanwhile, on reaching the more open crest of the hill, the skirmishers found the enemy. Lieutenant Simmons wrote that 'We were met by a regiment and kept

Major Gilmour, who commanded a wing of the 1st 95th Rifles at Sabugal.

skirmishing until the rest of the brigade came up.' While the Rifles were galling a battalion of the 4th French Light Regiment, the 43rd Light Infantry and the rest of the Caçadores were forming line from file. Captain James Ferguson wrote:

> ... as soon as each company gained the opposite bank of the river it moved rapidly forward in support of the riflemen, each company getting into line as it arrived [in the open]. We had scarcely formed when the riflemen were driven in and passed silently through our line; immediately two strong columns of the enemy approached. We were aware (by the peculiar noise of musketry when near) that they could not be far off. The 43rd Regiment stood alone to defend the ground, our 2nd Brigade not yet having passed the river.

What had happened is that the French battalion, having fallen back in confusion across the open ground onto the hill beyond where they had been rallied, and the rest of the 4th Light then advanced and drove the skirmish screen back. The 4th was, however, not the only enemy force in motion: a break in the fog revealed the approach of a column from the east. This was the leading battalion of General Heudelet's division of II Corps approaching from the direction of Quadrazais. On his own initiative, Captain Hopkins, commander of the 43rd's right flank company, saw the danger to the brigade's open flank and rear and promptly led

French officers, 4th Light Infantry.

No. 1 Company and some soldiers of No. 2 Company towards a commanding hillock half a mile to his right. From this eminence, provided he reached it first, he would dominate the French approach. He formed up his 100 men on the crest in time to confront the 17th Light and the 70th Line regiments, which duly halted, and several companies or an entire wing were sent against Hopkins' diminutive force. The veterans of No. 1 Company stood steady on their hilltop with muskets shouldered until the French were at a close range, and then Hopkins gave the orders 'Ready', 'Present' and 'Fire'. The resulting volley sent the French columns reeling back along the ridge in confusion where their officers rallied them, re-formed and advanced again, but for a second time they were sent running to the rear. This time they withdrew several hundred yards.

The fire effect of a company-plus of the 43rd's trained soldiers was outstanding for the day. Captain Cooper of the 56th Regiment's light company explained the contrast between the fire of light troops which regularly practised on targets and of centre companies that did so far less frequently:

> There is no doubt but that the fire of musquetry [sic] may be reduced to a theory; but far from that being the case, the soldier has no principle given him; for let the distance, or situation of the objects, be what they may, he fires at random. It is principally owing to the exercise of the target being so little practised that this ignorance, and deficiency of principle, is so severely felt.[7]

With Beckwith's congratulations, Captain Hopkins was told to act as he thought best and did so, remarkably holding back the leading elements of Heudelet's division until Drummond's 2nd Brigade arrived.

During this period of the battle, Lieutenant Colonel Elder deployed his musket-armed companies of 3rd Caçadores on the right flank of the 43rd. They and the 43rd were equally successful in halting the columns of the 4th Light with volley fire and, according to Lieutenant Ferguson, 'Immediately with a British cheer, we charged, and threw them back in confusion on the main body', which now included Sarrut's brigade.

Lieutenant Kincaid of the 95th recalled that the charge and subsequent pursuit that 'sent them flying at the point of the bayonet, and entering their position along with them, we were assailed by fresh forces.' Ferguson explained that

> ... in our charge, we discovered the enemy's main body strongly posted above, and cautiously retiring to our original ground, had scarcely gained it when three fresh columns of greater strength again advanced against us. The fog at this time in a degree clearing away, we discovered a wall in our front lined by a battalion of enemy, with a howitzer in rear which had been dealing destruction in our ranks.[8]

Simmons wrote of the French artillery section:

> Two guns opened on us and fired several discharges of grape.[9] The guns were repeatedly charged, but the enemy were so strong that we were obliged

The process of volley firing from being loaded in the shoulder arms position. On the word 'Ready', the musket is brought up and the cock is pulled back from half-cock (safe) to full-cock, i.e. ready to fire. At the command 'Present' the musket is brought down to the aim, which is quickly followed by the order to 'Fire'. After the volley the order 'Prime and load' would be given to repeat the process.

to retire a little. Three columns of the enemy moved forward with drums beating and the officers dancing like madmen with their hats frequently hoisted upon their swords. Our men kept up a terrible fire. They went back a little, and we followed. This was done several times.

General Erskine, having been cavalier earlier in committing Beckwith's brigade across the Côa, could hear if not see the fighting beyond the river, and now veered to caution, forbidding Colonel Drummond from crossing to support the 1st Brigade. At this point, however, he rode off with his staff to join the two cavalry brigades that had crossed the river further east. This left Beckwith and Drummond to make their own decisions.

Colonel Drummond's major of brigade Lieutenant Harry Smith, who had almost certainly been across the river, returned some forty minutes after the 1st Brigade had crossed the Côa, and reported that Beckwith's men were too closely locked in combat to withdraw without being overwhelmed. Consequently, Drummond ignored Erskine's instructions and sent his brigade across the river and into action.[10]

Colonel Sydney Beckwith.

The ford they found was further east and was probably the one that should have been used by the 1st Brigade earlier on. Captain Ewart of the 2nd 52nd recorded that it was '3 miles to the right of Sabugal', and 'only two feet deep'. Once across, the brigade headed uphill and the 1st 52nd formed line between the 43rd and Captain Hopkins' company. The newly-arrived 2nd 52nd were held back in reserve and 'kept in the rear by Colonel Drummond to cover the horse artillery'. The 1st Caçadores probably secured the ford to the battalion's rear.

Now, with a brigade of General Heudelet's division and Sarrut's division arriving, the French attacked again. Beckwith and Hopkins steadied their men, holding their fire until the enemy was at a range where volleys were devastating and then it was a cheer and the charge. The French ran in disorder down into a valley and up the other side with the 43rd and skirmishers of the 95th and Caçadores hard on their heels. On they went up to the wall and the French guns, which with their own infantry and the British intermingled, could not fire. The attackers swept over the wall and the 43rd captured a howitzer, but 'It was theirs only for a moment' before the French counter-attacked and drove Beckwith's brigade back:

> So much scattered were his men that twice at least he led no more than two companies of the Forty-Third to the charge, and twice, finding hostile columns in front and on both flanks, was forced to bring them back. He gave no regular word of command but signified his wishes by running conversation: 'Now, my lads, we'll just go back a little, if you please.'
>
> 'No, I don't mean that (as the men began to run), we are in no hurry – we'll just walk quietly back, and you can give them a shot as you go.'
>
> Then, when the men had reached their old position on the hill, 'Now, my men, this will do – let us show them our teeth again'; and shaking his fist in the face of the advancing columns, he dared them to come on.

In this manner the fight was maintained for an hour, during which Harry Smith recalled a French officer's fate, who in typical style was leading his men forward:

> A French officer on a grey horse was most gallant. Old Beckwith, in a voice like thunder, roared out to the Riflemen, 'Shoot that fellow, will you?' In a moment he and his horse were knocked over, and Sydney exclaimed, 'Alas! You were a noble fellow.'

With the Light Division regaining the ridge, the French counter-attacked again with a fresh column, this time supported by the light cavalry of Pierre Soult's brigade. A squadron each of the 1st Hussars and 22nd Chasseurs attacked the right flank and had the soldiers of the 52nd Light Infantry running for the cover of a stone enclosure on the crest of the ridge. The 52nd Light Infantry's historian recorded one of the incidents during the fighting:

> When the French cavalry thus dashed in upon the 52nd, Private Patrick Lowe, a well-known character for hardihood, was in advance with the skir-

'Fire and Retire'

Beckwith's riflemen from the 1st 95th Rifles and the 3rd Caçadores were trained to work in file pairs when skirmishing. This is a low-level tactic that modern soldiers would immediately recognize as a type of pairs fire and manoeuvre. The process could be used to advance or retire a skirmish line.

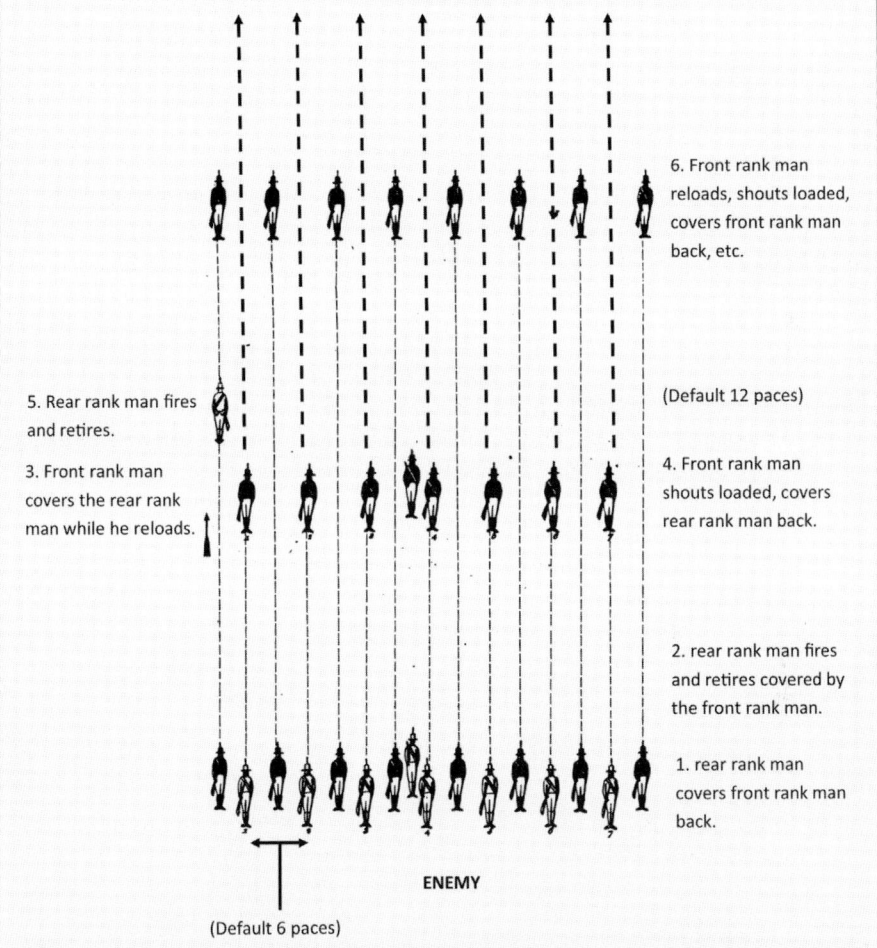

6. Front rank man reloads, shouts loaded, covers front rank man back, etc.

(Default 12 paces)

5. Rear rank man fires and retires.

3. Front rank man covers the rear rank man while he reloads.

4. Front rank man shouts loaded, covers rear rank man back.

2. rear rank man fires and retires covered by the front rank man.

1. rear rank man covers front rank man back.

ENEMY

(Default 6 paces)

The aim was to retire in a controlled manner, at the appropriate speed, keeping the enemy at a respectable distance while the skirmish line fell back, or drive the enemy back as they advanced. The officers would act as a marker for the soldiers of the firing line to align themselves on and the sergeants would control the line of men reloading muskets or rifles. Maintaining cohesive lines was important.

Targets would be selected by individual skirmishers while covering file partners back. These would normally be enemy officers, buglers and other skirmishers. Our light infantryman would aim and fire in his own time.

mishers, and being a little stout man, and not one of the fastest runners ... was soon almost overtaken by a French trooper. Finding that he had no time to get to the walls behind which the greater part of his comrades were now taking cover, he took refuge behind an old stump of a tree; came down on one knee, and deliberately covered the trooper with his piece on rest, and the butt to his cheek. The dragoon at once reined up, and not liking the look either of Pat or his muzzle, began to curvet[11] right and left, hoping to induce him to throw away his fire. Lowe, however, remained steady as a rock, and cool as on parade, still covering his man ... [When] the regiment in perfect order advanced, to the surprise of everyone Lowe allowed his friend to ride off unharmed. When he was roundly taxed by the leading officer for such conduct, as being 'a fool not to shoot him', the reply was irresistible. 'Sir! How could I shoot him when I wasn't loaded?'

At one point during the fighting the fog dispersed, and the sky brightened briefly before a very heavy rain shower swept in and made fire with black powder

'Rally Orb'

If threatened by cavalry while in skirmish order, as Beckwith's rifles and Caçadores were at Sabugal, ideally the light infantry would run for the cover of the line of formed supports. If, however, the cavalry was too close, then the officers and sergeants would order 'Rally orb', at which the skirmishers would form a tight knot around the officer. The orb would bristle with swords and bayonets, which should be sufficient to deter cavalry horses getting close enough for the cavalrymen to sabre the infantrymen.

A skirmish pair of riflemen.

Soldiers of the 1st French Hussars.

weapons impossible. In this situation steadiness, bayonet and sword were the greatest deterrent to the growing numbers of French troops that Reynier had sent marching to his corps' left flank. With the fog clearing, he would have seen that he could build a distinct numerical superiority and crush the isolated Light Division.

With Heudelet's columns being urged into action, disaster loomed for Beckwith and Drummond. Wellington wrote 'Reynier was placing a body of infantry

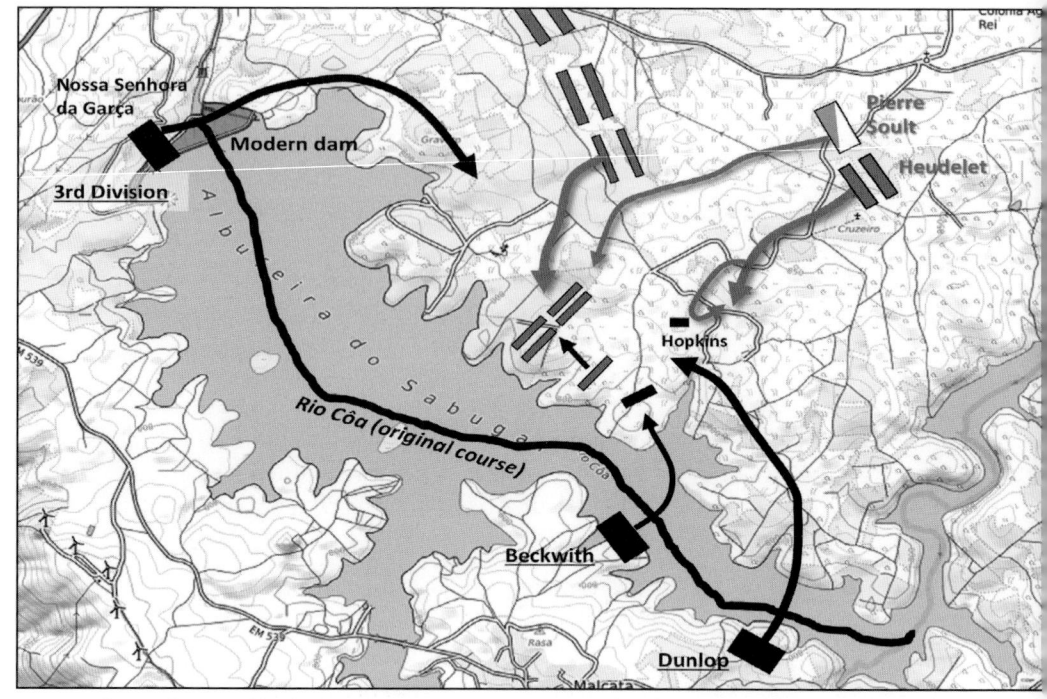

The combat of Sabugal on a modern topographic map.

on their left flank, which must have destroyed them, only that at that moment ...' the sound of the 3rd Division finally crossing the river changed the situation. Picton accounted for delays even earlier, seeking clarification from Wellington:

> The Light Division was to make its attack on the right, where the country became more level, and the banks of the river of easier access. The point where the 3rd Division was to penetrate was much more difficult, both with respect to the ford itself, as well as the means of approaching it. The Light Division easily effected its passage, and engaged the enemy, while the 3rd was perserveringly struggling with the local difficulties and untoward nature of the ground. However, after much labour at length they succeeded, and came up to the assistance of the Light Division, at a moment when it was nearly overwhelmed by numbers.

Wellington reported that

> The enemy were making arrangements to attack them [the Light Division] again in this post, and had moved a column on their left, when the light infantry of Major General Picton's division, under Lieut. Colonel Williams [5th 60th (Rifles)], supported by Major General the Hon. C. Colville's brigade, opened their fire upon them.

Initially the skirmishers of Colville's brigade were driven back, but as the numbers coming across the river grew, the brigade's four battalions were able to form line on its centre and advance up the slope into what was now the right rear of Reynier's deployment facing the Light Division. Picton's men led by the

5th Fusiliers brushed aside the French opposition. Private Donaldson of the 94th recalled the details of the action:

> When we had gained the edge of the river, the French columns were posted on the height above us. We passed the river under a heavy fire, and proceeded to ascend the hill. We could now see that more of our army had crossed, both to our right and left. As we advanced up the hill, we formed line. General Picton rode up in front of us, with his stick over his shoulder, exposed to the heavy fire of the enemy, as composedly as if he had been in perfect safety. 'Steady, my lads, steady!' said he; 'don't throw away your fire until I give you the word of command.' We were now close in them; the balls were whizzing about our ears like hailstones. The man before me received a shot in the head and fell. 'Why don't they let us give the rascals a volley?' said some of the men.[12]

Word that another British division was approaching Sabugal and would threaten his rear reached Reynier. Napier commented:

> Fortunately, the 5th Division got into action just in time, for the French at the moment were squeezing us awfully. The Light Division, under the shout of old Beckwith, rushed on with an impetuosity nothing could resist, for, so checked had we been, our bloods were really up, and we paid off the enemy most awfully. Such a scene of slaughter as there was on one hill would appal a modern soldier.[13]

The combat of Sabugal: the second phase.

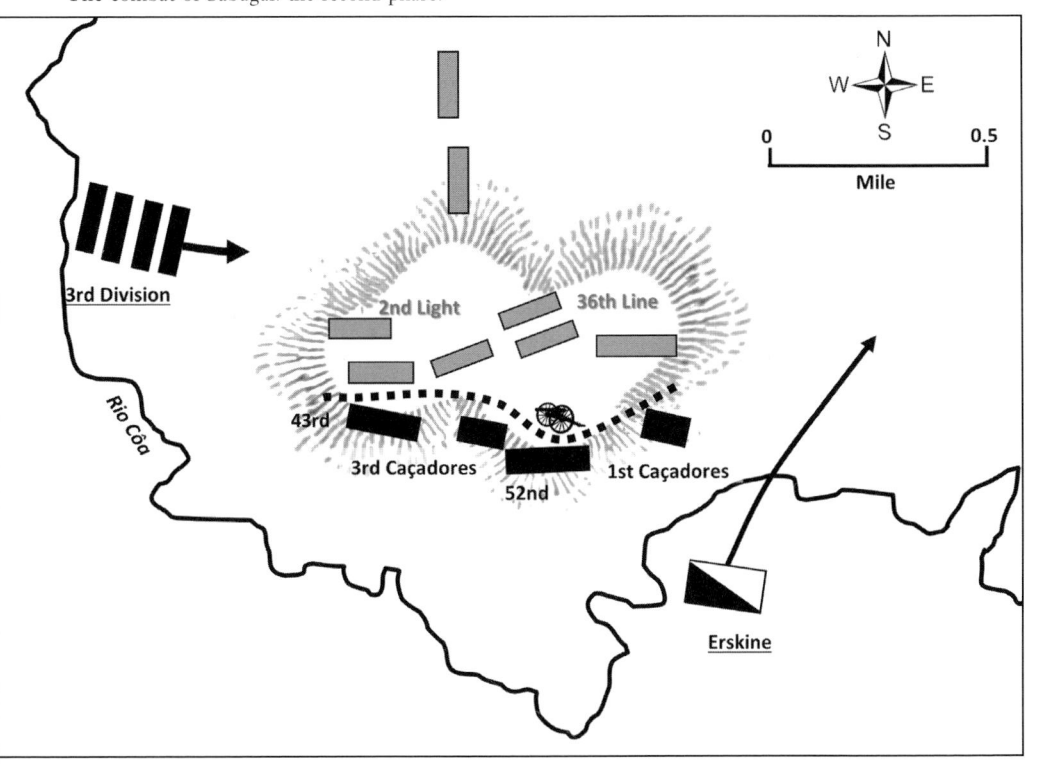

Line *versus* Column

Much has been written on the subject of the British two-deep line versus the French column. However, the performance of the Light Division, particularly the 43rd Light Infantry, against an attack by heavy enemy columns at Sabugal is one of the few occasions on which Wellington specifically mentions the issue in a letter to Marshal Beresford: 'Our loss is much less than one would have supposed possible, scarcely 200 men. The 43rd have 73 killed and wounded; but really these attacks in columns against our lines are very contemptible.' Wellington had three criteria for defeating the French columns:

(1) **Maximising fire power**. A British battalion deployed in two-deep line could bring more muskets to bear than a French battalion in column of either companies or divisions. A third rank could rarely fire effectively and was consequently reduced to the role of filling the first two files when casualties occurred. In the case of Sabugal the French were also up against the Light Division, which had marksmanship training during winter quarters and did not simply volley 'into the brown' but with the 1805-pattern musket, complete with a sight, aimed and fired.

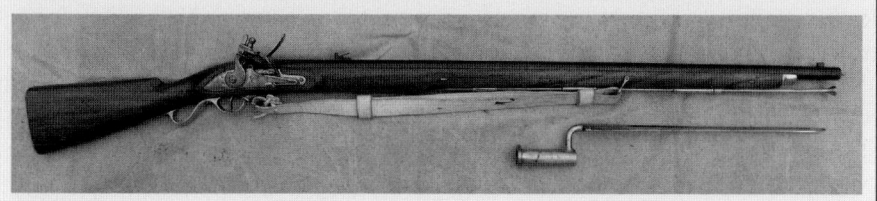

The 1805 New Land Pattern Light Infantry Musket. Note the sights and browned barrel. The latter not only prevented rust but stopped the soldiers wearing away the barrel, keeping it rust-free.

(2) **Protection from artillery fire**. A key part of French tactics was to soften up the defenders to be attacked with an artillery bombardment before the assault. By only having his artillery and skirmishers forward and placing his lines on a reverse slope where they were less vulnerable, Wellington reduced the effect of the French bombardment. Using the ground, he ensured that his battalions were as well screened as possible from shot and shell. On the hills of Sabugal only two French howitzers were able to fire on the allied infantry and thanks to the fog their opportunity to engage was reduced, but Simmons mentions that the grape was effective. The subsequent counter-attacks were not supported with artillery, as Reynier had earlier sent the majority of his guns to the rear. The Light Division similarly had no artillery until late in the fight due to the difficulty of getting the guns across the Côa. Sabugal was therefore in most respects a line *versus* column duel.

The ideal reverse slope position, with a plateau beyond the crest.

> (3) **Protection from Tirailleurs**. During the Revolutionary Wars most armies, Britain's included, were unable to effectively counter the swarms of French skirmishers deployed ahead of the columns, with either volley fire or the inferior numbers of their own light troops. By the time of the Peninsular War, Britain had responded to the enemy tactics by training whole battalions in light infantry tactics and eventually raising three battalions of the 95th Rifles. Add to this virtually every brigade across the army having a rifle-armed company and divisions a battalion of Caçadores, and Wellington was able to keep the French skirmishers from galling his line. In the fighting at Sabugal Beckwith deployed eight companies as skirmishers (4 × 95th Rifles, 3 × Caçadores and 1 × 43rd LI) and their supports. On this occasion, numbers combined with their fire effect kept Reynier's skirmishers well away from the line.
>
> The result of Wellington's measures was that the allied line was nearly always, as at Sabugal, steady and not half-beaten as it would have otherwise been when the heavy French columns bore down on them.

Reynier, in his attempt to destroy the Light Division, had stripped away troops from his centre and right and in consequence he had placed himself deeper in Wellington's trap than the Peer could have hoped for. Facing envelopment, he promptly called off the counter-attack and ordered a withdrawal, at some considerable pace. Sabugal was abandoned to the 5th Division and Merle's shattered brigade was quickly withdrawn behind the rearguard provided by the 17th Light and 70th Line of Heudelet's division. The vigour with which they were attacked, particularly by Picton's men, quickly overwhelmed them and the forward French battalions collapsed as Major Ridge's fusiliers volleyed and charged. Donaldson continued:

> The left of our brigade [5th and 83rd Foot], which was nearest them, now opened a heavy fire; and by the time the line was all formed, the French had taken to their heels. At this moment a severe rain storm commenced, and darkened the air so much that we lost sight of them completely; when the sky cleared up, they were discovered, about a mile forward, scrambling their way over hedge and ditch without any regularity. The ground which they had occupied now lay before us, strewed with the dead and wounded; and the Portuguese regiment belonging to our division were busy stripping them naked. In this barbarous action, however, they were joined by very few of the British. The division to our right and left had by this time succeeded in turning the flanks of the French army; and they were now retreating in great confusion.

The withdrawing French were vulnerable, but Erskine and the cavalry, who had been much delayed crossing their ford, were only now advancing towards Quadrazais; however, in the face of a speedy but well-executed retreat they achieved little except the capture of some of Reynier's baggage.

Portuguese caçadore battalions wore uniforms of a brown country cloth with distinctive-coloured collars and cuffs.

Clearly the weather conditions on the morning of 3 April had conspired against the British but William Napier, who was at the centre of events that day, described Sir William Erskine as 'a near-sighted old ass'. In contrast, Beckwith 'was the admired of all beholders'. It was emphasized how '… he rode first in the advance and last in the retreat, blood streaming from a wound on his temple, keeping the men in ranks, checking those who showed a tendency to quicken the pace and directing fires with perfect coolness.'[14]

In his dispatch of 9 April describing the events at Sabugal, Wellington wrote:

> Although the operations of this day were, by unavoidable accidents, not performed in the manner in which I intended they should be, I consider the action that was fought by the Light Division, by Colonel Beckwith's Brigade principally, with the whole of the 2nd Corps, to be one of the most glorious that British troops were ever engaged in.

During the ebb and flow of the fighting, the 6in howitzer originally captured by the 43rd changed hands several times, being finally secured by Lieutenant Love's company of the 52nd Light Infantry who held the area of the high ground where the guns were located at the end of the fighting. The question as to whether it was the 43rd or the 1st 52nd who had the greater claim to the prize howitzer became a *cause célèbre*. The essence of the argument was which battalion had the greater claim to the prize: the 43rd who originally captured but lost it, or the 52nd in whose possession the howitzer was at the end of the fighting.[15]

The following day Wellington reported to the ambassador in Lisbon from his headquarters in Sabugal:

> We beat Reynier here yesterday and forced the passage of the Côa at this place. The enemy retired upon Alfaiates, and this day are either entirely out

A contemporary sketch of Sabugal, looking across the Côa valley north-west towards the mountains and Guarda.

of Portugal, or at most at the frontier villages. I have not yet heard what they have done at Almeida.

On the same day as the disappointing outcome of the combat, he wrote to Beresford complaining about the movements of his divisions:

> In short, these combinations for engagements do not answer, unless one is upon the spot to direct every trifling movement. I was upon a hill on the left of the Côa, immediately above the town, till the 3rd and 5th divisions crossed, whence I could see every movement on both sides, and could communicate with ease with everybody; but that was not near enough.

As with the essence of campaigning, the coordination of marches, the British army still had to perfect the sequencing of battlefield manoeuvre.

Centre company French Line Infantrymen.

Chapter Seven

Back on the Border Lands

In the aftermath of the combat at Sabugal, II and VI corps pulled back to Alfaiates where the Army of Portugal was to concentrate. The following day, 4 April, Masséna ordered a forced march of 20 miles north-east to the borders of Spain, fearing that the allied army would force him into a major battle, pin him against the Sierra de Gata and cut his army off from their magazines at Ciudad Rodrigo. The allies only tentatively followed, and Wellington occupied Masséna's headquarters at Alfaiates, which the marshal had vacated only that morning.

Over subsequent days the French withdrew across the Rio Azaba, with their last toehold in Portugal being the fortress of Almeida. Wellington reported:

> I sent six squadrons of cavalry, under Sir William Erskine, on the 7th, towards Almeida, to reconnoitre that place, and drive in any [enemy] parties which might be in that neighbourhood, and to cut off the communication between the garrison [of Almeida] and the army. He found a division of the 9th Corps at Junça [3 miles south of Almeida], which he drove before him across the Turon [Rio Tourões] and Dos Casas; and he took from them many prisoners. Captain Bull's troop of horse artillery did great execution upon this occasion. The enemy withdrew in the night across the Águeda.[1]

Colonel Trant's Portuguese militia had been in the area since 3 April and rather than retire in front of the IX Corps they had been ordered to remain in place, but Erskine's force was delayed, only arriving just in time to prevent the militia from being overwhelmed by Drouet's Corps. Lieutenant Tomkinson was with one of the squadrons of the 16th Light Dragoons that day:

> One squadron (under Lieutenant Weyland) was left at Vilar Formoso to watch the enemy, and the remainder of the brigade moved with the 6th and 5th divisions towards Almeida, in which place the enemy had left a small garrison and were withdrawing their force. The horse artillery [Bull's troop] came up with their rear, composed entirely of infantry; and the left squadron of the 16th, led by Colonel Arentschildt, charged their rear of sixty-five infantry. They kept their fire until our men were close, but were broken and all made prisoners, we losing two men wounded, one of whom afterwards died.
>
> Our advance was in Val de la Mula, the enemy retiring on the Águeda.[2]

After the best part of a month's marching and fighting most of the army went into cantonments,[3] but the Light Division and Arentschildt's cavalry brigade found themselves on familiar ground, in the equally familiar role of providing the

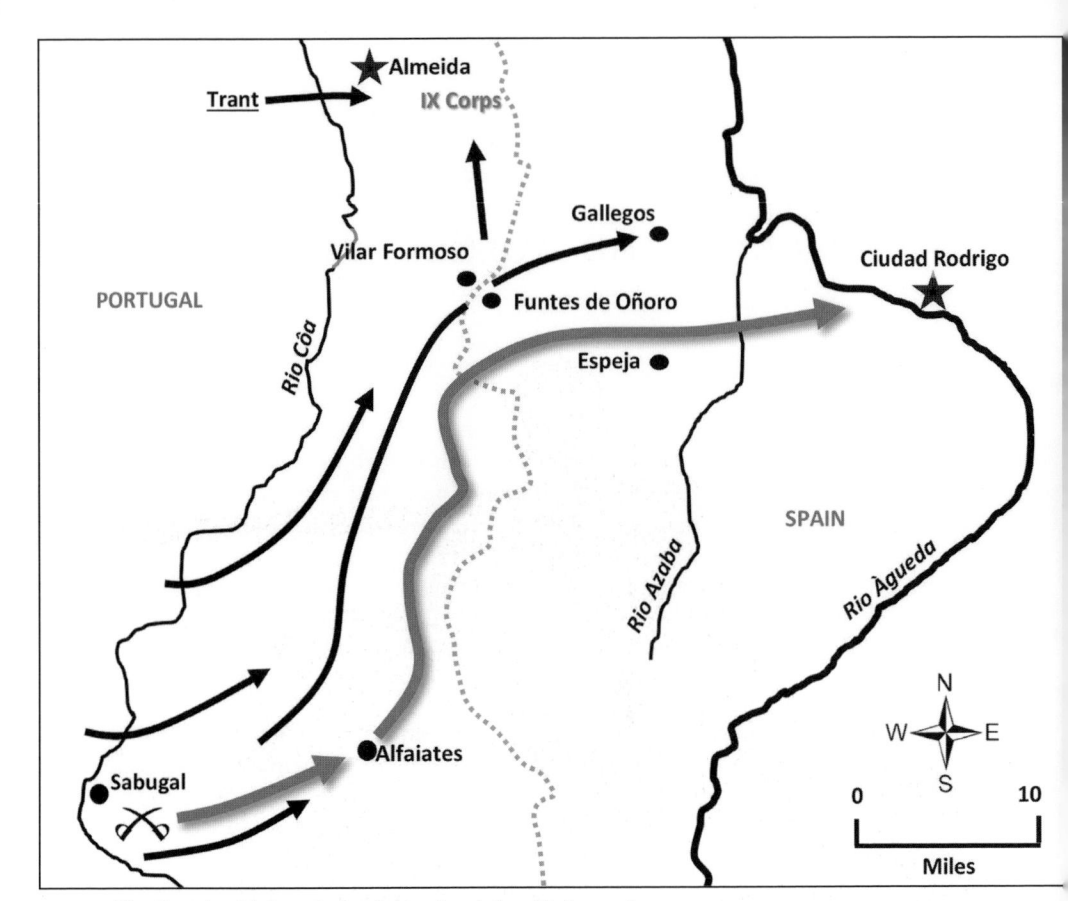

The French withdrawal after Sabugal and the allied pursuit.

army's outposts. On 9 April 1811 Captain Ewart recorded in his diary for that day: 'The Light Division marched at 8 a.m. 1st 52nd and 95th to Gallegos, with RHA [Ross's troop] and some cavalry; 2nd 52nd to Sao Pedro [de Rio Seco], a large village in Portugal, much destroyed.' The villages that had provided the division with shelter during the winter of 1809/10 now offered scant cover. Tomkinson wrote in his diary: 'We were now in our old quarters. The village, from being one of the nicest I ever saw, had been half unroofed for firewood, and many of the families obliged on that account to leave it.'

Wellington wrote to Lord Liverpool that

> The allied army have taken up the position upon the Dos Casas, which Brigadier General Craufurd occupied with his advanced guard in the latter part of the siege of Ciudad Rodrigo [in 1810], having our advanced posts at Gallegos, and upon the Águeda.
> The enemy have no communication with the garrison of Almeida, from whence they have lately withdrawn the heavy artillery employed in the summer in the siege of that place.

The Light Division, supported by the 5th Division, the latter from the area of the ruins of Fort Concepción, pushed forward piquets to the line of the Rio Águeda

Denis Dighton's picture of a brown-coated Portuguese caçadore.

and Rio Azaba, covering a frontage of nearly 20 miles from Barba del Puerco in the north to the ford of Molino de los Flores in the south.[4] Wellington was very clear that he did not want any permanent presence beyond the rivers but ordered cavalry patrols and guerrillas to watch and report. Dispatches were soon on their way to Wellington's headquarters at Vilar Formoso with news that the French had marched off east to Salamanca and as far afield as Toro and Valladolid, leaving garrisons in Almeida and Ciudad Rodrigo. Masséna deployed his least exhausted corps, Drouet's IX Corps,[5] as corps of observation. It had its headquarters at San Munzo, halfway between Ciudad Rodrigo and Salamanca, with two divisions covering the roads from Portugal.

Back in Spain, the Army of Portugal found that during its time isolated from a sustainable line of communication at Santarém, drafts of replacements numbering some 18,000 men, along with stores had been arriving on a regular basis from France. There was, however, far less food than reported due to the convoys being diverted to feed Marshal Bessières' Army of the North as they passed through northern Spain. Such men and stores as there were were quickly distributed and aided what was to be a remarkably quick reorganization and recovery of Masséna's army.

The allies had driven the French some 60 miles back to their magazines in Spain and Wellington believed them to be incapable of mounting offensive operations; however, his situation on the border was barely sustainable thanks to what were now extended lines of supply. From an easy static supply situation on the Rio Mayor at Santarém, the allies had marched over 150 miles in less than a month. Given the slow progress of the convoys, up the Mondego valley, the army had outrun its supplies. A new logistic base at Coimbra had to be established, stocked and a regular departure of convoys to the border lands organized. Being furthest forward, the Light Division felt the lack of food most keenly. Lieutenant Harry Smith explains the problem on the march north after Sabugal:

> This evening [4 April] we had a long march into Quadrazais but did not see a vestige of the enemy all day, nor of our commissariat either. We were literally starving. That old rogue Picton had seized the supplies of the Light Division for his 3rd. If he be now in the Purgatory that we condemned him to, he is to be pitied.[6]

This was not the first time that rations had been waylaid on their way to the front. Wellington had already had to issue a General Administrative Order on the subject of diverting supplies during the pursuit:

G. A. O.   Arganil, 20th March, 1811.

1. The Commander of the Forces is concerned to hear that some of the regiments coming up in the rear have forcibly seized on the supplies on the march for those in front, in consequence of which these last have been deprived of them.
2. Those who stopped and seized those supplies should reflect that it is most easy to supply the troops nearest to the magazine, while those nearest the enemy require the supplies with the greatest urgency. It is besides quite irregular, and positively contrary to the orders of this army, for any commanding officer to seize supplies of any description: there is a Commissary attached to every part of the army, and there is no individual, much less regiment, for whom some Commissary is not obliged to provide.
3. It is necessary that this practice should be avoided in future, otherwise it will become impossible to carry on any regular operation.

Food and forage were short for the British and, despite continuing attempts to induce the Regency in Lisbon to supply their troops, the Portuguese had virtually

Lieutenant Harry Smith, Colonel Dunlop's Major of Brigade.

158   *Masséna at Bay*

nothing to eat and were in an increasingly parlous state, with desertion rife. Wellington wrote of the overall supply situation on the border on 14 April:

> It is doubtful, however, that I shall be able to remain here, as I cannot feed the cavalry, owing to the difficulty of procuring means of transport to the army from our magazines on the Mondego, and nothing can be got in the country. I shall remain here, however, as long as I can.

Consequently, Wellington could not contemplate advancing into Spain to harry the Army of Portugal any further. In the event, however, he was able to remain in position on the border, with the army static and half of the light cavalry sent to the rear to recover condition.

Allied deployment, mid-April.

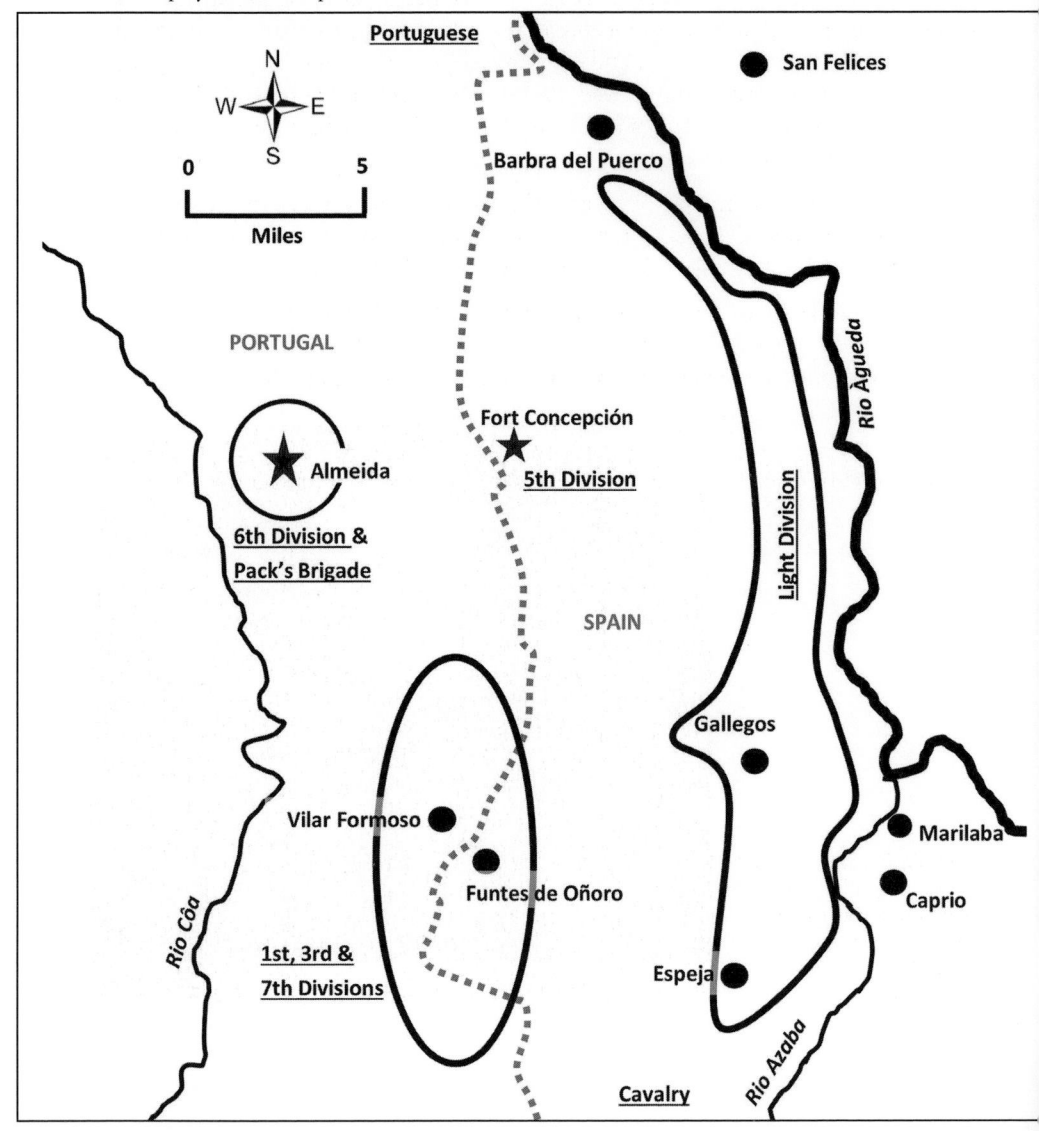

Observing Officers

At any one time Wellington had a number of capable, well-mounted British, Spanish and Portuguese officers gathering intelligence in French-held territory alongside the guerrillas and his secret correspondents. One of these officers was Captain Colquhoun Grant of the 11th Foot, but during this important period Wellington mentioned in his dispatches that 'I have not heard from Grant for several days.' Lieutenant Colonel Waters, one of Wellington's chief intelligence officers was, however, active on the Côa.[7]

Waters had distinguished himself during the crossing of the Douro the previous year and Wellington wrote of him:

> He has made himself extremely useful to the British army by his knowledge of the languages of Spain and Portugal, by his intelligence and activity. I have employed him in several important affairs, which he has always transacted in a manner satisfactory to me; and his knowledge of the language and customs of the country has induced me to send him generally with the patrols employed to ascertain the position of the enemy, in which services he has acquitted himself most ably.

On the morning of the combat of Sabugal, Waters was across the Rio Côa observing with his telescope when he was surprised and captured by four French troopers of the 1st Hussars. Wellington wrote to Lord Liverpool:

> I am concerned to have to report that Lieut. Colonel Waters was taken prisoner on the 3rd, before the action commenced. He had crossed the Côa to reconnoitre the enemy's position, as had been frequently his practice,

Captain Colquhoun Grant wearing a staff officer's uniform rather than his regimentals of the 11th (North Devon) Regiment.

without having with him any escort; and he was surrounded by some hussars and taken. He had rendered very important services upon many occasions in the last two years, and his loss is sensibly felt.

Wellington concluded, with tongue firmly in cheek, after reporting to Lord Liverpool the loss of Colonel Waters: 'To counterbalance the effect of this bad news, I announce to you the birth of the King of Rome,[8] on the 20th March. This event was announced to the Armée de Portugal on the 2nd instant, by the firing of 101 pieces of cannon.'

Napoleon, Marie Louise and their son Napoleon, King of Rome.

At least Napoleon had a son and heir to show for his absence from directing affairs in the peninsula in person.

Waters was not, however, captive for long. Major Napier recounted the story of his escape:

> Confident in his own resources, he had refused his parole, and, when carried to Ciudad Rodrigo, rashly mentioned his intention of escaping to the Spaniard in whose house he was lodged. This man betrayed him, but a servant, detesting his master's treachery, secretly offered his aid; Waters only desired him to get the rowels of his spurs sharpened, and when the French army was near Salamanca, he being in the custody of *gendarmes*, waited until their chief, who rode the only good horse in the party, had alighted, then giving the spur to his own beast, galloped off! An act of incredible resolution and hardihood, for he was on a large plain, and before him, and for miles behind him, the road was covered with the French columns. His hat fell off, and, thus distinguished, he rode along the flank of the troops, some encouraging him, others firing at him, and the *gendarmes*, sword in hand, close at his heels; nevertheless he broke at full speed, between two columns, gained a wooded hollow, and, having baffled his pursuers, evaded the rear of the enemy's army. The third day he reached headquarters, where Lord Wellington had caused his baggage to be brought, observing that he would not be long absent!

The Blockade of Almeida

For the security of northern Portugal and for future offensive operations Wellington ideally needed both Almeida and Ciudad Rodrigo in his hands, but his battering train was still at Lisbon.[9] It would take months, not weeks, to deploy it up to the border via Oporto and the Rio Douro. In that circumstance Wellington had initially hoped to be able to starve both fortresses into submission with Ciudad having been stripped of 200,000 rations by the withdrawing Army of Portugal. The plan was for Don Julián Sánchez's guerrillas to isolate it and give warning of attempts to resupply the city. To that end, on 10 April Wellington was reporting that:

> We have a distant blockade of Almeida, the works of which are as perfect as ever, and I mean that Don Julián should render the communication with Ciudad Rodrigo difficult by the left of the Águeda, while our cavalry shall do it by the right. Both places appear to have small garrisons, and provisions for about a month.

If the enemy approached Ciudad, the Light Division and cavalry would march to intercept the convoys. Within a few days, however, Wellington had to report that his plan had miscarried.

What happened was that despite Sánchez's warning of a convoy's approach and the Light Division's forward deployment, General Erskine was slow in putting

The classic defences of Almeida are one of the best-preserved in the peninsula.

the division in motion to block it. Consequently, convoys from Salamanca reached Ciudad on 14 and 16 April and without siege artillery and lacking sufficient supplies of all sorts himself, Ciudad Rodrigo was for the time being beyond Wellington's grasp. He wrote to Lord Liverpool telling him that

> The enemy having succeeded in getting provisions into Ciudad Rodrigo yesterday morning, it is useless to endeavour to blockade that place; and the extension which the attempt would give to the position of the army, would invite the enemy to make enterprises upon it. My opinion is, therefore, that we should confine ourselves to the blockade of Almeida, which operation should be given over to Major General Campbell's [6th] division, and General Pack's brigade; and that the remainder of the army should be so posted as to cover and protect that operation, to get green forage for the horses and cattle of the cavalry and artillery, and to be able to collect the whole in a short space of time as hereafter pointed out.

On 20 April, having been out of contact with the allies for nearly two weeks, General Marchand's division of VI Corps was sent forward on a reconnaissance to the Águeda/Azaba river line, particularly the direct route to Almeida. Here he was met by the outposts of the Light Division, who thanks to Erskine's bungling had sat and watched the reprovisioning of Ciudad Rodrigo days earlier, but on this occasion halted Marchand in his tracks.

On the road to Almeida the Marilaba bridge was piqueted by a company of the 52nd Light Infantry commanded by Lieutenant Dawson, reinforced by a sub-

Don Julián Sánchez or *El Charro* ('The Cowboy').

division of the 95th Rifles.[10] Captain Dobbs' company, also of the 52nd, was less than a mile south piqueting a ford at Molnos de Flores.

At about 0700 hours the enemy, consisting of a squadron of cavalry and two battalions of infantry, were assembled on the heights of Marilaba and sent a detachment to attack the piquet, who retired from the bridge, firing as they went. Hearing the action develop, Captain Dobbs, knowing that the overnight rain had made his ford impassable, left a corporal and three men to watch it and took the remainder of his company to the Marilaba bridge, arriving just as the enemy had forced their way across. The 52nd's historian recorded that

> Captain Dobbs without hesitation charged down on the enemy, who, supposing that his was only the advance of a much larger force, gave way, and re-crossed the bridge. On this the companies of the 52nd and the small party of the 95th placed themselves among the rocks on one side of the bridge and kept up such a fire upon it that the French were unable to force the passage a second time.[11]

The way in which the French officers inspired their men to attack was noted on this occasion as being 'rather singular':

> A drummer always led, beating what we used to nickname 'Old trowsers'; and as long as 'Old trowsers' encouraged them they continued to advance, but, as soon as the poor drummer fell, they immediately turned tail and ran back, till their officers stopped them and began the same process over again.[12]

A representation of a French attack.

This was a sharp little action in which an officer, a sergeant and fourteen other ranks of the 52nd were wounded, while 'Captain Dobbs received four shots through various parts of his clothing'. The French attacks on the bridge continued until the remainder of both the 1st and 2nd battalions of the 52nd arrived from Gallegos, 2 miles to the west, and effectually brought the affair to a conclusion.

Almeida had been devastated by the explosion of the main magazine at an early stage of the French siege during August 1810 and all the buildings inside the fortress had been badly damaged, losing their roofs and second storeys. The defences were, however, effective and where damaged the previous year, they had been repaired during the previous six months. The garrison of Almeida numbered 1,400 men under General Brenier, which amounted to a single battalion of the 82nd Line and a provisional battalion of artillerymen and engineers, with about thirty days' worth of food.

The two brigades of Major General Campbell's 6th Division and Pack's independent Portuguese Brigade were responsible for the blockade surrounding the fortress with a chain of piquets and posts deployed to contain the garrison and prevent food and messengers from reaching General Brenier's garrison.

Captain Jonathan Leach of the 1st Battalion, 95th Rifles recorded that 'Several companies of our regiment were also sent to shoot the cattle that were turned out to graze under the cover of the guns of the fortress. This frequently brought a cannonade on our men.'[13]

So effective had the blockade been that during late April General Brenier sent an ADC with a note to General Campbell, commanding the investment, requesting the exchange of prisoners. Wellington, however, saw through this, writing that

> The truth is, that this gentleman wants to get a little news. He has found that our men know little, or are but little communicative, and he wants to get some Frenchmen in exchange for them, from whom he thinks he will find out what is going on. It is as well to let him believe that we are good-natured gulls who will easily swallow.

Massena's Last Chance

With the situation appearing to be stable on the Beira front, on 15 April, leaving General Spencer in command, Wellington rode south with some of his staff to Estremadura where he joined Marshal Beresford. The situation here was far from satisfactory. Following the fall of Badajoz to Marshal Soult, the French had marched on Campo Mayor but Beresford's Anglo-Portuguese corps defeated General Mortier who then withdrew back across the Rio Guadiana. Problems in crossing the river delayed the allied follow-up and investment of Badajoz, but on 22 April Wellington carried out a reconnaissance of the fortress and issued orders for the siege.

Meanwhile, with information that Wellington had ridden south, Masséna, assuming that the Peer had taken a significant force with him, decided to salvage

Captain Jonathan Leach wearing a Tarleton helmet worn in the early days of the 95th Rifles.

Marshal Beresford in Portuguese uniform.

some of his reputation by relieving and resupplying Almeida. His army would, however, require further days in cantonments before it was recovered sufficiently to resume the offensive. Preparations for marching were, however, soon detected by Wellington's correspondents and passed on by General Spencer.[14] Wellington wrote from Castelo Branco on 26 April:

> 3 P.M. It appears by letters which I have received from Sir Brent of the evening of the 25th, that the enemy are in motion towards the Águeda, apparently intending to attempt to raise the blockade of Almeida. I go on immediately and shall be with the army to-morrow.[15]

This news had Wellington riding hard almost 80 miles back to the north, leaving Beresford to conduct the siege of Badajoz. This is a prime example of Wellington's strength and vigour.

To mount his offensive Masséna needed reinforcement and duly summoned help, particularly in the form of cavalry and artillery, from Marshal Bessières' Army of the North, which was itself struggling to hold down a large tract of northern Spain, let alone fulfil Napoleon's orders to secure Galicia. Despite assurances that he would send troops, as recalled by Major Marbot,

> ... they remained without result, and Almeida was known to be at the last gasp, Masséna no longer contented himself with writing to his colleague, whose headquarters were at Valladolid, but resolved to send an aide-de-camp, who could explain the gravity of the position, and press him to send support. The commander-in-chief selected me to discharge this duty. Having been severely wounded on March 14, I was, five weeks later, not exactly in condition to ride post-haste over roads covered with guerrillas. In any other circumstances I should have remarked as much to the marshal, but as he was cross with me, and as I had, through excessive zeal, asked leave to resume my duties (not expecting to have such a severe job in the course of the next few days) I did not care to throw myself on Masséna's pity, so I started in spite of the remonstrances of my comrades.[16]

Bessières finally agreed to send the Army of Portugal reinforcements, but his intransigence was not the only issue faced by Masséna; Napoleon's attempts to direct affairs in Spain once again came into play. Marbot recalled that Drouet and his IX Corps were essential to the relief of Almeida but were also ordered south by the Emperor to join Marshal Soult:

> Ordered thus in two contrary directions and knowing that his troops would be better off in fertile Andalusia than in sterile Portugal, d'Erlon was making ready to start for Seville. But as his departure would have deprived Masséna of two fine infantry divisions, and made it impossible for him to relieve Almeida, according to the Emperor's instructions, he declined to allow it. The other insisted, and the wretched squabbles which we had already witnessed in the past winter with regard to the corps were revived. At length, under pressure from Masséna, d'Erlon agreed to remain till the blockade of Almeida was raised. That a commander-in-chief should have thus to entreat his subordinate was quite unreasonable and could only injure military discipline.

Believing that Wellington had gone south with a strong detachment and that Bessières was on his way with a substantial reinforcement, Masséna decided to act. The Army of Portugal, with a strength of 42,000, marched to assemble at Ciudad Rodrigo, which Masséna reached on the 27th, with his army still strung out on the road from Salamanca.

General Jean-Baptiste Drouet, Comte d'Erlon.

On 30 April, north of the confluence of the Azaba and Águeda the French established a bridgehead at a ford, which had Lieutenant Simmons' company of riflemen on its way to confront them. He wrote, 'Marched to Sexmiro, as a strong piquet of French infantry was placed at a ford over the Águeda', but beyond an exchange of shots little happened. At the same time, however, the enemy's piquets again occupied the heights of Marilaba overlooking the Rio Azaba. Even though there was only skirmishing, it was clear that the Light Division would soon be under pressure and the 3rd Battalion of the 1st Foot was sent forward from the 5th Division to support the 'Light Bobs'.

The infantry soldiers in Masséna's divisions may have recovered quickly, but the same could not be said of the cavalry or the artillery's team horses.

Marshal Bessières in the uniform of a colonel of Chasseurs à Cheval of the Guard.

Consequently, the number of properly-mounted cavalry that could be put into the field in late April was just 3,000; half that of the 1810 invasion. When the army marched, no fewer than twelve batteries had to be left behind for want of horses and initially only thirty-two guns accompanied the army. As a result, the arrival of Bessières' reinforcement was keenly awaited. Marbot recalled that:

> Great was the joy of our soldiers, who, though they had lived some days on half rations of bread and less of meat, were yet eager to fight, when, on the

morning of the 2nd, they saw a weak column of Marshal Bessières' troops approaching, and took it for an advance guard. But the reinforcement so pompously announced, and so long awaited, was confined to 1,500 [*sic*] cavalry, six guns, and thirty good teams. Bessières was bringing neither ammunition nor provisions. It was a regular hoax. Masséna was horrified, but very soon grew angry at seeing that Bessières was himself in command of this feeble succour. Indeed, the presence of that marshal was calculated to annoy him. The Army of Portugal was, it is true, in a province subject to the jurisdiction of Bessières, but it was independent of him, and solely under Masséna's orders, nor was there any reason, because Bessières was lending a few soldiers, that he should come in person to control in some measure his colleague's actions. Masséna understood this.

The reinforcement of squadrons amounted to only four weak regiments of guard and light cavalry, plus a battery of horse artillery totalling just 1,700 men, not the 20,000 anticipated. Bessières later argued that despite having 70,000 men in the Army of the North, if he had sent more troops to Masséna's aid 'it would imperil the whole fabric of French supremacy in northern Spain', as guerrillas 'from the Guadiana to the Bay of Biscay, would blaze up in one general insurrection'.[17] Add to this the abysmal state of relations between the marshals and Bessières arguably had every selfish reason not to properly aid his fellow marshal.

French deserters were numerous during this period and contributed significantly to the intelligence picture that Wellington's staff were building. These deserters included eighty men from the battalion of the Irish Legion.[18] In a pre-arranged incident the party of Irish were 'captured' by Julián Sánchez's guerrillas including Colonel O'Mera.

Disillusioned with French corruption, Colonel O'Mera requested that he be allowed to return to Ireland. Wellington argued that he was disabused of his republican sympathies and wrote to Lord Liverpool that 'On these grounds I earnestly recommend to your Lordship that —— should be pardoned, and that he should be allowed to return to his native country.' Rather than face charges of treason, the colonel would be an example of someone who had seen at first hand the fruits of French republicanism.

Meanwhile, the allied army remained dispersed in its cantonments with half the cavalry and the Light Division forward. Wellington's instructions to be actioned if the enemy advanced further were as follows:

Vilar Formoso, 30th April, 1811.
In the event of the enemy passing the Águeda, and moving forward in force, the allied army will oppose his progress by occupying the high country, of which the left is between the Dos Casas and the Turones rivulets, and the right extends by Nave de Haver behind Almedilla, towards Furcalhos.

The body of the army will be drawn towards the right or towards the left of this line of country, or will be concentrated at any particular part of it,

A guerrilla from northern Spain.

according to the direction which the enemy appears to give to the principal part of his force.

It is not intended to dispute the country in front of the line of position above mentioned. (A full transcript of Wellington's instructions appears in Appendix IV.)

Wellington had meanwhile hurried the cavalry squadrons which had been sent to the rear up to the front. With them was Captain Edward Cocks of the 16th Light Dragoons, who recorded in his diary for 1 May that

> The enemy made a strong reconnaissance this morning and our cavalry was turned out; it occupies a chain of cantonments from Villa de Puerco[19] to Fuenteguinaldo. I must confess I find myself very happy being once again

with my regiment. If we fight soon I am confident we shall beat Masséna; there is neither union, confidence nor goodwill in the French army and all these in ours, but in this open country our want of cavalry will cramp all our movements and prevent us from gaining any material advantage. The object of contest is, however, whether or not Masséna will be able to relieve Almeida and if we prevent his doing this we ought to be very well satisfied.

On 2 May the Army of Portugal left Ciudad Rodrigo, crossed the Águeda and headed west towards the Azaba on two roads: one via Marelaba and Gallegos and the other via Carpio and Espeja. Cocks was again out with the vedettes:

Soon after daybreak as near as I could judge, 8,000 infantry and 1,200 cavalry passed the bridge of Ciudad Rodrigo and compelled our outposts to fall

Captain Charles Cocks of the 16th Light Dragoons.

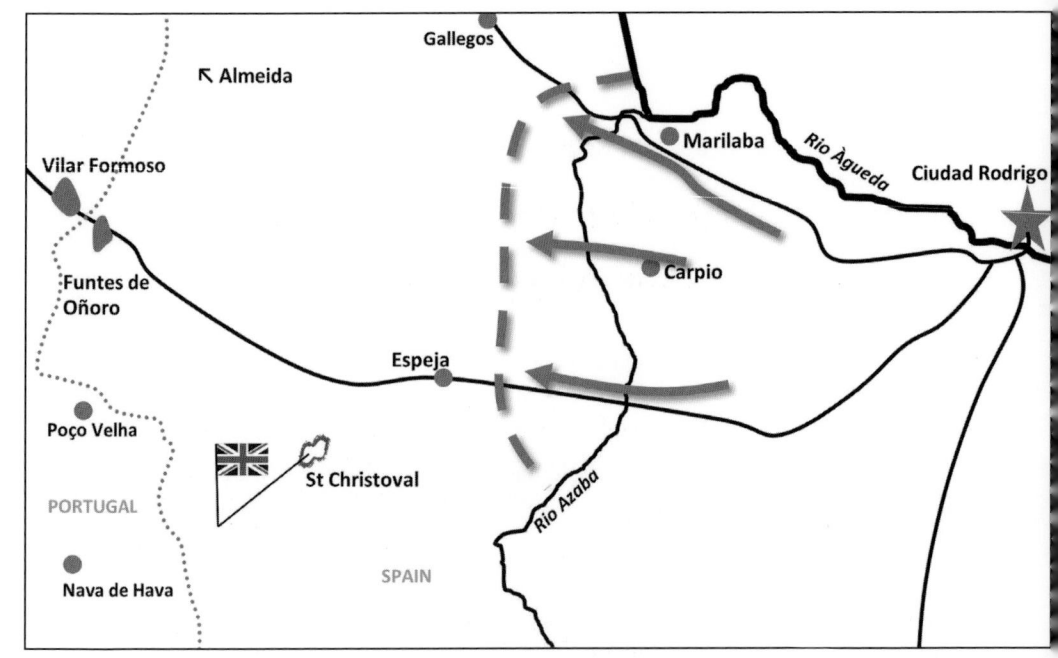

The French bridgehead across the Rio Azaba night 2/3 May 1811.

back. It is confidently reported in our army that Masséna has positive orders from the Emperor to fight and keep the position of the Côa … What Napoleon orders we cannot know but I think it is imprudent for Masséna, with an army not very superior in numbers, inferior in artillery, of late often beat, discontented and out of heart, to attack our army in the spirits it now is, and this imprudence is increased by his having two rivers in his rear. If he had not so much cavalry it would be madness. I think, therefore, his object is only to create a diversion and relieve Almeida.

This was a circumspect advance beyond the Azaba by the French, aimed at securing crossings of the river that had only started to fall after the rains of the previous week but nonetheless saw the Light Division and allied cavalry falling back steadily. Wellington, who had spent much of the day watching Masséna's manoeuvres from the Hill of San Cristoval, sent a dispatch to his divisional commanders at 1830 hours stating that 'It does not appear probable that the enemy's army will advance farther to-day than to the ridge between the Azaba and the rivulet of Espeja.' As daylight faded, the allied vedettes and piquets were deployed on the high ground that rose west of Gallegos and Espeja.

Chapter Eight

Fuentes de Oñoro, 3–4 May 1811

Wellington elected to give battle at Fuentes de Oñoro, his first general action since Buçaco in the September of the previous year, essentially to prevent Marshal Masséna's attempt to raise the blockade of Almeida and resupply the garrison. Knowing the reduced state of the Army of Portugal and a similarly reduced disparity in numbers between the armies, he decided that the risk of battle was low.

The British and Portuguese mustered 37,000 men versus Masséna's 48,000, including Bessières' reinforcement. The figure for the allied army does not include Pack's Portuguese Brigade or the 2nd Regiment of Foot, both of which were tasked to maintain the blockade of Almeida. The French, despite the appalling condition of the Army of Portugal's horses, with Bessières' cavalry still fielded three times the strength of the allied cavalry but the allies enjoyed a slight superiority in the number of guns: forty-eight versus thirty-six. With allied morale boosted by the pursuit of the French, Wellington believed that Masséna's advantage of 8,000 French infantry was more than cancelled out.

The ground chosen by Wellington had its strengths and weaknesses as a position on which to block Masséna's attempt to relieve Almeida. The strength was the Dos Casas which extended across a 9-mile front from Fort Concepción in the north to Nave de Haver in the south. For two-thirds of that distance from the north, the river ran in a deep rocky gully with but two bridges and a number of fords practicable only for infantry. However, in front of Fuentes de Oñoro and on to the south the river drains a shallow basin of marshy woods. West of the marshes lay an open plain, ideal for cavalry, broken only by the villages of Poço Velho and Nave de Haver, plus the odd stone wall. The plain extended 3 miles west to the next watercourse, the Rio Turon, which was only a minor hindrance to manoeuvre. Like the Dos Casas, however, further north along the Turons' course, its gully becomes deeper. North of Fuentes de Oñoro between the two streams, stretching north beyond Fort Concepción, is a ridge of broken high ground, which would become Wellington's main position.

The village of Fuentes de Oñoro is just to the west of the Dos Casas and down in the shallow valley, a little to the right of Wellington's centre. Most of the village was of single-storey stone buildings, with substantial dry stone garden walls, divided up by several streets and numerous narrow alleyways. The village chapel was on the western extremity of the village on rising ground adjacent to a rocky eminence.

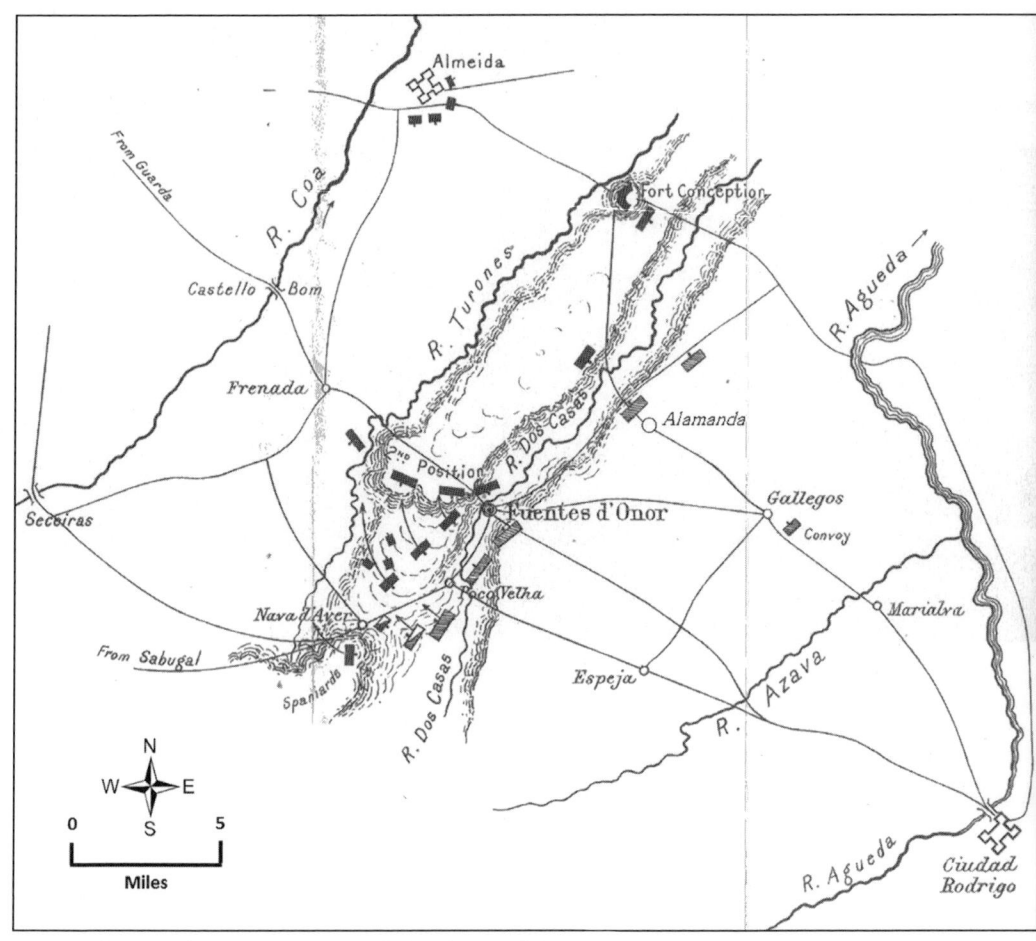

The general terrain between Ciudad Rodrigo and the Côa.

The Dos Casas where it is crossed by the road to Gallegos. The stream and valley are clearly an obstacle to manoeuvre but not as serious as often stated.

View of the Côa from the Castelo Bom bridge. It is a much more serious obstacle than the Dos Casas.

The big danger for Wellington in the case of a reverse was the lack of crossings of the deep gully of the Rio Côa for artillery and the army's baggage. Some 6 miles to the rear of the Dos Casas, the Côa had fords for the infantry and cavalry but at the time only four narrow bridges, with that at Castelo Bom being the only one conveniently sited, but it could not possibly take anything like the vehicles and baggage of the entire army. Further north the Almeida bridge had been broken by the French and though out of cannon shot of the fortress, it was uncomfortably close to the French garrison. The bridges at Ponte de Sequeiros[1] would require a 10-mile march off the battlefield to the south-west and the fourth bridge was way to the south at Sabugal.

Wellington's deployment adopted on the morning of 3 May was for the 5th Division[2] to remain where they were in the area of Fort Concepción, while also on the allied left the 6th Division would cover the road from Gallegos, on Masséna's direct route to Almeida. The 1st and 3rd divisions were on the heights behind the village of Fuentes de Oñoro, with the 7th Division and Ashworth's Portuguese Brigade in reserve. Don Julián Sánchez's Spanish guerrillas covered the right flank in the village of Nave de Haver. Fuentes de Oñoro and the immediate flanks were held by sixteen light companies of the 1st and 3rd divisions formed into four provisional battalions under the command of

> Lieut. Colonel Williams of the 5th Battalion 60th Regiment, in command of the light infantry battalion belonging to Major General Picton's division, supported by the [composite] light infantry battalion in Major General Nightingall's brigade [1st Division], commanded by Major Dick of the 42nd Regiment, and the light infantry battalion in Major General Howard's brigade [1st Division], commanded by Major McDonnell of the 92nd, and

the light infantry battalion of the King's German Legion, commanded by Major Aly of the 5th Battalion of the line [Low's brigade, 1st Division], and by the 2nd Battalion 83rd Regiment [3rd Division] under Major Carr.[3]

Captain Cocks of the 16th Light Dragoons reported that 'About eight o'clock the enemy was in motion and our army took up a position behind Fuentes.' The Light Division and much of the four regiments of cavalry were, however, still forward providing the army's outposts. During the hours of darkness they had already begun to move back from the high ground west of Gallegos and Espeja, fearing that the 4 miles of rolling wooded country would offer the enemy cavalry opportunities to manoeuvre into positions from where they could surprise the infantry battalions. The light infantrymen, rifles and cavalry duly retired skirmishing throughout the morning and into the afternoon.

Even though the French cavalry at times pressed them, the Light Division gave them no opportunity to attack with a chance of success. According to Captain Leach of the 95th Rifles:

> ... before daybreak we were again in motion; and having crossed the Dos Casas at Fuentes de Oñoro, without molestation from the French, took up the ground allotted to us on the heights above the village ... the Light Division near the centre, was a flying corps, ready to be despatched to any point of this extended position most menaced.

Troopers of the elite company of the 15th Chasseurs à Cheval skirmishing. The majority of the French corps' light cavalry were the green-coated Chasseurs à Cheval.

Despite his precipitate retreat to Spain, Masséna believed that in the face of an offensive and without a strong Buçaco-like defensive position, Wellington was unlikely to stand and fight to prevent the relief of Almeida, especially with the obstacle of the Côa behind him. Major Marbot expressed the view of Masséna's staff: 'I could never understand how Wellington consented to await the French in so unfavourable position ... which might have caused the loss of the army if it had been compelled to retreat.'

The French advanced in three columns preceded by their corps' light cavalry. Reynier's II Corps moved on the road from the Marilaba Bridge via Gallegos, while Solignac, the only division of Junot's VIII Corps present, marched via Allamanda to the adjacent bridge over the Dos Casas. VI Corps, with Ferey's division leading, used the road from Espeja to Fuentes de Oñoro, with the two divisions of Drouet's IX Corps following.

Captain Cocks, who was on the high ground, watched the French come into sight: 'At two o'clock the enemy's columns appeared and some skirmishing commenced [sic, continued] near the village of Fuentes. At half past three one 9-pounder was brought into action. At half past six the enemy advanced in close column beautifully at a run, charged the village.'

As the French columns closed on the Dos Casas, the skirmishing continued with Private Joseph Donaldson a witness to a curious event in front of Fuentes village:

> The skirmishers were covered in their advance by cavalry, in consequence of which ours were obliged to fall back, for greater safety, to some stone fences on the outskirts of the village, while a party of our German hussars covered their retreat. The cavalry now commenced skirmishing, the infantry keeping up an occasional fire. It was rather remarkable that the cavalry on both sides happened to be Germans. When this was understood, volleys of insulting language, as well as shot, were exchanged between them. One of our hussars got so enraged at something one of his opponents said, that raising his sword, he dashed forward upon him into the very centre of their line. The French hussar, seeing that he had no mercy to expect from his enraged foe, wheeled about his horse, and rode to the rear; the other, determined on revenge, still continued to follow him. The whole attention of both sides was drawn for a moment to these two, and a temporary cessation of firing took place; the French staring in astonishment at our hussar's temerity, while our men were cheering him on. The chase continued for some way to the rear of their cavalry. At last our hussar coming up with him, and fetching a furious blow, brought him to the ground. Awakening now to a sense of the danger he had thrown himself into, he set his horse at full speed to get back to his comrades; but the French, who were confounded when he passed, had recovered their surprise, and determined on revenging the death of their comrade; they joined in pursuit, firing their pistols at him. The poor fellow was now in a hazardous plight, they were every moment gaining upon him,

180   *Masséna at Bay*

and he had still a long way to ride. A band of the enemy took a circuit, for the purpose of intercepting him; and, before he could reach the line he was surrounded, and would have been cut in pieces, had not a party of his comrades, stimulated by the wish to save so brave a fellow, rushed forward, and just arrived in time, by making the attack general, to save his life, and brought him off in triumph.

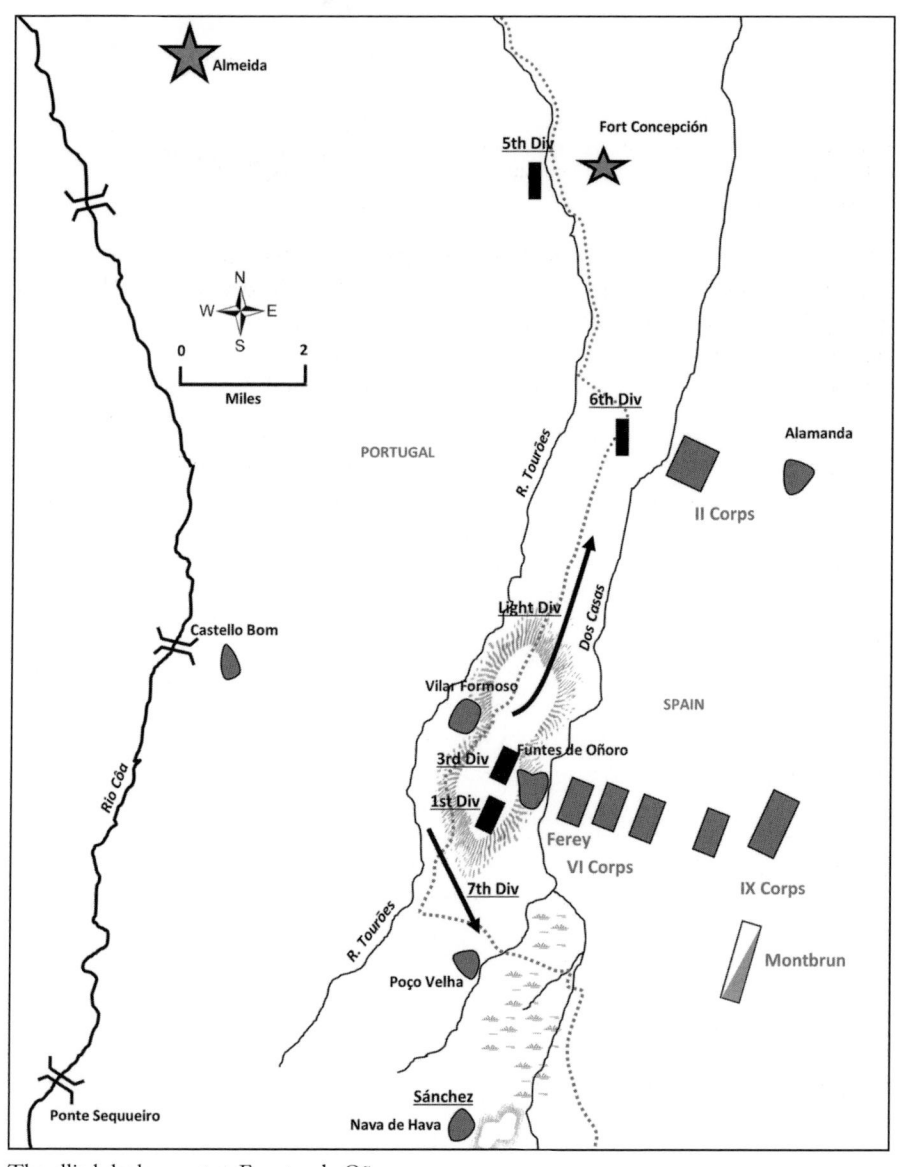

The allied deployment at Fuentes de Oñoro.

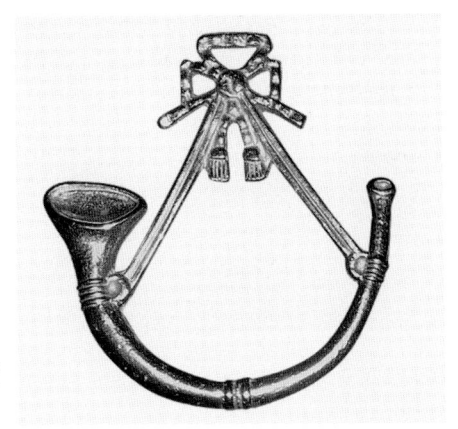

The bugle horn badge was used not only by light and rifle battalions but by the light companies of ordinary line battalions.

Of the defenders of Fuentes, the German riflemen of the four companies of the 5th 60th in the village were the first in action and 'understood light duties and appropriate use of cover; they also rapidly thinned the saddles of the French, who had ventured too boldly, without suffering any loss'.[4]

One of Masséna's ADCs, Major Marbot, recalled the beginning of the battle:

> Our troops were hardly in their respective positions when General Loison, without awaiting Masséna's orders for a concerted movement, charged the village of Oñoro,[5] occupied by the Highlanders and some picked battalions. Their attack was so brisk that the enemy, although entrenched in solid stone houses, were compelled to abandon the position.

The rush of overwhelming French numbers saw the companies falling back from their barricades and, as Donaldson recalled, 'the small number of troops which defended were obliged to give way'. They fought back uphill through the labyrinth of alleyways, firing from houses, walls and corners, with some groups being left behind in buildings until released later by a counter-attack. French soldiers fell but they pressed on, driving the light troops before them until they reached the chapel. 'The French now thought they had gained their point, but they were soon undeceived' as Colonel Williams rallied the light companies around the chapel and rocky eminence at the top of the village, from which the French could not dislodge them. During this period Colonel Williams fell seriously wounded and Colonel Cameron of the 79th Highlanders took over command with Major Woodgate of the 5th 60th commanding the 3rd Division's companies.

Wellington reported that

> ... having observed the repeated efforts which the enemy were making to obtain possession of the village, and being aware of the advantage which they would derive from the possession in their subsequent operations, I reinforced the village successively with the 71st regiment under Lieut. Colonel

The chapel at the top of the village, the square where hand-to-hand fighting took place and the memorial to the battle. Houses have now started to cover the rocky eminence to the left of the picture.

> the Hon. H. Cadogan, and the 79th under Lieut. Colonel Cameron, and the 24th under Major Chamberlain.
>
> I then withdrew the light infantry battalions, and the 83rd regiment, leaving the 71st and 79th regiments only in the village, and the 2nd battalion 24th regiment to support them.

As the French reached the chapel square the leading companies of the three British battalions from the 1st Division were launched in a counter-attack on Fuentes, falling on the now disorganized French whose attack had lost impetus. Private Thomas was with the 71st and wrote a remarkable personal account of the action:

> We stood under arms until ... a staff-officer rode up to our Colonel and gave orders for our advance. Colonel Cadogan put himself at our head, saying, 'My lads, you have had no provision these two days; there is plenty in the hollow in front, let us down and divide it.' We advanced as quick as we could run and met the light companies retreating as fast as they could. We continued to advance, at double-quick time, our firelocks at the trail, our bonnets in our hands. They called to us, 'Seventy-first, you will come back quicker than you advance.' We soon came full in front of the enemy. The Colonel cries, 'Here is food, my lads, cut away.' Thrice we waved our bonnets, and thrice we cheered; brought our firelocks to the charge and forced them back through the town.[6]
>
> How different the duty of the French officers from ours. They, stimulating the men by their example, the men vociferating, each chaffing each until they appear in a fury, shouting, to the points of our bayonets. After the first huzza the British officers, restraining their men, still as death. 'Steady, lads, steady,' is all you hear, and that in an undertone.
>
> In this affair my life was most wonderfully preserved. In forcing the French through the town, during our first advance, a bayonet went through between my side and clothes, to my knapsack, which stopped its progress. The Frenchman to whom the bayonet belonged fell, pierced by a musket

A pipe banner of the 71st LI. When converted to light infantry the regiment retained the bag pipes alongside the bugle.

> ball from my rear-rank man. Whilst freeing myself from the bayonet, a ball took off part of my right shoulder wing and killed my rear-rank man, who fell upon me. Narrow as this escape was, I felt no uneasiness; I was become so inured to danger and fatigue.
>
> The French had lost a great number of men in the streets. We pursued them about a mile out of the town, trampling over the dead and wounded; but their cavalry bore down upon us and forced us back into the town, where we kept our ground, in spite of their utmost efforts.

Masséna, who had by now arrived, ordered Marchand to send four battalions made up of grenadier companies to drive the 71st and 79th back, but as Thomas states they were only able to cross the Dos Casas and establish a foothold in the buildings in the lower part of the town. Thomas concluded that

> During this day the loss of men was great. In our retreat back to the town, when we halted to check the enemy, who bore hard upon us in their attempts to break our line, often was I obliged to stand with a foot upon each side of a wounded man, who wrung my soul with prayers I could not answer, and pierced my heart with his cries to be lifted out of the way of the cavalry. While my heart bled for them, I have shaken them rudely off.

The French were driven out of the village which was littered with dead and wounded men, but Marbot highlights a factor that probably prevented the recapture of the village:

> In Ferey's division there was a battalion of the Hanoverian legion in the French service. Their uniform was red, like the English, but they had the

usual grey overcoat of the French soldier, and accordingly their commander, who had had several men killed by our people at Buçaco, asked leave for his men to wear their greatcoats instead of rolling them up, as the order was. But General Loison replied that he must follow the order given to the whole corps. The result was a cruel blunder. The 66th regiment, having been sent to support the Hanoverians, who were in the fighting line, mistook them in the smoke for an English battalion, and fired into them, while our artillery, equally misled by the red coats, played on them with grape. I must do the brave Hanoverians the justice to say that, placed as they were between two fires, they endured them for a long time without recoiling a step, but after losing 100 men killed and many wounded, the battalion was compelled to retire, passing along one side of the village. Another regiment, which was entering the village at that moment, seeing the red coats on their flank, supposed that the position had been turned by an English column, and the enemy cleverly took advantage of the resulting confusion to recapture Fuentes de Oñoro, which would not have happened if the generals had followed Masséna's order to line the windows with infantry.

Wellington, observing the fighting ebb away, penned a dispatch to his divisional commanders:

Heights above Fuentes de Oñoro, 3rd May, 1811, 6 P.M.
It does not appear as if the enemy intended to make any serious attack upon the position this evening. The troops will, therefore, send for their camp kettles, and make their arrangements for the night.

The several divisions will throw out piquets along the ravine of the Dos Casas rivulet.

The divisions covered their respective fronts, less the Light Division, while the 7th Division redeployed south and established their piquets around Poço Velho, beyond the 1st Division's deployment.

That was not, however, entirely the end of the fighting at close quarters in the lower part of the village. Private Thomas recalled that

We kept up our fire until long after dark. About one o'clock in the morning, we got four ounces of bread served out to each man, which had been collected out of the haversacks of the Foot Guards. After the firing had ceased, we began to search through the town, and found plenty of flour, bacon and sausages, on which we feasted heartily, and lay down in our blankets, wearied to death. My shoulder was as black as a coal, from the recoil of my musket; for this day I had fired 107 rounds of ball-cartridge. Sore as I was, I slept as sound as a top till I was awakened by the loud call of the bugle an hour before day.

Meanwhile, the Light Division, in their role of 'a flying corps ready to be dispatched to any point in this extended position, most menaced' only had a short rest in the rear before they were set marching north to support the 5th and 6th divisions, which were threatened by II Corps. It, however, soon became apparent that the French intended nothing serious on this flank beyond skirmishing astride the Dos Casas and the division was ordered to halt and to remain where they were. This was a good, obvious position on the crest of the ridge and they were to remain in this position until the general redeployment on the 5th.

Soldiers of the Light Infantry Division on the march.

The madder red coat of a flank company soldier of the 94th Scotch Brigade,[7] showing the green facing colour, regimental lace and flank company wings.

4 May 1811

The 4th saw a lull in the battle but, as Thomas recalled,

> as soon as it was light the firing commenced and was kept up until about ten o'clock, when Lieutenant Stewart, of our regiment, was sent with a flag of truce for leave to carry off our wounded from the enemy's lines, which was granted; and, at the same time, they carried off theirs from ours. As soon as the wounded were all got in, many of whom had lain bleeding all night, many both a day and a night.

Donaldson added more detail: '... both sides were busily employed burying the dead and bringing in the wounded; French and English promiscuously mixed and assisted each other in that melancholy duty as if they had been intimate friends.'

A count of the dead revealed that there were 259 British and Portuguese bodies to be removed along with 652 French. Some 164 prisoners, mostly wounded, had already been sent to the rear. As recalled by Thomas, the remainder of the day had been spent in considerable contrast to the previous evening:

> The French brought down a number of bands of music to a level piece of ground, about 90 or 100 yards broad, that lay between us. They continued to play until sunset, whilst the men were dancing and diverting themselves at football. We were busy cooking the remainder of our sausages, bacon and flour.

Donaldson recorded the lack of bitterness between the two armies and that 'So far did this friendship extend, that two of our lads who spoke French, went up that night after dark to the enemy's picquet, and having conversed and wined with them, returned unmolested to their company.'

For the rest of the army it was a long day waiting on the ridge in the hot sun for action. During this day, much to the relief of the Light Division, General Craufurd returned from leave after an absence of three months and promptly resumed command of his division. Rifleman Costello witnessed the welcome the division gave a commander who only a year before they cordially loathed.[8]

> ... at an early hour General Craufurd made his re-appearance amongst us from England and was welcomed with much enthusiasm by the division; although a strict disciplinarian, the men knew his value in the field too well not to testify their satisfaction at his return. The Caçadores, particularly, caused much laughter among us, by shouting out in Portuguese the moment they caught sight of him, 'Long live General Craufurd, who takes care of our bellies!' meaning by this exclamation they got their rations regularly while under his command; the General seemed highly pleased, and bowed repeatedly with his hat off as he rode down their ranks.

This welcome return, had Craufurd lived into old age, would surely have been one of the greatest occasions of his life.

A post-1808 (when powdered hair was abandoned) miniature portrait of General Craufurd.

Masséna's Reconnaissance

Masséna and his staff were, however, busy throughout the 4th, having realized the strength of Wellington's position but above all the resolve of the allies to stand and fight. In short, he had to find an alternative way to force the allies to give way. Patrols were dispatched and soon identified that Wellington's right flank between Poço Velho and Nave de Haver was only lightly held by piquets and Julián Sánchez's mounted guerrillas. Marbot recorded: 'On hearing of this negligence through a cavalry patrol Masséna ordered everything to be got ready for crossing the marsh at daybreak the next morning, in order to take the enemy's right wing in the rear.'

Masséna himself carried out a reconnaissance, which was all too obvious and alerted Wellington to his intent. Captain Cocks recorded the activities of the day in his diary along with some old-fashioned courtesy:

> This day was spent in trifling skirmishing between the cavalry, which wearied our horses and answered no other end than ascertaining the enemy's force, but I should have thought we had known this already. Masséna reconnoitred our left. General Hay was too polite, and he would not allow Bull to fire on him when within range of case shot.

The French identified the wooded marsh and the upper reaches of the Dos Casas as a potential problem for deployment into the area between Poço Velho and Nave de Haver. Marbot recalled that 'Plenty of fascines were constructed during the night, and the 8th Corps with part of the 9th marched in silence towards Nave de Haver. Ferey's division remaining before Oñoro, which was still occupied by the enemy.'

Chapter Nine

Fuentes de Oñoro, 5 May 1811

'One of the finest movements which Masséna ever devised, the last flicker of an expiring lamp.' [Marbot]

Marshal Masséna's plan was to assemble a force overnight, under cover of the substantial hill immediately east of Nave de Haver, to turn Wellington's right flank. This consisted of the divisions of Marchand and Mermet (VI Corps) and Solignac's VIII Corps, plus General Montbrun's reserve cavalry and the light cavalry of VI and IX corps. Further north Ferey's division was to remain in front of Fuentes de Oñoro where, according to Masséna's orders, 'The IX Corps will be assembled before the day in front of Fuentes de Oñoro, where it will fight in two lines, leaving a large distance between regiments, to make the enemy believe that the VI Corps still occupies the same position.' (See Appendix V for a full translation.)

This was intended to fix Wellington away from his flanking move, but Ferey and Drouet were instructed 'not to risk anything'. Reynier's II Corps, with a similar role, remained deployed between Allamanda and the road to Fort Concepción. In the event of the expected allied withdrawal, Reynier was to cross the Dos Casas and attack the allied left flank.

Sadly for Masséna, the patrols and his presence out on the right flank the previous day had been observed by the allies and Wellington redeployed. He explained in his report to Lord Liverpool that

> From the course of the reconnaissance on the 4th, I had imagined that the enemy would endeavour to obtain possession of Fuentes de Oñoro, and of the ground occupied by the troops behind that village, by crossing the Dos Casas at Poço Velho; and in the evening I moved the 7th Division, under Major General Houston, to the right, in order, if possible, to protect that passage.[1]

The 7th Division was deployed near Poço Velho supported by three or four squadrons of cavalry from different regiments including squadrons of the 14th Light and Royal Dragoons. Major Brotherton of the 14th Light Dragoons recalled that

> I had been sent out the night before to the village of Nave de Haver, which was occupied by that humbug Don Julián Sánchez, with his corps of infantry

190 *Masséna at Bay*

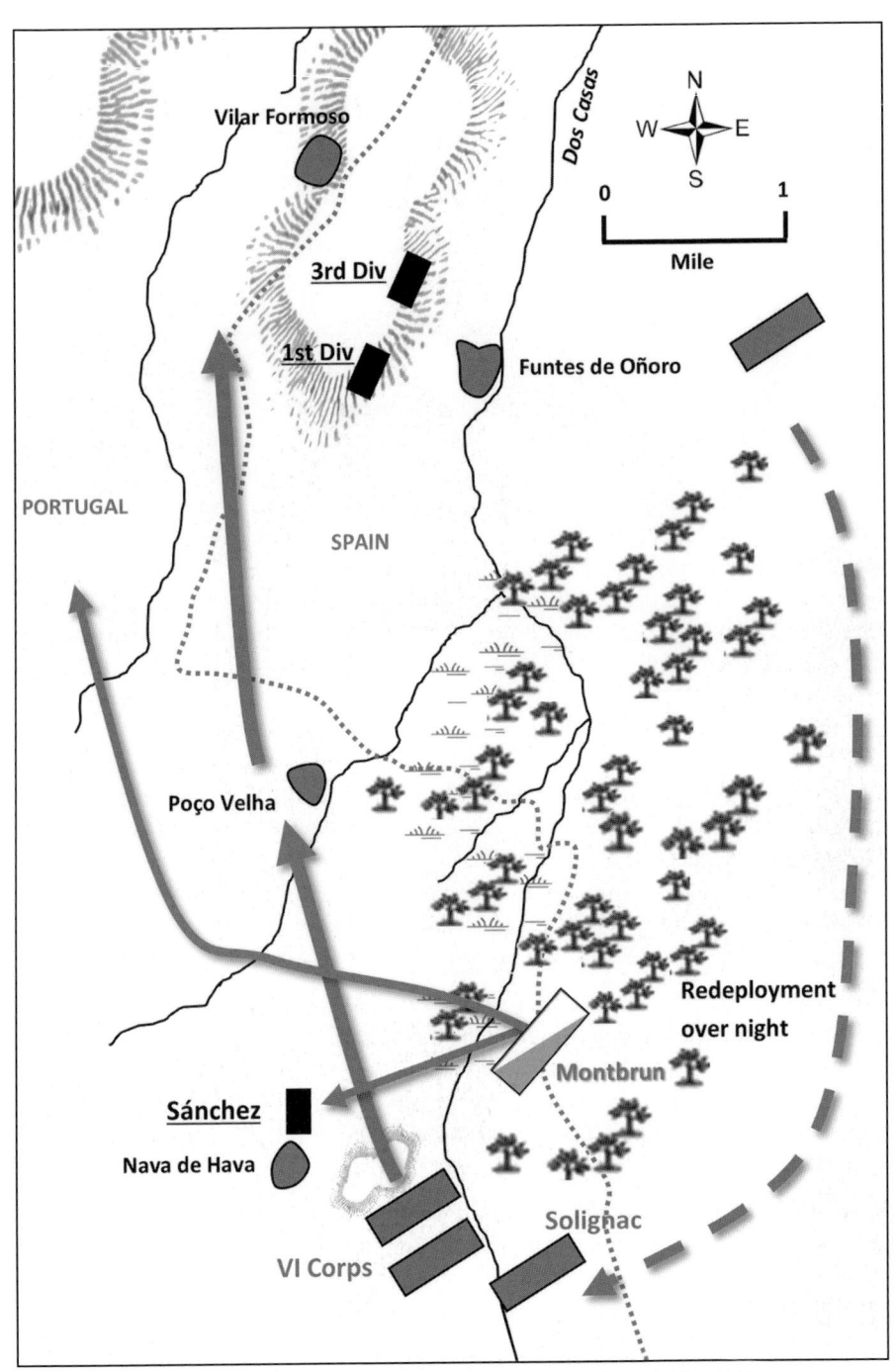

Masséna's redeployment and plan to attack Wellington's right flank on 5 May 1811.

An officer of the 14th Light Dragoons.

and cavalry ... I arrived there late at night and could not see what arrangements Don Julián had made for defence; but he assured me all was secure and that he meant to defend himself most obstinately.²

In front of them were the woods where, according to Marbot, 'At daybreak on 5 May a company of light infantry, slipping through the willows and reeds, crossed the marsh noiselessly, and, passing the fascines along, filled up the bad places, which turned out to be much fewer in number than we had supposed.'³

On the allied side of the line, as dawn broke, telescopes were trained on the woods to their right flank and soon movement of infantry and cavalry was to be seen and Wellington made further adjustments to his deployment to address what could develop into a dangerous situation. Wellington wrote:

> The Light Division, which had been brought back from the neighbourhood of Alameda, were sent with the cavalry, under Sir Stapleton Cotton, to support Major General Houston; while the 1st and 3rd divisions made a movement to their right, along the ridge between the Tourões and Dos Casas rivers.

The ruse to spread out Ferey's division to give the impression that the whole of VI Corps was still present before Fuentes de Oñoro failed in daylight and Wellington was able to redeploy the 1st and 3rd divisions, plus Ashworth's from reserve, from facing east to overlooking the plain to the south. If a withdrawal across the Côa became necessary, this redeployment effectively abandoned the lines of retreat to Sabugal and the Ponte de Sequeiros, placing reliance on the Castelo Bom bridge and the weak Almeida bridge. Wellington had had his right flank turned and he was in a potentially difficult situation.⁴ Lieutenant Colonel Gordon, a member of the Peer's staff wrote: 'Lord Wellington determined at once to give up the great road of communication to the rear through Nave de Haver [and Ponte de Sequeiros], on which our right rested, and drew his army more together to the left, which had been too much extended in the first instance.'⁵

Even though the distances involved in the redeployment were not great, it took some time to complete. Meanwhile, Captain Cocks was with the squadrons already deployed to the right:

> At six [am] the enemy advanced with the cavalry strongly supported by infantry and guns towards the morass, and the columns of infantry on Poço Velho and the surrounding woods. Two squadrons of our brigade had been advanced to the morass under Major Meyer of the 1st [KGL] Hussars to watch the enemy. Injudiciously and contrary to orders, they crossed the morass, charged the advance of the enemy and were overpowered by numbers. Capt Belli, 16th Dragoons, wounded and taken, Lt Blake killed with six men, Lt Weyland and Capt Krauchenberg [sic], 1st Hussars, with 30–40 men wounded.⁶

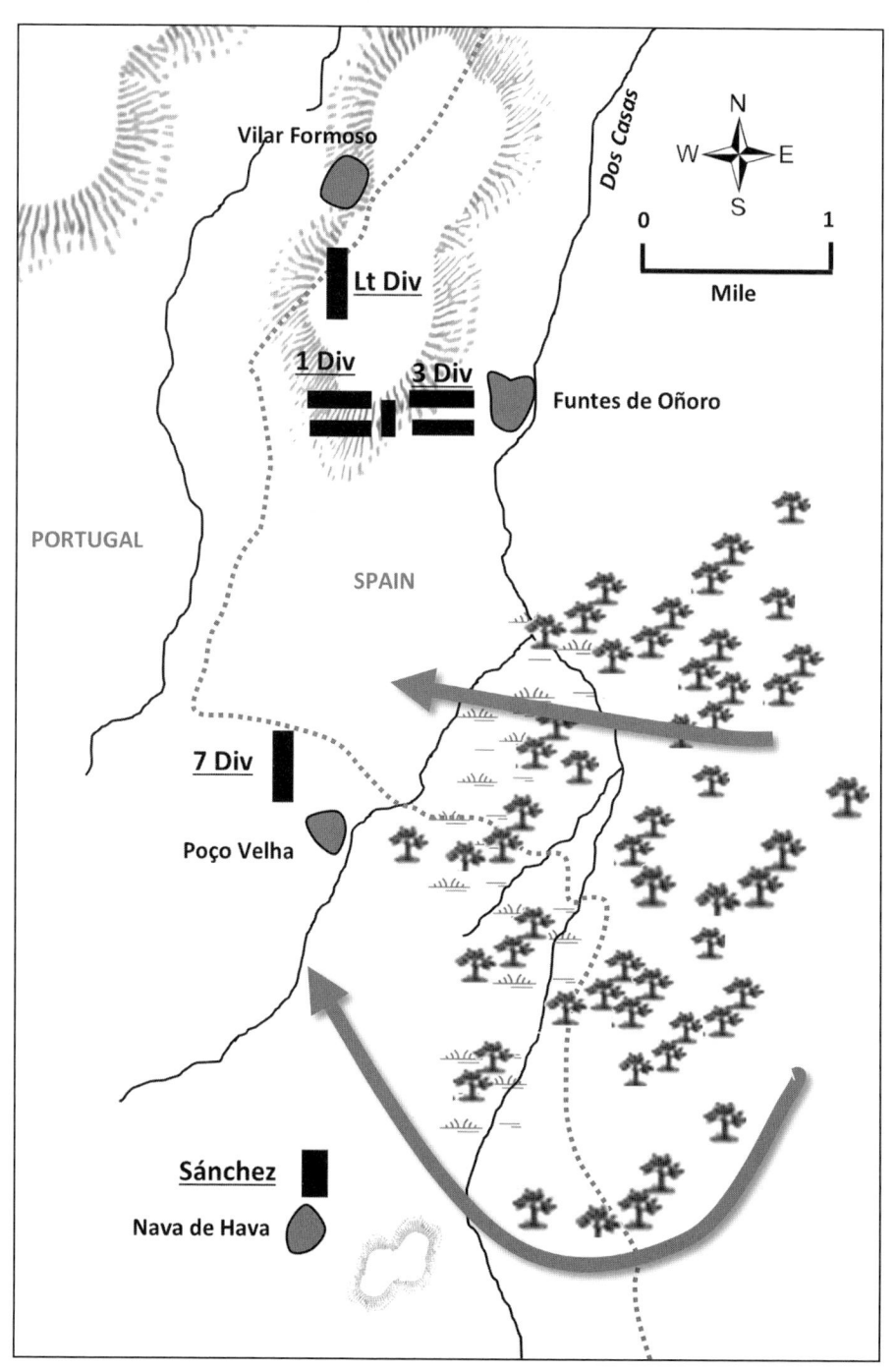

Wellington's redeployment on the southern half of the battlefield.

Sánchez's Guerrillas

Colonel Don Julián Sánchez's guerrillas were active between Poço Velho and Nave de Haver, where one of his lieutenants was gesticulating at the French as they made their way across the Dos Casas and the marsh. A guardsman on piquet duty with the 1st Division, mistaking him for a French officer, shot and killed him. Nonetheless, the main body of the guerrillas in Nave de Haver were surprised by the light cavalry of Fournier's Brigade. Brotherton recalled visiting the defences with Don Julián:

> Just at daybreak in the morning, however, having requested him to show me where his piquets were posted, he pointed out to me what he said was one of them, but I observed to him that it appeared to me in the dusk of the morning too large to be one of his piquets. However, the sun rising rapidly, as it does in these countries, dispelled the fog and the illusion the same moment, for what Don Julián pointed out to me as his piquet, proved to be a whole regiment of French cavalry dismounted. They mounted immediately and advanced.

Marbot wrote of this incident: 'Don Julián and his guerrillas deeming themselves secure behind the marsh, kept such a bad watch that our people found them asleep and killed thirty of them.' Major Brotherton confirms Marbot's opinion of this incident: 'It was a strong post, on an eminence, surrounded by stone wall enclosures, similar to those in Ireland, and no cavalry alone ought to have carried it.' Brotherton continued:

> I still believed the Spaniards would make a stand ... but the *brave* Don Julián, as the Spaniards called him, took himself off immediately with his whole force to the mountains, and left me with my two squadrons to shift for myself. The consequence was that I was pursued by the whole French cavalry towards the position at Fuentes de Oñoro, where the army was drawn up.[7]

Don Julián in fact retired behind the relative safety of the Rio Turon where he continued to cover the right flank until ordered towards Almeida.

The Cavalry Outnumbered

The French corps' light cavalry was initially still making its way through the woods to the plain with its leading elements pursuing Sánchez's guerrillas and Brotherton's squadrons, which were outnumbered four to one. Thus Brotherton wrote that he '... began the battle by running away' and was pursued across the plain towards Poço Velho

> ... which, as I approached, I saw was occupied by red-coats, and began to breathe and feel secure. As I approached I found our infantry posted with great regularity and steadiness, but as they did not commence firing on the French cavalry that were closely pursuing me, I rode up to the first officer

An idealized image of Don Julián Sánchez's lancers. In reality they would have worn a mix of civilian and military clothing and carried a range of weapons.

I could approach, and asked him why he did not fire and stop the progress of the enemy. He replied with astonishment, 'Are those the French?' I told him I knew it to my cost, having sustained considerable loss from them during my retreat. He immediately commenced firing on them, and most effectively checked them, bringing down numbers of men and horses.

The British battalion was the 85th (County of Dublin) Regiment, which had only just joined the army, and this was the first time they had been in contact with the enemy.[8] They did not panic and according to Brotherton they '... gave me the liberty of retiring leisurely'.

With the French cavalry thus engaged, it was up to an hour before the French turned their attention to the rest of Stapleton Cotton's horsemen who had by this time arrived and deployed near the 7th Division around Poço Velho. Cotton's task was to relieve pressure on the 7th Division and allow them to withdraw to a safer position, and a general but still unequal melee resulted. Captain Cocks enumerates the disparity in numbers:

> The enemy showed about forty squadrons or near 4,000 cavalry;[9] we had Anson's [sic, Arentschildt's] and Slade's brigades forming 1,010 men, serjeants included. Of these, two squadrons of Slade's had been detached to the left and two of Anson's [sic] had been nearly annihilated. On the right we had not above 800 cavalry, they were drawn up fronting outward to the right echelon.

The French drove in the foremost British squadrons and seeing two guns of Captain Bull's battery of horse artillery halting to fire canister, attempted to capture them.[10] Captain Ramsay, as the second captain commanding this section of guns, could not see the approaching enemy through the smoke but was altered just in time by Major Brotherton who 'sent an officer to warn him and saw him cease loading his grape as I knew he had just seconds left at the scene.'

Limbering up and just avoiding capture by the chasseurs, the guns were on the move but soon surrounded and isolated by the French cavalry. Major William Napier of the 43rd Light Infantry described what happened next:

> ... a great commotion was observed in their main body. Men and horses there closed with confusion and tumult towards one point, a thick dust arose, and loud cries, and the sparkling of blades and the flashing of pistols, indicated some extraordinary occurrence. Suddenly the multitude became violently agitated, an English shout pealed high and clear, the mass was rent asunder, and Norman Ramsay burst forth at the head of his battery [sic],

The 1796-pattern British cavalry sabres. Above, the light cavalry sabre; below, the controversial heavy cavalry sabre.

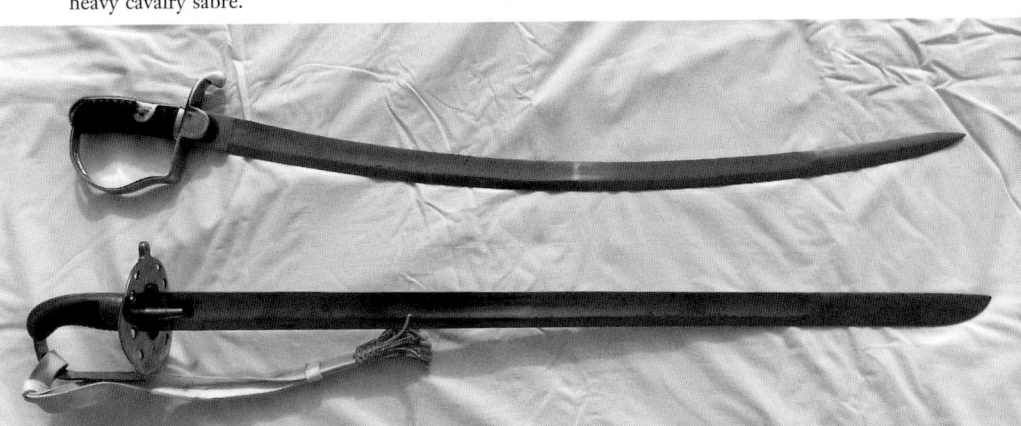

Captain Ramsay and the saving of the guns at Fuentes de Oñoro.

his horses breathing fire, stretched like greyhounds along the plain, the guns bounded behind them like things of no weight, and the mounted gunners followed in close career.

Major Brotherton's squadrons of the 14th Light and Royal Dragoons having recovered from their earlier exertions, on seeing the drama playing out in front of them, charged the pursuing French horsemen. 'General Charles Stewart joining the charge, took the enemy General Lamotte, fighting hand to hand.' The enemy, however, counter-attacked and the British cavalry along with Ramsay's guns were forced to disengage and re-form behind the approaching Light Division.

The 7th Division Under Pressure

Meanwhile, the 7th Division, with the Light Division still deploying onto the plain, were out on their own threatened by the approach of Marchand's division followed by Mermet's, both of which were marching out from the cover of the hill at Nave de Haver. They advanced in column of double-companies preceded by a cloud of *voltigeurs* north towards Poço Velho, thrusting back the 7th Division's skirmish line, and pushed on through the scrub into the village. The 85th Regiment and 2nd Caçadores fell back, struggling to maintain order as the French cavalry regiment fell on them, inflicting 150 casualties. The toll would have been higher but for the intervention of the German Hussars who moved up on their right flank and covered the 85th's withdrawal to their division's main position a mile further back.

A canister or grapeshot round consisting of a wooden sabot base, with a light metal container packed with musket balls (light canister) or larger shot (heavy canister).

The 7th Division was deployed in two lines on some high ground, with the 51st Light Infantry, the division's only other British battalion forward sheltered in a dip. Private Wheeler of that battalion wrote:[11]

> Our position ... was about twenty paces under the brow of a gentle descent, beyond which was a large plain covered with the enemy. A little distance in our rear the ground began to rise rather abruptly, it was covered with cork trees, rocks and straggling bushes, there was also a long wall behind us. On the high ground this was occupied by the Chasseurs Britanniques Regiment and the Portuguese brigade. We had some men in our front skirmishing, but they were soon driven in and formed with us; thus situated we anxiously awaited the attack.
> An officer of [French] hussars soon shewed himself on the brow, he viewed us with much attention then coolly turned round in his saddle and waved his sword. In an instant the brow was covered with cavalry. This was a critical moment; the least unsteadiness would have caused confusion. This would have been followed with defeat and disgrace. The enemy had walked to the brow, and their trumpeter was sounding the charge, when Colonel Mainwaring gave the words 'Ready, Present, Fire'. For a moment the smoke hindered us from seeing the effect of our fire, but we soon saw plenty of horses and men stretched not many yards from us.

Fuentes de Oñoro, 5 May 1811 199

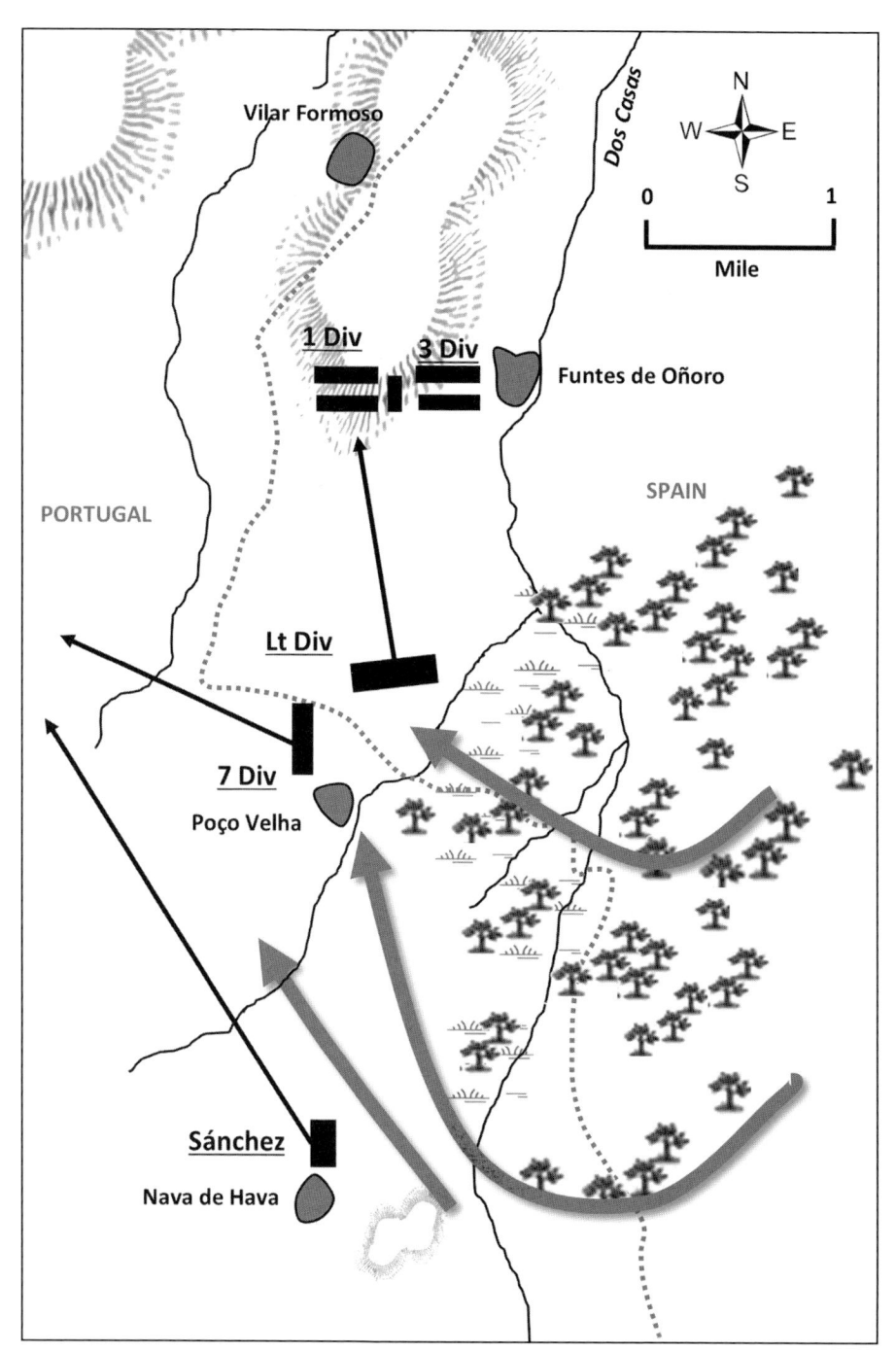

The withdrawal of Wellington's right flank.

The view looking south-east across the plain towards Poço Velho from the N332 international border road. The country is typical of the terrain fought over south of Fuentes de Oñoro.

During the 7th Division's withdrawal, the Chasseurs Britanniques distinguished themselves with their steadiness and from behind the stone walls, together with the Portuguese, volley-firing.[12] As they were on higher ground to the rear of the British battalion, they fired over the heads of the 51st who were lying down and checked the French advance at a crucial moment. Marbot describes their fire as being 'no less well sustained than aimed'. Wheeler continued:

> The confusion amongst the enemy was great, and as soon as the fire could be stopped a squadron of the 1st Royal and of the 14th Light Dragoons gallantly dashed in amongst the enemy and performed wonders, but they were soon obliged to fall back – for the enemy outnumbered them twenty to one or more; we now sorely felt the want of artillery and cavalry.[13]
>
> The enemy had formed again and was ready for another attack; our force was not sufficient to repel such a mass, so the order was given to retire independently by regiments. We retired through the broken ground in our rear, crossed the wall, and were pretty safe from their cavalry, but they had brought up their guns to the brow and were serving out the shot with a liberal hand.

During this period, with the French at times seeming certain to overwhelm the 51st, Lieutenant Colonel Mainwaring ordered his battalion's colours to be ripped off their staves and burned rather than have them fall into enemy hands. Ensign Mainwaring, nephew of the colonel, wrote:

> Colonel Mainwaring of the 51st was placed in a position in which he thought he was certain to be surrounded by the French. So, he called his officers and said, we are sure of being taken or killed; therefore, we'll burn the Colours. Accordingly, they brought the Colours and burnt them with all funeral pomp and buried the ashes or kept them.

Fuentes de Oñoro, 5 May 1811 201

The uniform, weapons and equipment of the Chasseurs Britanniques was standard British but with light blue facings, a colour generally reserved for foreign corps.

Private Wheeler continued his account:

> We continued retiring and soon came to a narrow rapid stream [Ribeira de Tourões]; this we waded up to our armpits and from the steepness of the opposite bank we found much difficulty in getting out. This caused some delay so the regiment waited until all had crossed, then formed line and continued our retreat in quick time; it was now the division was suffering much from the enemy's fire, the Portuguese in particular, the Chasseurs Britanniques came in for their share.
>
> Thanks to Colonel Mainwaring we came off safe, although the shot was flying pretty thick, yet his superior skill baffled all the efforts of the enemy, he took advantage of the ground and led us out of a scrape without loss. I shall never forget him, he dismounted off his horse, faced us and frequently called the time 'right, left' as he was accustomed to when drilling the regiment.
>
> His eccentricity did not leave him; he would now and then call out 'That fellow is out of step, keep step and they cannot hurt us.'
>
> Another time he would observe such a one, calling him by name, 'cannot march, mark him for drill, serjeant major.'
>
> 'I tell you again they cannot hurt us if you are steady, if you get out of time, you will be knocked down.'

A cross-belt plate of the 51st Light Infantry.

He was leading his horse and a shot passed under the horse's belly which made him rear up. 'You are a coward,' he said, 'I will stop your corn three days.'

The 7th Division crossed the Rio Turon to cover Freineda and Wellington's withdrawal route should the enemy attacks succeed on his right flank. Wheeler's praise of Colonel Mainwaring is, however, in stark contrast to Wellington's view of what he regarded as the unnecessary burning of the king's colours:

> Lord Wellington was exceedingly angry when he heard of it, as he knew well enough where he had placed the Regiment. So, he ordered Mainwaring under arrest and tried him by court martial. An old Colonel, who undertook his defence, said, 'I believe it was something to do with religious principles.' 'Oh,' said Lord Wellington, 'if it was a matter of religious principles, I have nothing more to do with it. You may take him out of arrest; but send him to Lisbon.'

The 51st's commanding officer was relieved of his command for what was perceived as 'panicking' while under pressure during the withdrawal. He was replaced in command by Colonel Mitchell in June.

Nonetheless, for a new formation, placed out on a flank where Wellington must have believed that they would not be sorely tested, the Anglo-Portuguese 7th Division's withdrawal was a feat of arms that gladdened Major General Houston. It was, however, to be shortly eclipsed by a similar withdrawal by the veteran Light Division.

Bessières' Betrayal

General Montbrun, who was being urged forward at a specific point when the French cavalry could have created the conditions for victory, had a dispute with General Loison. Marbot recalled that Montbrun 'stayed the march of the Reserve Cavalry under the plea that the battery of the Guard which had been promised to him had not yet come up'. It was, in fact, much worse: Marshal Bessières was not to be found and General Lepic, who was commanding the Imperial Guard light cavalry, to his eternal shame replied that he was personally willing to attack but he was under orders not to without Bessières' orders. Eventually Bessières was found and even then, it is alleged that the marshal still refused to commit the guard cavalry.

Marbot explained that with Montbrun's cavalry 'stayed' and Lepic's brigade remaining at the rear:

> The delay, however, was doubly fatal to us, first because Loison's infantry, seeing that it was no longer supported by Montbrun's cavalry, hesitated to engage in the plain, while in the second place this disastrous halt gave Wellington time to bring up all his cavalry to support Houston's and Craufurd's divisions, which alone were as yet in position before us.

French cavalry commanders General of Division Montbrun and General of Brigade Lepic.

Major Napier argued that the 1st but particularly the Light and 7th divisions would have been in greater peril if Marchand's and Mermet's divisions had immediately followed their cavalry, destroying the allied divisions in an all-arms fight. Instead, they drew up in front of Wellington's left centre, to the south of Fuentes village.

March of the Light Division

Having held the enemy cavalry, immediately after the saving of Ramsay's guns, it was now the turn of Craufurd's Light Division to retire more than 2 miles in the presence of the enemy; one of the most difficult phases of the war. With no fewer than five brigades of cavalry, as Thomas Garrety of the 43rd recalled, '5,000 French cavalry with fifteen pieces of artillery, close at hand, [were] impatient to charge ...' Captain Leach of the 95th Rifles recounted:

> The British right being turned at Nave de Haver, the mass of French cavalry, with artillery, continued to advance along the plain, threatening to cut off the Light Division from the position on the heights. We were, therefore, directed to retire from the wood, to form squares of battalions, and to fall back over the plain on the 1st Division.

Having defeated the first cavalry attacks in square, to conduct his retirement Craufurd ordered his five battalions into close column of companies.[14] From this formation, squares, with an impenetrable hedge of bayonets that horses refused

Major William Napier fought in the battle with the 43rd Light Infantry and was one of the early historians of the Peninsular War.

to charge, could be quickly formed by halting and facing outwards to form an all-round defence. In addition, the battalions were also echeloned so that when they halted to face the cavalry, they could volley fire without hitting each other. As the French advanced, they chased the riflemen from copses near Poço Velho, 'the last of them having to run at speed to obtain the shelter of the nearest square – one of the 52nd's'. The Light Division's columns began their march, with Colonel Elder's 3rd Caçadores out on the division's right flank. Leach continued:

> The steadiness and regularity with which the troops performed this movement, the whole time exposed to a cannonade, and followed across a plain by a numerous cavalry, ready to pounce on the squares if the least disorder

The Light Division's squares at Fuentes de Oñoro supported by Bull's troop and Slade's cavalry. ('Masterly Manoeuvre' by Christa Hook)

should be detected, has been acknowledged by hundreds of unprejudiced persons (unconnected with the Light Division), who witnessed it from the heights, to have been a masterpiece of military evolutions. We sustained a very trifling loss from the cannonade and reached our station in the position near the 1st Division.

Throughout the retirement the columns had to maintain their formations; any gaps would have been exploited by the enemy. Whenever the French cavalry approached, the battalions halted, faced outwards, volleyed, and emptied saddles in any squadrons that came too close. The Royal Dragoons, plus the 14th and 16th Light Dragoons and the 1st German Hussars launched squadron charges against vulnerable enemy horsemen. Having charged and overthrown enemy squadrons, before French numbers could come to their comrades' aid, they then fell back behind the division to re-form and await another chance to charge. The 95th's historian acknowledges that the British cavalry's action was a 'fine feat of arms, in the face of overwhelming odds' but stops short of saying that it made the retirement possible or even, uncharitably, more readily achievable.[15] The same could be said of Bull's troop who were still deployed in sections, providing support from the flank of the division's columns.

This was an example of the experienced soldiers of the Light Division, working under Craufurd, at their best under the eyes of the rest of the army, and was a seminal moment in the history of the division. They had already proved that

St Clair's painting of the Battle of Fuentes de Oñoro, 5 May 1811. This is the view during the cavalry battle looking south towards the hill of Nave de Haver, with the wooded marsh to its left.

they were masters of the outposts, had shown their steadiness under pressure at Buçaco Ridge and now they had demonstrated that they could manoeuvre in a general action with considerable nerve and precision in the face of a dauntingly large enemy force. Sir John Moore's concept of the universal soldier developed at Shorncliffe Camp and with Craufurd's standing orders were both thoroughly tested in the heat of battle.

There are, however, also French failures of co-operation and lack of activity to consider. Not only was there General Lepic's failure to join the battle, but Loison's reluctance to help Montbrun's attempt to destroy the Light Division. There is no starker example of relations between French commanders being so bad that they would not willingly assist each other. Consequently, Montbrun's cavalrymen could only impotently swear and gesticulate at the columns while they circled around the Light Division just out of musket shot, awaiting an opportunity to charge. Where possible, riflemen and Caçadores left the shelter of the squares to harass the enemy. Firing from patches of wood and walls, they kept the enemy wary of approaching the division. Although there was little toe-to-hoof fighting for the Light Division during this action, with just sixty-seven casualties, the steadiness of the British and Portuguese light battalions was remarkable. Of Craufurd and his division, Fortescue goes further: 'No more masterly manoeuvre is recorded of any general; no grander example of triumphant discipline is recorded of any regiment in the history of the British Army.'[16]

When the Light Division arrived on the ridge in front of the 1st Division, companies of the guards wheeled back and cheered as Bull's guns and the Light Division's columns came through and into reserve. They were not at rest long before a French column attempted to turn the British flank via the Rio Turon valley. A wing of four rifle companies under Captain O'Hare was sent to block them and firing from the cover of rocks, the French advance was duly checked by the riflemen. Lieutenant Cope of the 1st 95th Rifles later recalled:

> While the battalion were in position near Tourões, and the French infantry which threatened them kept out of rifle range, Flinn ... was observed to leave the ranks, and with his comrade, advance towards the enemy. The officer in immediate command, fancying they were deserting, asked the Sergeant of the Company what it meant. 'Oh no, sir,' he replied, 'they are only gone for some amusement.' Accordingly ... after stopping to drink at the Tourões (for the May day was hot) they crept up to the French and taking good aim, brought down each his man. Then putting their caps on their rifles to receive the return fire, while they were well under cover, they deliberately walked back and fell into their places in the Battalion.

On the ridge the 1st and 3rd divisions and Ashworth's Portuguese prepared to receive the enemy, but Wellington's superiority in artillery came into play and the French guns were outmatched and Loison's divisions largely confined themselves to skirmishing.

Riflemen deployed for skirmishing.

The Fate of the Guards' Light Companies

During this period of the battle, the Guards' three light companies and No. 5 Company of the 5th 60th Rifles were deployed as skirmishers in front of the 1st Division's new line, under the command of Lieutenant Colonel Hill of the 1st 3rd Guards. They had just beaten back a frontal attack when the French 13th Chasseurs took them in the flank in a surprise charge. Donaldson's 94th Scotch Brigade commented that the enemy's

> ... efforts were now chiefly confined to partial cannonading, and some charges with their cavalry, which were received and repulsed by the piquets of the first division in one instance; but as they were falling back, they did not perceive the charge of a different body in time to form and many of them were killed, wounded and taken prisoners including Colonel Hill.

Major Hall recounted that 'The enemy made a dart at the pickets of the 1st Division, with the expectation of sweeping off the line before our cavalry could support them.' Lieutenant Grattan of the 88th Connaught Rangers (3rd Division) was, as he explains, an impotent onlooker:

> Our division was posted on the high ground just above the plain: a small rugged ravine separated us from our comrades [in the 1st Division]; but although the distance was short, we were in effect, as far from them as if we

210   *Masséna at Bay*

were placed on the Rock of Lisbon: we felt much for their situation, but could not afford them the least assistance, and we saw them rode down and cut to pieces, without being able to rescue them or even discharge a musket in their defence.

Losses in these companies were heavy, but Major Hall recalled that

> They succeeded in part by coming up unexpectedly, but when they were perceived the men, by collecting into knots (or 'hiving' as they called it), repulsed them with the bayonet. A troop of the 14th Light Dragoons and some of the Royals were ordered out to the skirmish and suffered some loss.[17]

It is estimated that almost 100 of the 1st Division's losses in the battle this day, including prisoners, were suffered during this attack. Montbrun's men, eventually supported by infantry, however, continued to probe the allied position with little effect, Donaldson recalled:

> ... the 42nd regiment also, under Lord Blantyre, gallantly repulsed another charge made by the enemy's cavalry. The French then attempted to push a strong body of light infantry down the ravine to the right of the first division, but they were driven back by some companies of the Guards and 95th Rifles.[18]

The Fight for the Village Renewed

On the evening of 4 May:

> After dark a deserter from the French told us that there were five regiments of grenadiers picked out to storm the town. In the French army, the grenadiers are [grouped] all in regiments by themselves. We lay down, fully accoutred as usual, and slept in our blankets. An hour before day we were ready to receive the enemy.

As the 7th Division reached safety and the Light Division withdrew, Masséna saw that his plan to turn Wellington's right flank had failed, but he was not yet ready to concede and would resume the battle with a revised plan. Ferey's division and Drouet's pair of divisions were to attack the village of Fuentes de Oñoro and Reynier's II Corps was to advance by in the north. Once these attacks were making progress the three divisions to the south of the village – Merle's, Mermet's and Solignac's – were to attack Wellington's new line. At this point, however, as Marbot recalls:

> General Eblé, commanding the artillery, hurried up with the news that he had, at the artillery park, not more than four cartridges per man, which, with those left in their pouches, gave not more than a score to each soldier. This was an insufficient supply with which to renew the struggle against a foe who was sure to resist desperately, and Masséna ordered every wagon to be sent instantly to Rodrigo for ammunition. But the commissary-general reported

Fuentes de Oñoro, 5 May 1811 211

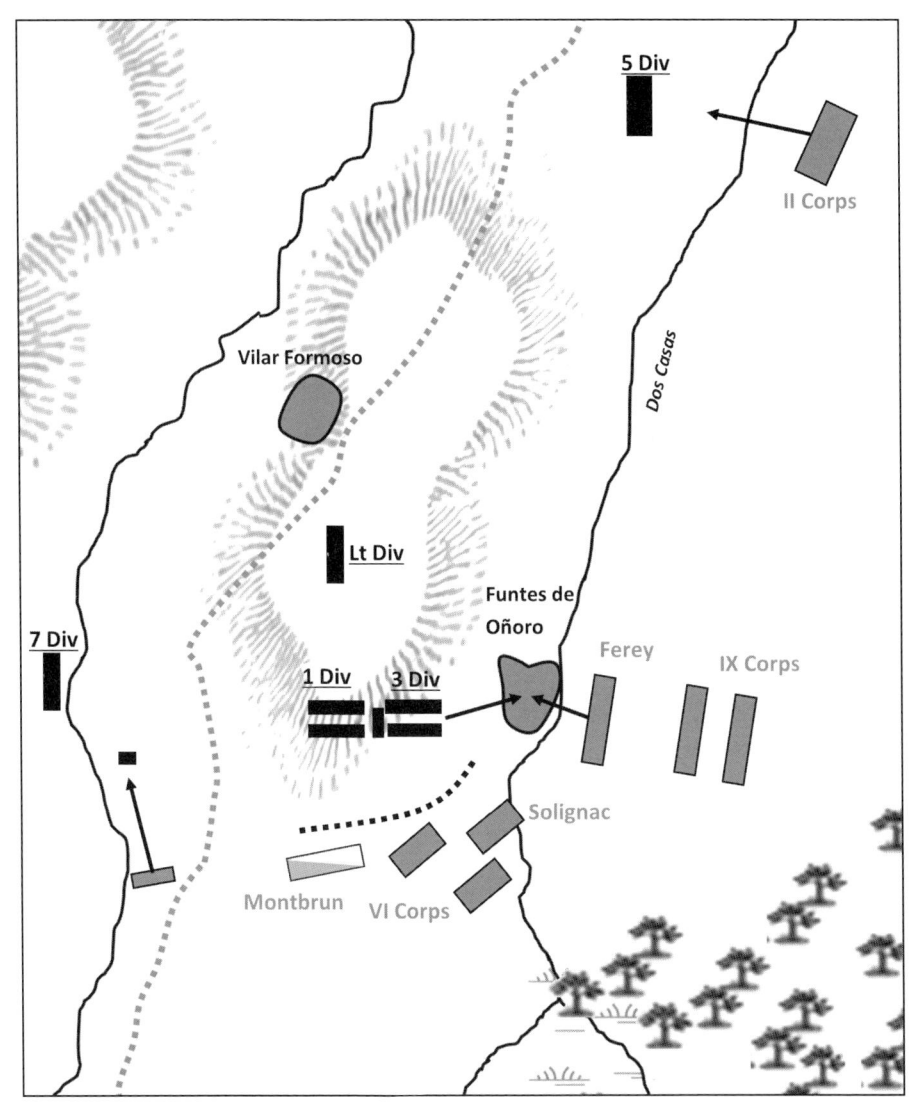

The final phases of the battle.

that he had made use of them to fetch from the same place the bread required for the morrow's supply. Having no other means of transport, Masséna asked Bessières to lend him the Guard's ammunition-wagons for a few hours; but he replied that his teams were already tired, and that a night march over bad roads would finish them – he could not lend them till the next day. Masséna flew into a rage, exclaiming that victory was being snatched from him a second time; but Bessières maintained his refusal, and a violent scene took place between the two marshals.

Consequently, the French battalions that were already prepared to attack Fuentes became the focus of French operations. Thomas of the 71st Light Infantry continued his account:

> About half-past nine o'clock a great gun from the French line, which was answered by one from ours, was the signal to engage. Down they came, shouting as usual. We kept them at bay, in spite of their cries and formidable looks. How different their appearance from ours! Their hats set round with feathers, their beards long and black, gave them a fierce look. Their stature was superior to ours; most of us were young. We looked like boys; they like savages. But we had the true spirit in us. We foiled them in every attempt to take the town until about eleven o'clock when we were overpowered and forced through the streets, contesting every inch.

The 71st and 79th were driven back, as Ferey's division was reinforced by Drouet, including the 9th Light Regiment. The defenders were in turn reinforced by the 2nd 24th and by the light companies of the 1st and 3rd divisions. The fighting ebbed and flowed around the village, but as Thomas wrote:

> Notwithstanding all our efforts, the enemy forced us out of the town, then halted and formed close column betwixt us and it. While they stood thus, the havoc amongst them was dreadful. Gap after gap was made by our cannon, and as quickly filled up. Our loss was not so severe, as we stood in open files. While we stood thus, firing at each other as quick as we could, the 88th Regiment advanced from the lines.

Wellington had now committed Mackinnon's Brigade (45th, 74th and 88th Foot) of the 3rd Division to the fight in the village. Lieutenant Grattan of the 88th Connaught Rangers takes up the story:[19]

> The Highlanders were driven to the churchyard at the top of the village, and were fighting with the French grenadiers across the tombstones and graves; while the 9th French Light Infantry[20] had penetrated as far as the chapel, distant but a few yards from our line, and were preparing to *debouche* upon

In the defence of the village both the Brown Bess musket and Short Infantry Rifle were used.

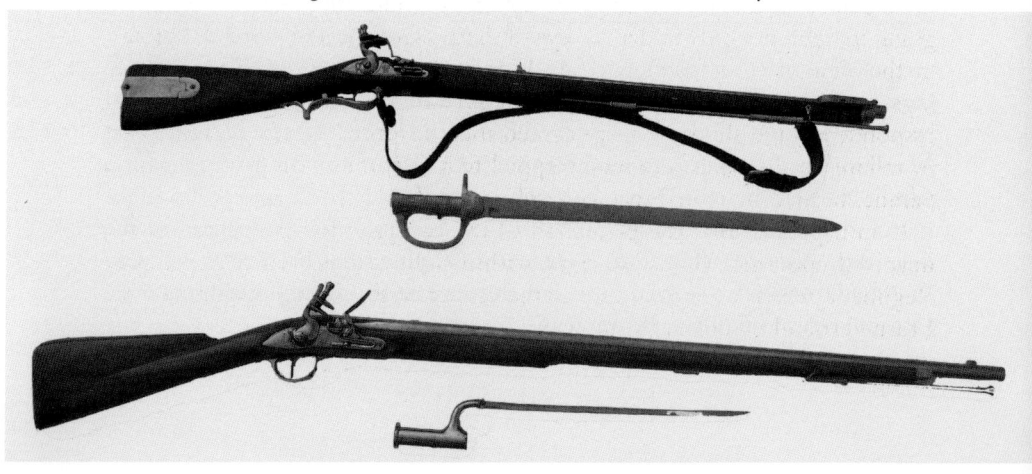

The view across the Dos Casas to the village of Fuentes de Oñoro.

our centre. Wallace with his regiment, the 88th, was in reserve on the high ground which overlooked the churchyard, and he was attentively looking on at the combat which raged below, when Sir Edward Pakenham galloped up to him, and said, 'Do you see that, Wallace?'

'I do,' replied the colonel, 'and I would rather drive the French out of the town than cover a retreat across the Côa.'

'Perhaps,' said Sir Edward, 'his lordship don't think it tenable.' Wallace answering said, 'I shall take it with my regiment, and keep it too.'

'Will you?' was the reply, 'I'll go and tell Lord Wellington so; see, here he comes.'

Colonel Mackinnon rode up and, leaving the 45th in position above Fuentes, he led the Connaught Rangers followed by the 74th Foot down towards the village accompanied by Sir Edward Pakenham who bravely remained mounted throughout, an obvious target:

> This battalion advanced with fixed bayonets in column of sections, left in front,[21] in double-quick time, their firelocks at the trail. As it passed down the road leading to the chapel, it was warmly cheered by the troops that lay at each side of the wall, but the soldiers made no reply to this greeting – they were placed in a situation of great distinction, and they felt it; they were going to fight, not only under the eye of their own army and general, but also in the view of every soldier in the French army; but although their feelings were wrought up to the highest pitch of enthusiasm, not one hurrah responded to the shouts that welcomed their advance, – there was no noise or talking in the ranks, the men stepped together at a smart trot, as if on a parade, headed by their brave colonel.
>
> It so happened that the command of the company which led this attack devolved upon me. When we came within sight of the French 9th [Light] Regiment, which were drawn up at the corner of the chapel, waiting for us, I turned round to look at the men of my company, they gave me a cheer that

General Sir Edward Pakenham, a member of Wellington's staff.

a lapse of many years has not made me forget, and I thought that that moment was the proudest of my life. The soldiers did not look as men usually do going into close fight – pale; the trot down the road had heightened their complexions, and they were the picture of everything that a chosen body of troops ought to be.

The enemy were not idle spectators of this movement; they witnessed its commencement, and the regularity with which the advance was conducted

Fuentes de Oñoro, 5 May 1811 215

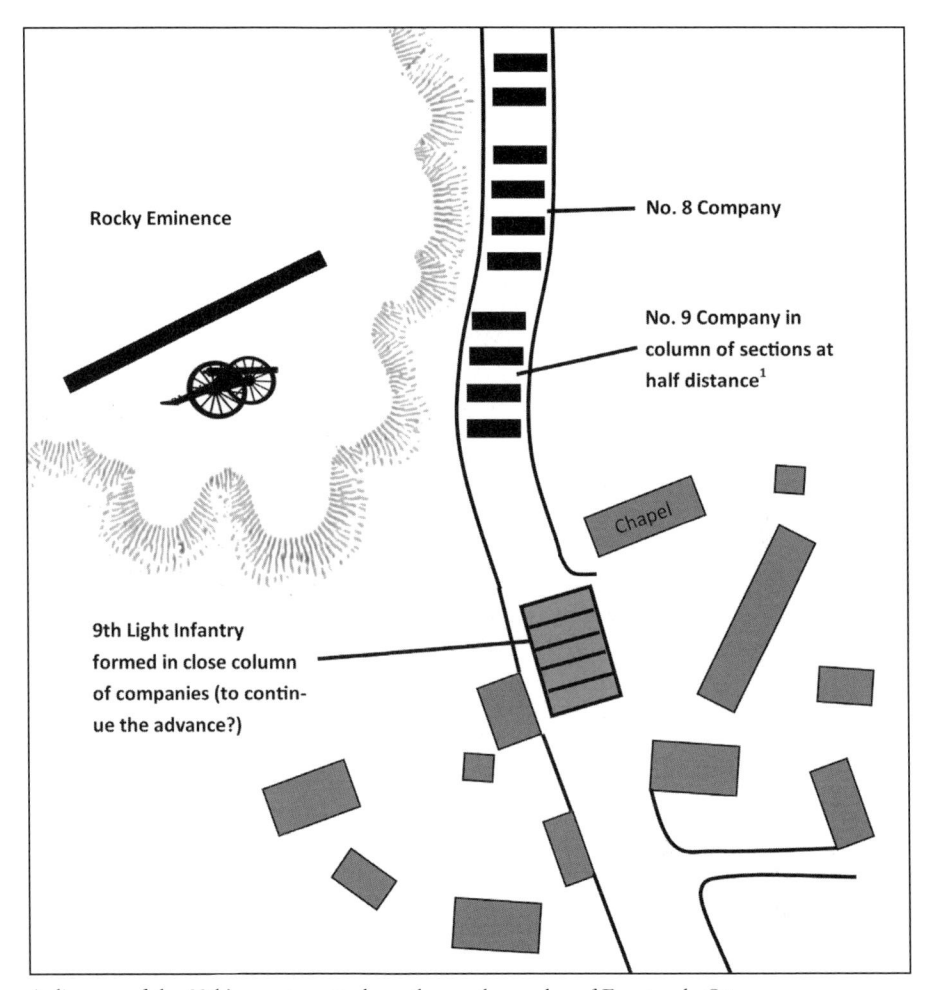

[Diagram labels: Rocky Eminence; No. 8 Company; No. 9 Company in column of sections at half distance¹; Chapel; 9th Light Infantry formed in close column of companies (to continue the advance?)]

A diagram of the 88th's counter-attack on the northern edge of Fuentes de Oñoro.

made them fearful of the result. A battery of eight-pounders advanced at a gallop to an olive-grove on the opposite bank of the river, hoping by the effects of its fire to annihilate the 88th Regiment, or, at all events, embarrass its movements as much as possible; but this battalion continued to press on, joined by its exhausted comrades, and the battery did little execution.

On reaching the head of the village, the 88th Regiment was vigorously opposed by the 9th Regiment, supported by some 100 of the Imperial Guard,[22] but it soon closed in with them, and, aided by the brave fellows that had so gallantly fought in the town all the morning, drove the enemy through the different streets at the point of the bayonet, and at length forced them into the river that separated the two armies. Several of our men fell on the French side of the water.

A soldier of a French light infantry regiment.

Drouet had fed further reinforcements into the battle to support Ferey and some 150 of his grenadiers were driven down a street that had been barricaded and, arriving at the bottom, they found themselves 'shut in'. The Rangers were

> flushed with victory and had no great time to deliberate as to what they will do; the thing is generally done in half the time the deliberation would occupy. In the present instance, every man was put to death; but our soldiers, as soon as they had leisure, paid the enemy that respect which is due to brave men.

Private Donaldson of the 94th was one of those original defenders that joined the counter-attack and

> charged the enemy and forced them to give way. As we passed over the ground where they had stood, it lay two and three deep of dead and wounded. While we drove them before us through the town, in turn they were reinforced, which only served to increase the slaughter. We forced them out and kept possession all day.

Wellington wrote in his post-action report: 'The contest again lasted in this quarter till night, when our troops still held their post; and from that time the enemy have made no fresh attempt on any part of our position.'

An officer of the 4th Battalion, 9th Light Infantry, Sub Lieutenant Cardon, commanding the battalion's No. 2 Company, who had in 1810 been so dismissive of the Allied army, had now revised his opinion writing that[23]

> ... I cannot go without saying about an event which came a little too close for comfort. I mean the meeting I had with Messrs the English. It was the first time I had fought against them, and although many call them poor soldiers on dry land, they proved on this occasion, as in many others, they deserve the esteem of the French rather than their sarcasm and bad jokes. For my personal account, I have to be pitied in admiring them somewhat. The first time we had a full affair together, they wanted to deprive me of two limbs! Fortunately they succeeded poorly, because the first embrace was from only a small bullet which hit me above right breast, near the shoulder and which, to my good fortune, having lost its force, did not penetrate at all, but rendered me all black and so swollen I was incapable of using the arm, which I had to carry in a sling for a month. Another ball attacked my opposite extremity at the same moment. It cut the third phalanx of the little toe on my left foot. I want to believe this blow was sent with good intentions, because it relieved me of an ingrown nail which had made me suffer a lot.[24]

The battle ended with the fighting gradually dying down across the battlefield. Further to the north on the Dos Casas General Reynier completed Masséna's discomfort when his lacklustre attack by II Corps was sharply repulsed by the 5th Division.

A French centre company shako (left) and the 1805-pattern British regimental cap.

Over three days, Masséna had failed at Fuentes de Oñoro in his attempt to break Wellington's line and re-provision Almeida.

At dusk, Colonel Beckwith's brigade of the Light Division marched down to the village to relieve the exhausted men of the 1st and 3rd divisions. Beckwith's men found 'the village and the ground near it covered with killed and wounded'. Donaldson of the 94th recorded his regiment's casualties: 'In these affairs we lost four officers and two taken prisoners, besides 400 men killed and wounded. This statement, more than any words of mine, will give an idea of the action at Fuentes de Oñoro.' Captain Leach wrote of that evening:

> We had been but a short time at Fuentes de Oñoro, when a flag of truce came in, requesting permission to send into the village unarmed parties to bring away their wounded, who filled the streets and houses. During this

truce, several French officers came down to the little bridge over the Dos Casas, at the foot of the village, on which happened to be posted a file of men of my own company, whilst two French grenadiers were on sentry at the other end of it. On the centre of the bridge three French officers met and conversed a considerable time with the officers of my Company and were politeness itself. After offering us a pinch of snuff, by way of prelude, the events which had taken place during the day were discussed. They paid many compliments to the gallant conduct of our army and declared that to-morrow would be a great and decisive day, and full of glory for one of the two.

The MGSM, finally awarded to Private Brant of the 5th 60th Rifles in 1848. The bar for Fuentes de Oñoro was one of nine to which he was entitled.

In expectation that the French would attack again on the following day, there was little rest that night for Lieutenant Simmons and his riflemen in Fuentes de Oñoro:

> The remainder of the night was occupied in knocking down many an honest man's garden wall and making strong breastworks to fire over as soon as the day dawned. Only a few random shots were fired during the night. Before day every man stood to his arms and carefully watched it dawning.

However, no attack came, and the 6th was spent with both sides removing the dead and the allies entrenching on the ridge and erecting barricades in the village. Marbot explained why the battle was not renewed:

> At daybreak on the 6th, Bessières' wagons started for Rodrigo; but they moved so slowly that the cartridges did not come till the afternoon, and Wellington had employed the twenty-four hours in entrenching his new position, especially the upper part of the village of Fuentes de Oñoro. It could not now be taken save at the expense of torrents of French blood, and the opportunity of victory was hopelessly lost to us.

Of casualties, Wellington wrote home that

> We have had warm work in this quarter, but I hope we shall succeed in the end. The French, it is said, lost 5,000 men, we 1,200, in the affair of the 5th; on the 3rd we lost about 250; the French left 400 dead in the village of Fuentes de Oñoro. We lost the prisoners by the usual dash and imprudence of the soldiers.

Masséna's report to Napoleon described the battle in terms of a victory and Fuentes de Oñoro numbers among those victories on the Arc de Triomphe in Paris. Debate over Wellington's mistakes and French misfortune went on for many years, but Wellington candidly wrote to Marshal Beresford: 'If *Boney* had been there, we should have been beat.'

Chapter Ten

Aftermath

When the expected attack failed to materialize during 6 May 1811, it became apparent that Marshal Masséna was not going to renew the battle against a now well-prepared defensive position. The marshal wrote in his dispatch on the 7th:

> The enemy has passed the night after the battle in fortifying the crest of the plateau he occupies. There are five large works, much artillery is visible, and trenches for the firing line. He has put *épaulements*[1] in the ravines and behind rocks; he has barricaded the upper part of Fuentes de Oñoro village, and Vilar Formoso; thus he has called to his aid all the resources of fortifications against an attack that would need to be made by main force.

Masséna, with little possibility of successfully attacking the allies on the ridge behind Fuentes de Oñoro and having issued the supplies in the convoy intended for Almeida for want of rations, was unable to keep his army concentrated. He only delayed long enough to issue orders for a retreat back into Spain and to get instructions through the blockade to General Brenier in Almeida. Private Donaldson remained with the garrison in Fuentes de Oñoro:

> On the 7th we still remained quiet; but on this day the whole French army were reviewed on the plain by Masséna. On the night of the 7th, some companies of our regiment were detached on piquet to the ravine on the left of the town, and during the night I was placed on one of the outpost sentries. The French piquets occupied the opposite side, and the distance between us was but trifling. The night was very dark, and the place where I was posted was amongst bushes and trees, near the river's edge. All was still, save the river gurgling over its rocky bed, or when a slight breeze set the leaves in motion, and the *qui vive* of the French sentinels could be distinctly heard.
> On the 8th the French sentries were withdrawn at daylight, the main body of the enemy having retired during the night, to the woods between Fuentes and Gallegos.

That day Wellington wrote to Marshal Beresford from Vilar Formoso:

> From the 5th to this day the two armies have been not only in sight, but literally within shot of each other. The French, however, withdrew in the night and this morning towards the Azaba, and I cannot tell yet how far they are going, or what shape they will take. Almeida still holds.

The Army of Portugal was now back across the border, but this was only the first stage of Masséna's withdrawal, which Wellington followed with cavalry patrols.

A French infantryman on sentry duty.

Break-Out from Almeida

Having failed to reprovision Almeida and with the certainty of its garrison being starved into submission by the blockade, Masséna took the decision to slight the fortress's defences and for General Brenier's men to break out. The problem, however, was how to get orders to General Brenier. The solution was to offer a reward of 6,000 francs for delivery of the message. Marbot recalled that

> Three brave men, whose names deserve to be recorded in our annals, volunteered for the perilous duty of passing through the enemy's camp, and carrying to General Brenier instructions with regard to the evacuation. These three intrepid soldiers were Pierre Zaniboni, corporal of the 76th, Jean Noel Lami, a canteen-man in Ferey's division, and André Tillet of the 6th Light Infantry. They had all taken part in the siege of Almeida the year before and knew the surrounding district thoroughly. They were to take different roads, and each bore a letter in cipher to the governor. They started at nightfall on the 6th; Zaniboni, disguised as a Spanish pedlar, for he spoke the language well, slipped into the English bivouacs on the plea of selling tobacco and buying dead men's clothes; Lami, as a Portuguese peasant, played much the same role at another part of the English lines. This kind of

petty trade is common in all armies, and the two Frenchmen went from line to line without awaking any suspicion. Just as they were drawing near the gates of Almeida, however, the trick was discovered – in what manner has never been explained – the poor fellows were searched, and being convicted by the letters found on them, were shot as spies, according to the law of war which punishes with death every soldier who lays aside his uniform when on duty. Tillet, with better judgement than his unhappy comrades, started in uniform, with his sword. Following at first the deep gorge of the Dos Casas stream, up to his waist in the water, he crept slowly from rock to rock, hiding himself behind them at the least sound, until he was near the ruined Fort Concepción. There, leaving the stream, he crawled on all fours through the full corn, and at length reached the outworks of Almeida, being received there at dawn by the French outposts.

The arrival of the message in Almeida was duly signalled by firing the fortress's heavy cannon, at which Masséna started to issue the orders for the withdrawal to Ciudad Rodrigo. It would, however, take some days for Brenier to prepare the demolition of the fortress walls. Mines were dug into the ramparts and the chambers charged, while all ammunition, gun-carriages and barrels were rendered useless. As Marbot noted: 'The two armies remained facing each other for four days without any further action.' Reynier's II Corps retired via Barba del Puerco to San Felices in order to be positioned to cover the latter stage of Brenier's break-out.

Suspecting that Almeida's garrison would attempt to break out, on 10 May Wellington sent Major General Campbell's 6th Division to reinforce Pack's Portuguese Brigade. The division's three brigades were deployed in villages 3 to 4 miles from the fortress, with a chain of piquets between the villages, completing encirclement. As a deception measure, during the days before his break-out, Brenier's men were to be seen on the walls making preparations well away from where the actual break-out was to take place.

Sometime after 2300 hours on the night of 10 May, the 1,300 men of the garrison left the fortress in two columns to cover the 10 miles to the Águeda at Barba del Puerco. They were personally led by General Brenier who 'guided himself by the moon and the direction of the streams'. According to Marbot, thus 'he had come within a short distance of General Heudelet's division [II Corps], which Masséna had sent to meet him, when he fell in with a Portuguese brigade. He attacked and dispersed it.'

Brenier was lucky: his columns had struck the junction between Pack's and Burn's brigades, where the thinly-spread piquets of the 1st Portuguese and the 2nd Queen's were simply charged down by the escaping French columns. Shortly afterwards the fuses that had been left burning in the fortress reached the demolitions.

Wellington's measures to blockade Almeida had failed; his instructions and orders had not been actioned. Lieutenant Colonel Iremonger had simply stood

224 *Masséna at Bay*

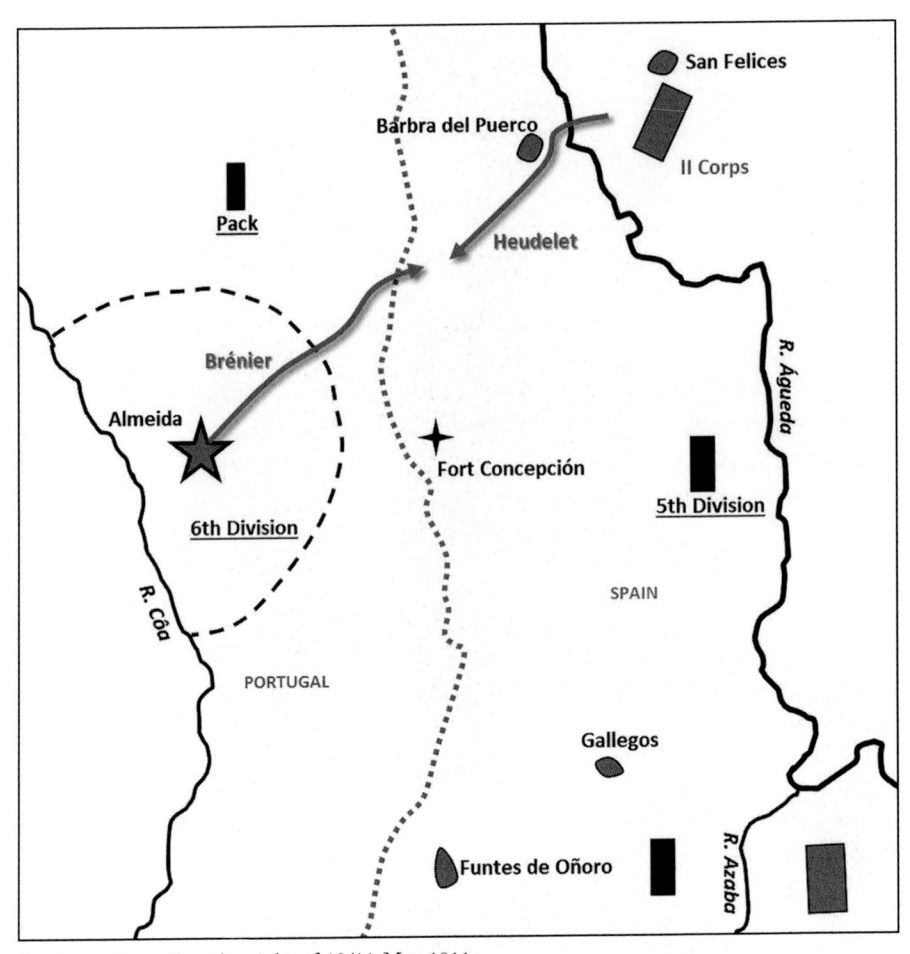

Break-out from Almeida, night of 10/11 May 1811.

the Queen's to arms and dispatched patrols, even though he was best placed to take immediate action against Brenier. General Erskine now commanding the 5th Division had that afternoon received orders to extend the division's front to Barba del Puerco, but as he was about to sit down to dine, he put it in his pocket and delayed forwarding instructions to the 4th King's Regiment. Even so, the message is said to have reached Lieutenant Colonel Bevan by early evening, but he decided that his battalion should stay where it was until the following morning. In the event it only moved after midnight when it was already too late to intercept the break-out column. Bevan later claimed, however, that he received no orders from Erskine until midnight. The deployment of the 4th King's to Barba del Puerco could have delayed or prevented General Heudelet from crossing the Águeda to meet Brenier and the latter's columns escaping. Pack's Portuguese and some of Slade's cavalry did, however, pursue and by dawn had

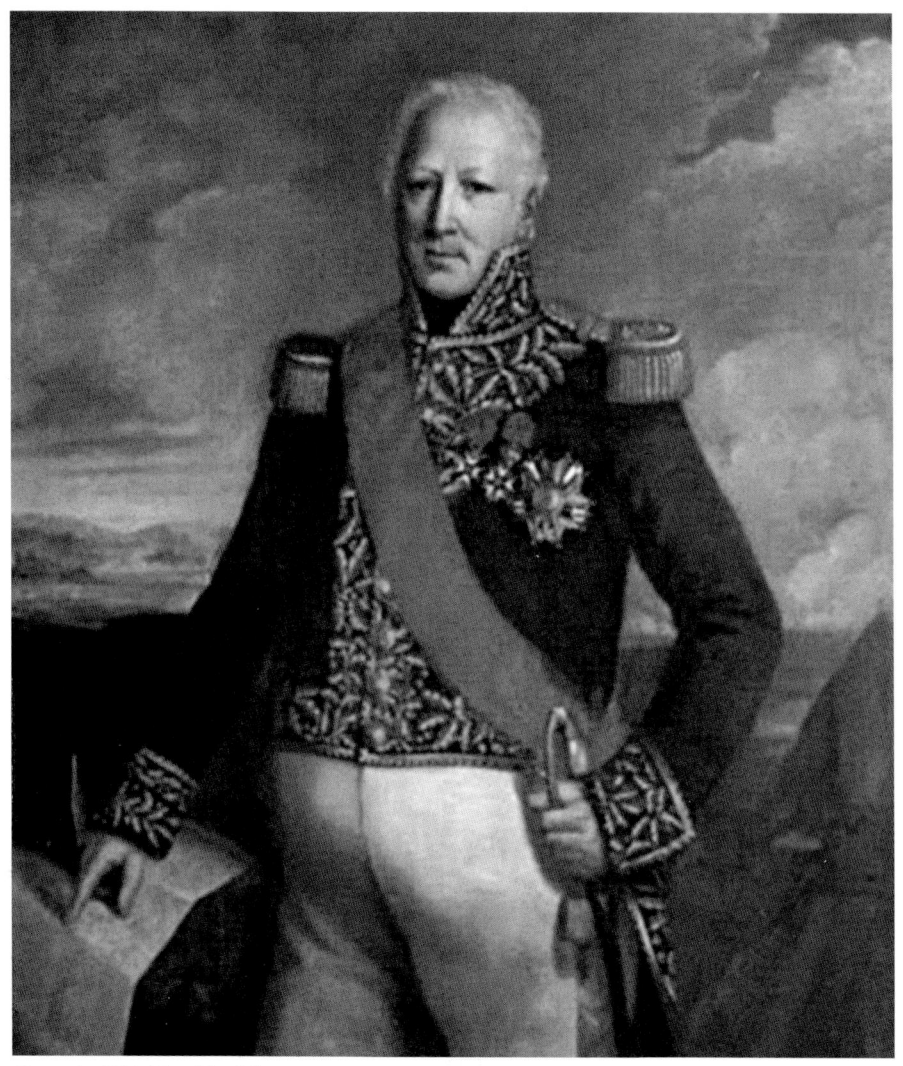

General of Division Heudelet.

inflicted casualties, taken some prisoners and captured the baggage, but the majority of the garrison and Heudelet's division escaped.

Wellington was furious at 'the most disgraceful military event' and he later wrote: 'They had about 13,000 to watch 1,400. There they were all sleeping in their spurs even; but the French got off. I begin to be of the opinion that there is nothing on earth so stupid as a gallant officer.'

Lieutenant Colonel Bevan was arrested and was to be court-martialled, but he shot himself before he came to trial. Brenier, however, was promoted to general of division by Napoleon.

French line infantry. The soldier on the left wears the pre-1812 uniform and the man on the right the post-1812 habit and shako.

Masséna Relieved of his Command

With Major Pelet arriving in Paris bearing news of Masséna's dismissal of Marshal Ney, Napoleon ordered the recently-created Marshal Marmont, Duke of Ragusa, to the peninsula to take over command of VI Corps. However, with news arriving of the scale of the Army of Portugal's reverse and Masséna admitting to Napoleon that he had lost the confidence of a dispirited army, the emperor had little choice but to relieve him of his command.

Marmont had arrived in Ciudad Rodrigo on 8 May, and General Foy bearing revised orders for Marmont to take command of the Army of Portugal two days later. Marmont protested that he knew nothing of Napoleon's change of mind,

Marshal Marmont, Duke of Ragusa.

Marshal André Masséna, Duc de Rivoli and Prince d'Essling.

but Masséna was furious at his dismissal. While being relieved of his command was inevitable for Masséna, there were those who believed it to have been harsh; among them was artilleryman Captain Noël who wrote:

> Even if there were some who were gratified by this disgraceful incident, this was not true of most of the officers and soldiers, who gave full credit to the strength of character displayed by our commander-in-chief throughout this difficult war. They did not blame him either for our failure or for our sufferings. His departure did nothing to appease an unhappiness that verged on anger. If, by striking at him, Napoleon had wished to turn him into a scapegoat, then he was mistaken for it was he himself whom the army blamed for its troubles.

This was the end of Masséna's active career. After reporting to Napoleon, he was sent to Marseilles as garrison commander. During the 'Hundred Days' in 1815, he did his best to sit on the fence and after the Second Restoration he was a member of a court martial that refused to try his young competitor, Marshal Ney. He died in 1817.

British line infantry volley fire at a barricade in Fuentes de Oñoro during a re-enactment of the battle.

Hamilton Smith's illustration of highlanders of the period.

Appendix I

Welington's Memorandum to Lieutenant Colonel Fletcher

Memorandum for Lieutenant Colonel Fletcher, Commanding Royal Engineers

Lisbon, 20th October, 1809.

The plan was altered after this memorandum was written, as it was found that the plain of Castanheira could not be occupied with advantage; the right was therefore thrown back on Alhandra. But this memorandum is the foundation on which the whole work was commenced and completed. It was written after a detailed reconnaissance of the ground, and a personal visit to every part of it.

In the existing relative state of the allied and French armies in the Peninsula, it does not appear probable that the enemy have it in their power to make an attack upon Portugal. They must wait for their reinforcements; and as the arrival of these may be expected, it remains to be considered what plan of defence shall be adopted for this country.

The great object in Portugal is the possession of Lisbon and the Tagus, and all our measures must be directed to this object. There is another also connected with that first object, to which we must likewise attend, *viz.* – the embarkation of the British troops in case of reverse.

In whatever season the enemy may enter Portugal, he will probably make his attack by two distinct lines, the one north, the other south of the Tagus; and the system of defence to be adopted must be founded upon this general basis.

In the winter season the river Tagus will be full and will be a barrier to the enemy's enterprises with his left attack, not very difficult to be secured. In the summer season, however, the Tagus being fordable in many places between Abrantes and Salvaterra, and even lower than Salvaterra, care must be taken that the enemy does not, by his attack directed from the south of the Tagus, and by the passage of that river, cut off from Lisbon the British army engaged in operations to the northward of the Tagus.

The object of the allies should be to oblige the enemy as much as possible to make his attack with concentrated corps. They should stand in every position which the country could afford, such a length of time as would enable the people of the country to evacuate the towns and villages, carrying with them or destroying all articles of provisions and carriages, not necessary for the allied army; each corps taking care to preserve its communication with the others, and its relative distance from the point of junction.

In whatever season the enemy's attack may be made, the whole allied army, after providing for the garrisons of Elves, Almeida, Abrantes and Valence, should be divided into three corps, to be posted as follows – one corps to be in Beira; another in Alentejo; and the third, consisting of Beira; another in Alentejo; and the third, consisting of the Lusitanian legion, eight battalions of Caçadores, and two of militia, in the mountains of Castello Branco.

In the winter, the corps in Beira should consist of two-thirds of the whole numbers of the operating army. In the summer, the corps in Beira and Alentejo should be nearly of equal numbers.

I shall point out in another memorandum the plan of operations to be adopted by the corps north and south of the Tagus in the winter months.

In the summer, it is probable, as I have above stated, that the enemy will make his attack in two principal corps, and that he will also push one through the mountains of Castello Branco and Abrantes. His object will be, by means of his corps south of the Tagus, to turn the positions which might be taken up in his front on the north of that river; to cut off from Lisbon the corps opposed to him; and to destroy it by an attack in front and rear at the same time. This can be avoided only by the retreat of the right centre, and left of the allies, and their junction at a point at which, from the state of the river, they cannot be turned by the passage of the Tagus by the enemy's left.

The first point of defence which presents itself below that at which the Tagus ceases to be fordable is the river of Castanheira, and here the army should be posted as follows: – 10,000 men, including all the cavalry, in the plain between the Tagus and the Hills; 5,000 infantry on the left of the plain; and the remainder of the army, with the exception of the following detachments, on the height in front, and on the right of Cadafoes.

In order to prevent the enemy from turning, by their left, the positions which the allies may take up for the defence of the high road to Lisbon by the Tagus, Torres Vedras should be occupied by a corps of 5,000 men; the height in the rear of Sobral de Monte Agraço by 4,000 men; and Arruda by 2,000 men.

There should be a small corps on the height east by south of the height of Sobral, to prevent the enemy from marching from Sobral to Arruda; and there should be another small corps on the height of Ajuda, between Sobral and Bucelas.

In case the enemy should succeed in forcing the corps at Torres Vedras, or Sobral de Monte Agraço, or Arruda; if the first, it must fall back gradually to Cabeo de Montachique, occupying every defensible point on the road: if the second it must fall back on Bucelas, destroying the road after the height of Ajuda: if the third, it must fall back upon Alhandra, disputing the road particularly at a point one league in front of that town.

In case any one of these three positions should be forced, the army must fall back from its position as before pointed out, and must occupy one as follows:

5,000 men, principally light infantry, on the hill behind Alhandra; the main body of the army on the Serra or Serves, with its right on that part of the Serra

Appendix I: Welington's Memorandum to Lieutenant Colonel Fletcher

which is near the Cazal de Portela, and is immediately above the road which crosses the Serra from Bucelas to Alverca; and its left extending to the pass of Bucelas. The entrance of the pass of Bucelas to be occupied by the troops retired from Sobral de Monte Agraço, &c., and Cabeca de Montachique, by the corps retired from Torres Vedras.

In order to strengthen these several positions, it is necessary that different works should be constructed immediately, and that arrangements and preparations should be made for the construction of others.

Accordingly, I beg Colonel Fletcher, as soon as possible, to review these several positions.

1st. He will examine particularly the effect of damming up the mouth of the Castanheira river; how far it will render that river a barrier, and to what extent it will fill.

2nd. He will calculate the labour required for that work, and the time it will take, as well as the means of destroying the bridge over the river, and of constructing such redoubts as might be necessary on the plain, and on the hill on the left of the road, effectually to defend the plain. He will state particularly what means should be prepared for these works. He will also consider of the means and time required, and the time it will take, as well as the means of destroying the bridge over the river, and of constructing such redoubts as might be necessary on the plain, and on the hill on the left of the road, effectually to defend the plain. He will state particularly what means should be prepared for these works. He will also consider of the means and time required, and the effect which might be produced by sloping the banks of the river.

3rd. He will make the same calculations for the works to be executed on the hill in front, and on the right of Cadafoes, particularly on the left of that hill, to shut the entry of the valley of Cadafoes.

4th. He will examine and report upon the means of making a good road of communication from the plain across the hills into the valley of Cadafoes, and to the left of the proposed position, and calculate the time and labour it will take.

5th. He will examine the road from Ota by Abrigada, Labrugeira to Merciana, and thence to Torres Vedras; and also from Merciana to Sobral de Monte Agraço. He will also examine and report upon the road from Alenquer to Sobral de Monte Agraço.

6th. He will entrench a post at Torres Vedras for 5,000 men. He will examine the road from Torres Vedras to Cabeça de Montachique; and fix upon the spots at which to break it up as might stop or delay the enemy; and if there should be advantageous ground at such spots, he will entrench a position for 400 men to cover the retreat of the corps from Torres Vedras.

7th. He will examine the position at Cabeça de Montachique, and determine upon its line of defence, and upon the works to be constructed for its defence, by a corps of 5,000 men; of which he will estimate the time and the labour.

8th. He will entrench a position for 4,000 men on the two heights which command the road from Sobral de Monte Agraço to Bucelas.

9th. He will entrench a position for 400 men on the height of Ajuda, between Sobral and Bucelas, to cover the retreat of the corps from Sobral to Bucelas; and he will calculate the means and the time it will take to destroy the road at that spot.

10th. He will construct a redoubt for 200 men and three guns at the windmill on the height of Sobral de Monte Agraço, which guns will bear upon the road from Sobral to Arruda.

11th. He will ascertain the points at which and the means by which the road from Sobral to Arruda can be destroyed.

12th. He will ascertain the labour and time required to entrench a position which he will fix upon for 2,000 men to defend the road coming out of Arruda towards Villa Franca and Alhandra, and will fix upon the spot at which the road from Arruda at Alhandra can be destroyed with advantage.

13th. He will construct a redoubt on the hill which commands the road from Arruda, about one league in front of Alhandra.

14th. He will examine the estuaries at Alhandra, and see whether, by damming them up at the mouths, he could increase the difficulties of a passage by that place; and he will ascertain the time and labour and means which this work will require.

15th. He will fix upon the spots, and ascertain the time and labour required to construct redoubts upon the hill of Alhandra on the right, to prevent the passage of the enemy by the high road; and on the left, and in the rear, to prevent by their fire the occupation of the mountains towards Alverca.

16th. He will determine upon the works to be constructed on the right of the position upon the Serra de Serves, as above pointed out, to prevent the enemy from forcing that point; and he will calculate the means and the time required to execute them. He will likewise examine the pass of Bucelas, and fix upon the works to be constructed for its defence, and calculate the means, time, and labour required for the execution.

17th. He will calculate the means, time, and labour required to construct a work upon the hill upon which the windmill stands, at the southern entrance at the pass of Bucelas.

18th. He will fix upon spots on which signal posts can be erected upon these hills, to communicate from one part of the position to the other.

19th. It is very desirable that we should have an accurate plan of the ground.

21st. Examine the effect of damming up the river which runs by Loures and calculate the time and means required to break up the bridge at Loures.

WELLINGTON

Appendix II

Wellington's Orders for Operations against Guarda

Arrangement for the Movement of the Army on 29 March 1811

Celorico, 28th March, 1811.

The Light Division will march at daybreak exactly from Maçal do Chão along the great road towards Alverca and will turn off to the right hand when it arrives at the road leading to the village of Recammodo, and proceed to that village. From Recammodo it will move in the direction of Guarda, keeping on the left bank of the rivulet of Maousa, which passes between Recammodo and Avelãs d'Imbom, and runs by Avelãs da Ribeira towards Alverca. When the division gets about halfway from Recammodo to Guarda, it will occupy the heights that look towards the latter place, and wait for further orders, putting itself in communication, however, on the right with the 6th Division, and sending out patrols and piquets to the front, and also to the left flank towards the roads that lead from Guarda to Pinhel, and to Almeida. Captain Bull's troop of horse artillery and Major General Anson's brigade of light cavalry will move with the Light Division. Colonel Barbacena's brigade of Portuguese cavalry, and the Portuguese troops (militia) under Colonel Wilson, will take post at Alverca and at Avelãs da Ribeira, and will observe the enemy towards Freixedas, keeping up a communication, also, with the Light Division through the village of Recammodo.

The troops (Portuguese) under the orders of Colonel Trant will advance to Granja and Ervastendras, and will observe the enemy towards Pinhel, Souro Pires and Freixedas, communicating on the right with the troops at Alverca.

The 6th Division will cross the Mondego at the Ponte do Ladrao (near Lagiosa) and at the ford of Porto de Came, and will move afterwards, partly through Sobral da Serra and partly by Cabadoide, towards Guarda. It will halt upon the high grounds which look towards Guarda, about half a league from that town, and will put itself in communication, on the left, with the Light Division, and on the right, with the 3rd Division. If the artillery of the 6th Division cannot be got up the hills by either Sobral da Serra or Cabadoide, Major General Campbell will order it to proceed up the great paved road to Guarda, following the artillery of the 3rd Division; and Major General Campbell will give to the artillery of his division, in its movement up the paved road, such assistance and protection as may be necessary beyond that afforded by a battalion of the 3rd Division, which is ordered to march by the same route. The 6th Division will begin to move one hour after daybreak.

The right and centre brigades of the 3rd Division, with the mountain guns attached to that division, will march at daybreak, the former by Trinda and Crujeiro, the latter by Mazinha towards Guarda, and will endeavour to gain possession, as soon as possible, of the road which leads from the village of Porcos to Guarda, and of the old fort, or redoubt, near that road, called the Fort d'Alorna.

The left brigade of the 3rd Division will march one hour after daybreak, and will move by the road which leads from the Ponte de Faia (near Miserelha) through Covo to Guarda, sending one battalion, however, to accompany the artillery of the division, by the great paved road which goes from Porto de Came to Guarda.

The left brigade of the 3rd Division will be in communication with the battalion which is detached to move with the artillery; and it will also observe the progress of the 6th Division and regulate its own advance accordingly.

The 5th Division will move from Linhares at daybreak, by the mountain roads which lead from thence into the Val de Mondego (the artillery going round, however, by Cortiçô and Lagiosa), and the division will be in reserve upon the left bank of the Mondego, at Porco, and at Miserelha.

The brigade of cavalry, commanded by Colonel Hawker, will be in reserve near Sueiro.

The 1st Division will move forward at daybreak, by brigades, from its present cantonments, along the great road towards Celorico, and will halt upon the open ground just before entering that town, and there wait for further orders.

The 7th Division will move at daybreak from the neighbourhood of Pinhanços to Cortiçô, Linhares, Mesquitela and Carrapichana; and if Colonel Ashworth's Portuguese brigade is with the 7th Division, it will occupy Villa Cortez.

Captain Lawson's brigade of 9-pounders, and the Portuguese brigade of 3-pounders along with it, will move from Vinho to Cortiçô.

The baggage of the Light Division, and of Major General Anson's brigade of cavalry, will remain at Maçal do Chão till further orders.

That of the 6th Division will, in like manner, remain at Lagiosa; and that of the 3rd Division in the Val de Mondego.

Appendix III

Wellington's Orders for Sabugal

Arrangement for the Attack of the French Corps at Sabugal on 3 April 1811

Marmeleiro. 2nd April, 1811.

Major General Sir William Erskine will have the troops under his orders formed in close columns behind the top of the heights which form the left bank of the Côa above Sabugal, so as to be prepared at 8 o'clock a.m. to move down towards the river (if so ordered), and to pass it about one mile above the little chapel which is on the left bank of the Côa a mile higher up than the bridge of Sabugal. If Sir William Erskine is directed to pass his infantry at the place here mentioned, he will make the cavalry pass further up the river, so as to cover the right of the infantry and gain the open country, by leaving the woods upon the opposite side of the Côa to their left.

As circumstances may, however, render it desirable that the cavalry and the Light Division should turn the enemy by even a wider circuit, Sir William Erskine will be prepared, in that case, to move to his right, along the left bank of the Côa, in order to pass it as far up as Quadrazais, or at any intermediate point that may be ordered. He will be so good, therefore, as to have the roads in that direction reconnoitred as soon as possible.

Major General Picton will move forward the 3rd Division at 6 o'clock in the morning, and will have it in readiness to move down from the heights forming the left bank of the Côa at 8 o'clock (if so ordered), and to cross the river near the little chapel which is about one mile above the bridge of Sabugal.

All the artillery with the 3rd Division will move forward by the road leading towards Sabugal, so that it may be at hand to protect the passage of the troops if necessary, and, if not, to move forward and pass the Côa by a ford a little below the bridge.

The 5th Division will move so as to be formed by 8 o'clock, each brigade in close column near the artillery of the 3rd Division, a little off the great road leading from Pega to Sabugal.

6th Division will remain at Martin de Pega till further orders; but Major General Campbell will have the roads to the right reconnoitred, so as to be able to move his division in that direction if ordered, either to Sabugal or to any of the fords of the Côa between Sabugal and Rapoula de Côa.

The 1st Division will move at daybreak by the road from Serdeira to Quinta de Gonzalez Martinez (which is between Marmeleiro and Martin de Pega), and from thence will march to Val Mourisco, which is on the great road from Guarda through Pega to Sabugal.

The 7th Division and Colonel Ashworth's Portuguese brigade will move at daybreak to Serdeira, and from thence will follow the route of the 1st Division.

Sir Brent Spencer will be so good as to leave the posts which he may have established to-day in view of the enemy, near the Foote Sequeiros, until they can be relieved by a battalion of the 7th Division, which Major General Houston will allot for that purpose, as soon as his troops have come forward.

The whole of the cavalry of Major General Anson's and Colonel Hawker's brigades, not already with Sir William Erskine, will move at daybreak to join him, leaving only a party of a serjeant and twelve dragoons with the 6th Division at Rapoula de Côa.

Colonel Barbacena [Portuguese Cavalry Brigade] will place the headquarters of his brigade at Serdeira, and will observe the passages of the Côa at Castelo Bom and Castelo Mendo, and in the neighbourhood of the Ponte de Sequeiros; he will send his reports to the right of the army in the neighbourhood of Sabugal.

It is desirable that the columns near Sabugal should be kept as much as possible out of the view of the enemy until they receive orders to move down to the points where they are to pass the river. All the divisions are to move by the right.

INSTRUCTIONS FOR THE ADVANCE OF THE ARMY
April 3, 1811.

The right column, after having passed the Côa, will march across the country direct towards the village of Quadrazais, keeping as far to the right as the nature of the country will permit.

The 3rd Division will also march across the country towards Quadrazais, keeping to the right of the great road all the way till it comes near to Quadrazais. The artillery will move by the great road.

The 5th Division will march through Quinta da Torre and Casas de Suano, leaving the great road to its right. Its artillery must go by the great road.

The 1st Division will march by the great road.

All the baggage of the army is to remain on the left bank of the Côa till further orders.

INSTRUCTIONS FOR THE ATTACK OF THE ENEMY'S POSITION ON THE CÕA

3rd April, 1811, near Sabugal.

As soon as the Light Division and 3rd Division have moved down to paw the river, the light infantry of the 5th Division will drive in the enemy's posts which are upon the left bank of the Côa opposite Sabugal.

The battalion of the 5th Division which is attached to the 9-pounders will assist in this operation by moving forward along the tongue of land that turns the left of the enemy's posts on this side of the Côa; and the 9-pounders will follow that battalion till they can be placed advantageously to cannonade the enemy on the opposite side of the river.

Appendix III: Wellington's Orders for Sabugal 239

A British 9-pounder field gun.

As soon as the enemy begins to give way at the town and the bridge, in consequence of the movements of the Light and 3rd divisions around his left and rear and of the fire of the 9-pounders and will follow that battalion until they can be placed advantageously to cannonade the enemy on the opposite side of the river.

As soon as the enemy begins to give way at the town and the bridge, in consequence of the movements of the Light and 3rd Divisions round his left and rear, and of the fire of the 9-pounders upon his front, the 5th Division will move forward and pass the river.

The infantry of the division will pass the bridge of Sabugal, if it remains entire, and will march round the town, leaving it to the left hand.

The artillery will pass at the ford below the bridge of Sabugal, and will go round the town, leaving it to the right hand.

Major General Dunlop will allow the two brigades of 9-pounders to get across the river as soon as they are no longer necessary on this side; and will also get his own brigade of guns across as soon as the infantry of his front brigade has passed. The remainder of the artillery will not pass the river until the whole of the infantry of the 5th Division has crossed.

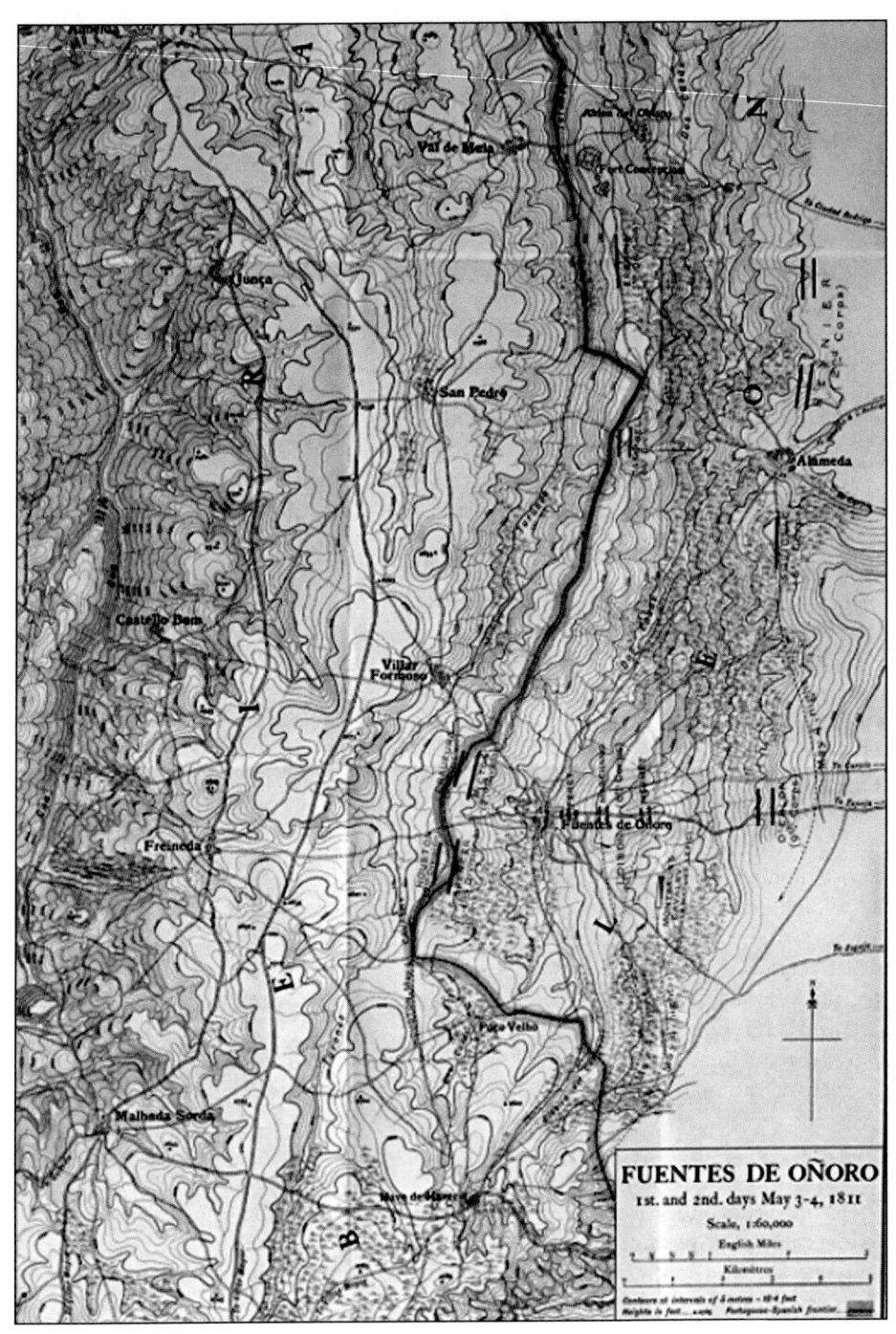

Fortescue's map of Fuentes de Oñoro.

Appendix IV

Wellington's Orders for Fuentes de Oñoro

Vilar Formoso, 30th April, 1811.

In the event of the enemy passing the Águeda, and moving forward in force, the allied army will oppose his progress by occupying the high country, of which the left is between the Dos Casas and the Turones rivulets, and the right extends by Nave de Haver behind Almeida, towards Furcalhos.

The body of the army will be drawn towards the right or towards the left of this line of country, or will be concentrated at any particular part of it, according to the direction which the enemy appears to give to the principal part of his force.

It is not intended to dispute the country in front of the line of position above mentioned. When it appears that the enemy is decidedly moving forward in force, therefore, Sir Stapleton Cotton will give orders to the troops in front to retire, the Light Division falling back from Gallegos and Espeja, by the direct roads from these two places, to Fuentes de Oñoro, and the cavalry falling back towards the line of position in such direction as circumstances may at the time require; continuing, however, to watch and delay the progress of the enemy's columns, but without committing themselves or harassing the troops. The order for the retreat of the 38th Regiment from Barba del Puerco is also to be given by Sir Stapleton Cotton, as soon as he finds that the enemy is advancing in such force as to make it expedient to withdraw the troops from Gallegos, and from the posts upon the Águeda, to the left of that village.

The blockade of Almeida (under the circumstances of the enemy advancing in force) will be entrusted to a greater or less portion of the troops now allotted for that service, according as may appear at the time to be requisite.

It is very necessary that the staff officers attached to the several divisions should make themselves acquainted with the general line of the position above pointed out, with all the roads in its neighbourhood, and with the names of the villages; in order that no mistake or delay may occur in the execution of any movement that may be directed.

Vilar Formoso, 1st May, 1811.

As soon as intelligence is received of the advance of the enemy in any considerable force, the following arrangement is to take place.

The 5th Division is to assemble upon the high ground between the Dos Casas and the Turones rivulets, near where the road passes from the village of Alameda to Val de la Mula.

Sir William Erskine will observe the roads that come from Vilar de Ciervo, Barquilla and Gallegos, and cross the Dos Casas river in front of his alarm post. He will be prepared also to detach to his left to favour the march of the 38th Regiment along the line of retreat pointed out for it in a former instruction.

Captain Bull's troop of horse artillery will fall back from Alameda, with the infantry of the 5th Division cantoned there, and will continue in reserve with the 5th Division until otherwise ordered.

Sir William Erskine will not evacuate entirely the villages of Castillejos and Alameda until obliged to do so by the advance of the enemy in force upon these points.

The 6th Division will assemble at San Pedro, leaving its piquets in front of Almeida, and one battalion between Almeida and San Pedro, to support the piquets until further orders.

Major General Campbell will apprise Brigadier General Pack of the movement of the 6th Division to San Pedro, as also of any other arrangements afterwards ordered which may affect the blockade of Almeida.

The 3rd Division will remain in the cantonments it at present occupies and will be prepared to get under arms and move to any point ordered with the least possible delay.

The 7th Division and Colonel Ashworth's brigade will repair to the alarm posts already assigned them upon the Caril road, the former between Aldea da Ribeira and Nave de Haver,[1] the latter between Malhada Sorda and Nave de Haver.

The 1st Division will be prepared to get under arms and move from its cantonments as may be ordered with the least possible delay.

Instructions respecting the movements of the troops in advance, upon the enemy's moving forward in force, have been already given.

The following arrangements are to be observed in regard the conveyance of intelligence of the enemy's advance, or of any other circumstance of general importance:-

Sir Stapleton Cotton will order immediate reports to be sent in such cases, from Gallegos and from Barquilla, to Lieutenant General Sir Brent Spencer, *or officer commanding* at Alameda.

The officer commanding at Alameda will forward the intelligence he receives without delay to Sir William Erskine at Aides do Bispo, and also to Major General Campbell, or officer commanding at Val de la Mula.

The officer commanding at Espeja will report to Quinta da Aguila, where Major General Picton will station a small party, under the command of an officer, to receive these reports, and to forward them without delay to Nave de Haver, sending a copy at the same time to Fuentes de Oñoro.

The officer commanding the cavalry outposts upon the right of the line will report to the officer commanding at Almeida and will send a report also to the officer commanding at Albergueria.

Major General Picton and Major General Houston will establish joint posts of communication halfway between Nave de Haver and Malhada Sorda, and also halfway between Nave de Haver and Vilar Mayor; and Major General Picton will transmit by that means to Malhada Sorda and to Vilar Mayor the intelligence forwarded to him from the front, of the enemy's movements.

The same mode of communication is to be established between Nave de Haver and Almeida, and Major General Nightingall will make arrangements in a similar manner for the speedy circulation of intelligence, and of orders, betwixt the cantonments of the 1st Division.

In addition to the above communications, in the event of a decided forward movement of the enemy's army, the intelligence is to be circulated from the points above mentioned, by means of mounted officers, with the least possible delay.

INSTRUCTIONS RESPECTING THE BAGGAGE OF THE ARMY
Hill of San Cristoval, behind Espeja, 2nd May, 1811, 3 P.M.

The baggage of the army is to be sent to the rear to-night as follows: That of the troops under Brigadier General Pack is to go to Pinhel; that of the 5th and 6th Divisions, and of the cavalry, to Castello Mendo; that of the 3rd Division and of the 7th Division, including Colonel Ashworth's brigade, is to go to the village of Bismula; and that of the 1st Division to Alfaiates. Instructions will be given hereafter respecting the *baggage* of the Light Division. The reserve ammunition of the several divisions is to remain with them.

The camp kettles are also to remain; and cattle sufficient to furnish two days' meat in advance are to be retained near the divisions. Whatever bread there may be in reserve is to be issued to the men, and the Commissariat mules are to be sent to the rear for a fresh supply.

The baggage of headquarters is to be in readiness to move to-morrow on the shortest notice.

INSTRUCTIONS PREPARATORY TO THE BATTLE OF FUENTES DE OÑORO
Hill of San Cristoval, 2nd May, 1811, 6½ P.M.

It does not appear probable that the enemy's army will advance farther to-day than to the ridge between the Azaba and the rivulet of Espeja. Sir Stapleton Cotton will be so good, therefore, as to place the cavalry in the country between the Espeja rivulet and Fuentes de Moro. Colonel Beckwith's brigade of the Light Division is to be in the woods on the right of the cavalry, and the remainder of the division in the woods on the left of the cavalry. Colonel Beckwith will endeavour to keep a piquet on the hill of San Cristoval; and he will have a post at Quinta da Aguila, to enable him to communicate with Nave de Haver and with Poço Velho. The left of the Light Division will in like manner put itself in communication with the infantry of the 5th Division, which occupies the village of Alameda; and also with the troops at Fuentes de Oñoro.

Sir Stapleton Cotton will continue to keep small posts of observation at Puebla de Azaba and towards Fuenteguinaldo and will cause reports to be made from the posts in the latter direction to the officer commanding at Nave de Haver, as well to himself. He will also make arrangements for being in direct communication with the officer commanding at Fuentes de Oñoro, to which place any further orders there may be for the cavalry or for the Light Division will be transmitted. Head-quarters will remain at Vilar Formoso.

INSTRUCTIONS ISSUED TO MAJOR GENERAL CAMPBELL PREVIOUS TO THE BATTLE OF FUENTES DE OÑORO
Vilar Formoso, 2nd May, 1811, 9½ A.M.

Major General Campbell will move the 6th Division tomorrow morning at daybreak, and will take post to the right of the 5th Division, near that part of the general line of position which overlooks the bridge over the Dos Casas river, coming from the village of Alameda towards San Pedro. One battalion of the division and two guns are to be left, however, near Val de la Mula, as a support to Brigadier General Pack.

Brigadier General Pack will take upon himself the blockade of Almeida, with his own brigade of infantry, and one regiment of Colonel Barbacena's cavalry, having the further support of the battalion and guns above mentioned.

INSTRUCTIONS RESPECTING THE POSITION OF THE TROOPS AT FUENTES DE OÑORO
Heights near Fuentes de Oñoro, 3rd May, 1811, 10 A.M.

The troops which are to occupy that part of the position which looks towards Fuentes de Moro are to be formed as follows:

The 1st Division, in two lines, is to form the right; and the 3rd Division and Colonel Ashworth's brigade, in two lines, are to form the left.

The 7th Division is to be in reserve behind the right of the 1st Division, and the Light Division is to be in reserve behind the left of the 3rd Division.

Each brigade of the two divisions in reserve is to be formed in close column where the ground admits of it, that they may be the better prepared to make any movement which may be directed.

Captain Lawson's brigade of British 9-pounders is to be with the 1st Division; and Major Arentschildt's brigade of Portuguese 9-pounders is to be with the 3rd Division.

The light infantry are to dispute the village of Fuentes de Oñoro, and the gardens, enclosures, and broken ground along the left bank of the Dos Casas rivulet.

The line of infantry is to occupy, and maintain as its position, the higher parts of the ridge which is between the Dos Casas and the Turones rivulets.

And the officers of the artillery will place their guns in the most advantageous manner for annoying the enemy in his advance up the slopes to attack that position.

The cavalry will be placed as circumstances may require.

INSTRUCTIONS ISSUED AFTER THE REPULSE OF
THE FRENCH ATTACK
Heights above Fuentes de Oñoro, 3rd May, 1811, 6 P.M.

It does not appear as if the enemy intended to make any serious attack upon the position this evening. The troops will, therefore, send for their camp kettles, and make their arrangements for the night.

The several divisions will throw out piquets along the ravine of the Dos Casas rivulet. These piquets are to communicate with each other and are to form a connected chain along the whole line of the front of the army.

Sir William Erskine will push his look-out posts to a considerable distance beyond the left flank of the army; and he will put himself in communication, likewise, with Brigadier General Pack, through Val de la Mula.

Major General Houston will push forward strong piquets into the wood between Fuentes de Oñoro and Poço Velho, which latter place he will occupy in considerable strength.

Sir Stapleton Cotton will support the infantry piquets by posts of cavalry, where the ground is open; and he will also put himself in communication with Don Julián Sánchez, who is at Nave de Haver.

A complete line of connected posts is to be established, likewise, along the whole of the ridge which forms the position now occupied by the troops, that orders may be passed with certainty and with rapidity, from one division to another, even during the night. The whole of the troops are to be under arms half an hour before daybreak to-morrow morning.

INSTRUCTIONS IN THE EVENT OF A RETREAT
Vilar Formoso, 3rd May, 1811, 8 A.M.

In the event of any advantage being obtained by the enemy, which may induce the Commander of the Forces to order the army to retire, it will fall back as follows, unless other instructions are given at the time:

The two divisions of the right (the 1st and 7th) will fall back by the road leading by Nave de Haver to Aldea da Ribeira.

The two divisions of the centre (the 3rd and the Light Division) will fall back by the Caril road to the turn near where the road to Vilar Mayor branches off from the Caril road; and if necessary to retire farther, these divisions will pass the rivulet behind them by the fords between Aldea da Ribeira and Vilar Mayor.

The two divisions of the left (the 5th and 6th) will fall back through San Pedro, Frenada and Malhada Sorda, to the heights above Vilar Mayor, upon this side of the rivulet, and they will cross the rivulet to Vilar Mayor when it becomes necessary to do so.

The cavalry will retire along the Caril road, following the two divisions of the centre, and covering the march of the infantry.

The two brigades of horse artillery will join and move with the cavalry.

Brigadier General Pack will withdraw the troops under his orders either towards Pinhel or by the fords of Junoca, and the bridge of Castelo Bom, as he may find most expedient under the circumstances of the moment.

Appendix V

Masséna's Orders for 5 May 1811

Arrangements for the day of 5 May 1811

The 6th Corps [Loison] will be in motion tomorrow at 2 a.m. with the exception of the 3rd Division [Ferey], which will remain in the position it currently occupies: the two other divisions, 1st and 2nd [Marchand and Mermet], will move in the evening, below the great hillock of Nave de Haver, and in front of Poço Velho. They will be ready to march obliquely on the enemy line. The two divisions will have their artillery with them, and will move at dawn, in column by divisions, on the village of Poço Velho, to attack the enemy in the position which he occupies. Ferey's division, which occupies a part of the village of Fuentes de Oñoro, will make arrangements as if it was to attack the enemy at this point, but, however, is to do nothing.

The 8th Corps [Solignac's division] will move to the heights of Fuentes and will follow the 2nd Division of the 6th Corps, to fight as per the orders for 6th Corps; he will have all his artillery with him.

The 2nd Corps [Reynier] will observe on its right the important route from Alameda which leads to the Fort de la Concepción: it will, however, assist the attack of the army, by making a general demonstration on this line; he will follow the enemy in all his movements, that is to say that if the forces he has before him come to the aid of the main body of the enemy army, which is in the direction of Fuentes de Oñoro he is to follow him on his march and attack him on his left: while the main body of the army, which will have advanced on the enemy via Poço Velho, will attack him on his right. General Reynier will have the road to Fort de la Concepción covered, if he deems necessary, by cavalry.

If it happens, which is not to be presumed, that the Poço Velho attack does not have all the success expected, and that it is repulsed, General Reynier is to retire to Gallegos. The General-in-Chief, who will be on his left, will let him know when to move. In case he does not receive an order, having made sure that the bulk of the army has already retreated, he will still march on Gallegos.

The 9th Corps [Drouet] will be assembled before the day before Fuentes de Oñoro, where it will fight in two lines, leaving a large distance between the regiments, to make the enemy believe that the 6th Corps still occupies the same position.

The army is informed that the Prince General-in-Chief will be with the 8th Corps.

M. le General Montbrun, having under his orders the reserve of dragoons, the Fournier brigade [IX Corps], and the Wathier brigade [Bessières' light cavalry], will place himself to the left of the 6th Corps, to turn the positions of the enemy and attack its right.

The Imperial Guard, which arrived this evening, will co-operate tomorrow with all army movements.

MASSÉNA

Appendix VI

Order of Battle
Fuentes de Oñoro

Allied Army – Lieutenant General Viscount Wellington

1st Division – Lieutenant General Spencer
  1st Brigade (Colonel Stopford): 1st Coldstream Guards, 1st/3rd Guards, 1 company 5th/60th Rifles
  2nd Brigade (Major General Nightingall): 2nd/24th Foot, 2nd/42nd Foot, 1st/79th Foot, 1 company 5th/60th Rifles
  3rd Brigade (Major General Howard): 1st/50th Rifles, 1st/71st Foot, 1st/92nd Foot, 1 company 5th/60th Rifles
  4th Brigade (Major General Baron Löwe): 1st, 2nd, 5th, 7th Line Battalions, King's German Legion, 2 companies KGL Light Battalion

3rd Division – Major General Picton
  1st Brigade (Colonel Mackinnon): 1st/45th Foot, 1st/74th Foot, 1st/88th Foot, 3 companies 5th/60th Rifles
  2nd Brigade (Major General Colville): 2nd/5th Foot, 2nd/83rd Foot, 2nd/88th Foot, 94th Foot
  Portuguese Brigade (Colonel Power): 1st & 2nd/9th and 1st & 2nd/21st Portuguese Line Regiments

5th Division – Major General Erskine
  1st Brigade (Colonel Hay): 3rd/1st Foot, 1st/9th Foot, 2nd/38th Foot, 1 company Brunswick Oels
  2nd Brigade (Major General Dunlop): 1st/4th Foot, 2nd/30th Foot, 2nd/44th Foot, company Brunswick Oels
  Portuguese Brigade (commanded by Brigadier General Spry): 1st & 2nd/3rd and 1st & 2nd/15th Portuguese Line Regiments, 8th Caçadores

6th Division – Major General Alexander Campbell
  1st Brigade (Colonel Hulse): 1st/11th Foot, 2nd/53rd Foot, 1st/61st Foot, 1 company 5th/60th Rifles
  2nd Brigade (Colonel Burne): 1st/36th Foot (2nd with Pack at Almeida)
  Portuguese Brigade (Brigadier General Baron Eben): 1st & 2nd/8th and 1st & 2nd/12th Portuguese Line Regiments

7th Division – Major General Houston
  1st Brigade (Brigadier Sontag): 2nd/51st Light Infantry, 85th Light Infantry, Chasseurs Britanniques, 8 companies Brunswick Oels[1]

250   *Masséna at Bay*

Portuguese Brigade (Brigadier General Doyle): 1st & 2nd/7th and 1st & 2nd/19th Portuguese Line Regiments, 2nd Caçadores

Light Division – Brigadier General Craufurd
   1st Brigade (Lieutenant Colonel Beckwith): 1st/43rd Foot, 4 companies 1st/95th Rifles, 1 Company 2nd/95th Rifles, 3rd Caçadores
   2nd Brigade (Colonel Drummond): 1st/52nd Foot, 2nd/52nd Foot, 4 companies 1st/95th Rifles, 1st Caçadores
   Doyle's Portuguese Brigade (Colonel Doyle): 1st & 2nd, 7th & 1st, & 2nd/19th Portuguese Line Regiments, 2nd Caçadores
   Ashworth's Portuguese Brigade (Colonel Ashworth): 1st & 2nd/6th and 1st & 2nd/18th Portuguese Line Regiments

Cavalry
   1st Brigade (Major General Slade): 1st Royal Dragoons and 14th Light Dragoons
   2nd Brigade (Lieutenant Colonel von Arentschildt): 16th Light Dragoons & 1st KGL Hussars
   Portuguese Brigade (Brigadier General Barbacena): 4th & 10th Portuguese Dragoons[2]

Artillery – Brigadier General Howorth
   (48 guns) Ross's and Bull's troops, Royal Horse Artillery,
   Lawson's & Thompson's Batteries,
   Von Arentschildt's, da Cunha's & Roize's Portuguese batteries

---

Army of Portugal – Marshal André Masséna, Prince d'Essling

II Corps – General Reynier
   1st Division (General Merle): 2nd, 4th & 36th Légère each of 3 battalions
   2nd Division (General Heudelet): 17th & 31st Légère, 47th & 70 Line each of 3 battalions
   Pierre Soult's Cavalry Brigade: 1st Hussars, 22nd Chasseurs, 8th Dragoons

VI Corps – General Loison
   1st Division (General Marchand): 6th Légère, 39th, 69th & 76th each of 3 battalions
   2nd Division (General Mermet): 25th Légère, 27th, 50th & 59th each of 3 battalions
   3rd Division (General Ferey): 26th, 82nd & 86th Line (each of 3 battalions) & Midi and Hanoverian Legions, 1 battalion of each
   Lamotte's Cavalry Brigade: 3rd Hussars, 15th Chasseurs

VIII Corps – General Junot, Duke of Abrantes
   2nd Division (General Solignac): 15th, 65th 86th (each of 3 battalions and 1 Battalion Irish Legion

IX Corps – General Drouet, Comte d'Erlon
  1st Division (General Claparède): 1 battalion from each of the 21st & 28th Légère, 54th, 40th, 63rd, 88th, 64th, 100th, 103rd Line
  2nd Division (General Conroux): 1 battalion from each of the 9th, 16th & 27th Légère, 8th 24th, 45th, 94th, 95th 96th Line
  Fournier's Cavalry Brigade: 7th, 13th & 20th Chasseurs
Reserve Cavalry – General Montbrun
  Cavrois' Brigade: 3rd, 10th & 15th Dragoons
  Ornano's Brigade: 6th, 11th & 25th Dragoons
  Artillery (32 guns)
Army of the North – Marshal Bessières, Duke of Istria
  Cavalry of the Imperial Guard (General Lepic): 1 Squadron each of Chasseurs à Cheval, Grenadiers à Cheval, Polish Lancers, Mamelukes
  Light Cavalry Brigade (General Wathier): 5th Hussars, 11th, 12th & 24th Chasseurs
  Artillery (6 guns)

Notes

Chapter 1: The Storm Clouds Gather

1. The fourth of the 1801 War of the Oranges is included. France supported the Spanish in that war.
2. Marbot, translated by Butler, *Memoires of Baron de Marbot* (Kesinger Legacy Reprints, 1892).
3. Lacking a navy capable of taking on the British fleet and invading Britain, Napoleon issued the Berlin Decrees in 1806 to close the ports of Europe to British trade. The aim was to break Britain economically.
4. Gurwood, Lt Col (ed), The Dispatches of Field Marshal the Duke of Wellington, Vol. 4 (John Murry, 1837). Memorandum on the Defence of Portugal, 7 March 1809.
5. Andrew Leith Hay was ADC to General Sir James Leith, General Officer Commanding 5th Division.
6. In 1807 General Junot had sent the best Portuguese troops to join the *Grande Armée* and disbanded the remainder, demilitarizing Portugal.
7. Oman, Sir Charles, *A History of the Peninsular War*, Volume III (The Clarendon Press, 1908).
8. Cadiz, Spain's main naval port, was successfully defended and was a distraction that tied down a significant number of French troops until the middle of 1812.
9. Twenty-four infantry regiments of two battalions, six Caçadore battalions and twelve regiments of cavalry. The latter arm suffered from a shortage of horses.
10. Six British and one Portuguese divisions.
11. This and the Thames ice fairs during this period were due to some violent volcanic activity in south-east Asia.
12. Including 800 of Don Julián Sánchez's mounted guerrillas.
13. Saunders, Tim, *The Sieges of Ciudad Rodrigo 1810 and 1812* (Pen & Sword, 2018).
14. Saunders, Tim and Yuill, Rob, *The Light Division in the Peninsular War, 1808–1811* (Pen & Sword, 2020).
15. Schaumann, August, *On the Road with Wellington* (N&M reprint). At this time he was at this time the unit commissary to the 4th Dragoons.
16. There is debate over the presence of defensive works at Ponte de Murcela. By the time the French reached that point at the end of September, Pelet refers to them as the 'dismantled works'.
17. Henriette Leberton (née Renique), sister of one of Masséna's earlier ADCs, was a ballet dancer aged 18 when she first met the 50-year-old marshal. By 1810 she was married to a dragoon captain who she abandoned to follow the marshal as an additional ADC, allegedly dressed as an officer of dragoons. The marshal's fourteen other ADCs were not happy. What eventually became of Henriette is not known.
18. Pelet, Jean Jaques, *The French Campaign in Portugal, 1810–18* (translated by Donald D. Howard) (Minnesota, 1973).
19. Quoted by Levine, Sir Augustus, *Historical Record of the Forty-Third Regiment – Monmouthshire Light Infantry* (Naval & Military Press reprint of the 21867 edition).
20. Kincaid, *Tales from the Rifle Brigade* (Pen & Sword, 2007). He added that 'The commissariat some years afterwards, called for a return of the men who had received shirts and shoes on this occasion, with a view to making us pay for them.'
21. Nicholas Trant held the rank of lieutenant colonel in the British army and brigadier general in the Portuguese.
22. Kincaid, John, *Random Shots from a Rifleman* (Pen & Sword, 2005).

23. Gurwood, Lt. Col. (ed.), *The Dispatches of Field Marshal the Duke of Wellington*, Vol. 4 (John Murry, 1837). Memorandum on the Defence of Portugal, 7 March 1809.
24. Obituary, Lieutenant Colonel George Elder (*The United Services Journal* and *Naval and Military Magazine*, 1837, Part II).

Chapter 2: The Lines of Torres Vedras

1. Jones, General Sir John, *Memoranda Relative to the Lines Thrown up to Cover Lisbon in 1810* (Privately published, 1829).
2. Quoted by Fortescue, *History of the British Army, 1809–10*, Vol. VII.
3. Gurwood, *Dispatches*.
4. The only other time Wellington returned to inspect the Lines was in February 1810. Otherwise the Engineers got on with the work supervised at a distance by Colonel Fletcher.
5. Jones commented on the use of militia and *ordenanza*: 'militia, ill-organised peasantry and gunners who, though totally unfit to act in the field, still being possessed of innate courage, were equal to defend a redoubt and work its artillery.'
6. Work on the Lines continued until 1812 as an insurance policy, with the number of guns increasing to 648 in 152 redoubts.
7. Gurwood, *Dispatches*.
8. Gurwood, *Dispatches*.
9. The identification of the 95th Rifles is almost certainly incorrect, as the Light Division and the 95th were occupying Aruda and the Pass of Mattos. The 1st Division's order of battle, however, had two companies of green-jacketed 5th/60th Rifles and detachments of the 1st and 2nd Light Battalions of the King's German Legion. The latter also had uniforms very similar to that of the 95th including black facings.
10. Pococke, Thomas, *Journal of a Soldier of the 71st, or Glasgow Regiment, Highland Light Infantry, From 1806–1815* (Balfour & Clark, 1819).
11. Pelet, writing in 1816–18 without the benefit of the passage of time that Marbot enjoyed, could only hint that 'They had contrary desires or interests ...'
12. Gurwood, *Dispatches*.
13. Jones, General Sir John, *Account of the War in Spain and Portugal, and in the South of France, from 1808 to 1814* (Egerton Bookseller, 1818).
14. The 6th Division under Major General Alex Campbell had recently been formed on the arrival of another British brigade in Portugal.
15. Gurwood, *Dispatches*.
16. Noël, Colonel Jean-Nicholas-Auguste, *With Napoleon's Guns* (Frontline Books, 2016).
17. Delagrave, Colonel Charles, *Campagne du Portugal, 1810–11* (Paris).
18. Kincaid, Captain Sir John, *Adventures in the Rifle Brigade* (third edition, 1837).
19. Grattan, William, *Adventures of the Connaught Rangers from 1808 to 1814* (Henry Colborne, London, 1847).
20. In military parlance of the day a 'banquette' was a fire-step that allowed a soldier to fire from behind a defensive feature.
21. Montgomery shared the same views regarding officers' dress during the Second World War.

Chapter 3: Winter at Santarém

1. General Jean-Baptiste Drouet, Comte d'Erlon.
2. General Clausel reported that 'The majority of the men are absent foraging to the rear ... The last detachment that came back to camp had been nine days away.' These foraging parties travelled between 30 and 50 miles from their units.
3. Noël, Colonel Jean-Nicholas-Auguste, *With Napoleon's Guns* (Frontline Books, 2016).
4. Pococke, Thomas, *Journal of a Soldier of the 71st, or Glasgow Regiment, Highland Light Infantry, From 1806–1815* (Balfour & Clark, 1819).
5. Gurwood, *Dispatches*.

6. The French had been thinning out for some days and even the rearguard had a head start of some eighteen hours.
7. 'The Peer' was Wellington's nickname among senior officers and his headquarters staff.
8. Hay, William (ed. Wood), *Reminiscences 1808–1815 under Wellington* (Simpkin, Marshal, et al., London, 1901).
9. Simmons, George (ed. Verner), *A British Rifleman* (London, A. & C. Black, Soho Square, 1899).
10. See Saunders and Yuill, *The Light Division, 1808–1811* (Pen & Sword, 2020).
11. Robert Craufurd's nickname probably had as much to do with his dark 'five o'clock shadow' as his domineering character.
12. Today El Vallé is known as Vale de Santarém.
13. Today the causeway and bridge are known as the Ponte d'Asseca, which carries the N3 north to Santarém.
14. Drouet's IX Corps was located as far back as Valladolid and its commander was reluctant to act on either Masséna's requests or Napoleon's instructions.
15. Colonel Arentschildt was an old and much-respected friend of the Light Division, having commanded the German Hussars with the division for much of the period from early 1809 onwards. He took command of the brigade during the absence of General Slade. The 16th Light Dragoons were also comrades from the border lands during the same period.
16. Four companies were green-coated riflemen, with the remainder being armed with muskets. The rifle companies were subsequently distributed among the other divisions, while the musketeers served with the 7th Division.
17. Five light 6-pounders and one 5.5in howitzer. Now known as the Chestnut Troop RHA.
18. Ross to Dalrymple. Quoted by Lipscombe in *Wellington's Guns* (Osprey, 2014).
19. Only sufficient boats were captured for a bridge over the Rio Zêzere at Punhete.
20. Cavalrymen of the piquets riding in a circle was a signal that the enemy were advancing.
21. General Junot was shot in the nose and an ADC was killed.
22. General Erskine remained with the Light Division until the return of Craufurd during Fuentes de Oñoro and survived in various other appointments until 1813 when he was declared insane and was to be sent home. He committed suicide in Lisbon by jumping out of a window; reputedly his last words were 'Now why did I do that?'
23. This episode was the inspiration for Bernard Cornwell's story in the *Sharpe* series.
24. Quoted by Oman.
25. The reinforcement of 6,000 men did not even replace Masséna's losses during the campaign thus far and was insufficient to alter the balance of forces in the French favour. Another 6,000 remained on the Spanish border.
26. Six weeks of bad weather meant that they only landed on 2 March 1811.

Chapter 4: Withdrawal to the Rio Mondego

1. Charles Beckwith was nephew of Colonel Beckwith, commanding the Light Division's 1st Brigade.
2. The division included Pack's Portuguese Brigade and Arentschildt's and Slade's brigades of cavalry.
3. They were probably an elite company of dragoons who wore a tall grenadier-style bearskin cap. The Grenadiers à Cheval were in the Army of the North at this time.
4. Quoted by Beamish in *The History of the King's German Legion*.
5. Napier, William, *History of the Peninsula War*, Vol. III (Thomas and William Boone, London, 1833).
6. Cooper, John Spencer, *Rough Notes of Seven Campaigns 1809–1815* (Spellmount, 1996).
7. Colonel Williams was commander of the 5th 60th Rifles, whose companies were attached to brigades across the army, three of which were in the 3rd Division. In this case he not only commanded his riflemen but the light companies of the division's line battalions.

Chapter 5: Pursuit to Spain

1. Gurwood, *Dispatches*.
2. They were a reconnaissance patrol from the 1st KGL Hussars, not an advance guard. They reported the presence of the French at Fuente-Cuberta and the regiment duly moved forward as described by Marbot.
3. Marbot, *The Memoirs of Baron de Marbot* (Kissinger Legacy Reprints, 2005).
4. This is disputed by Marbot who points out that marshals did not wear feather plumes. They did, however, have white feather trimming to their cocked hats.
5. This is the only time Henriette is mentioned in accounts after Buçaco.
6. Commanding officer of the 52nd Light Infantry.
7. These officers were William Napier and Jonathan Dobbs. The latter's brother, Captain John Dobbs, was a part of a reinforcement on its way to join the Light Division with his company of the 2nd Battalion, 52nd Light Infantry. He is the author of *Recollections of an Old 52nd Man*.
8. Napier, General George, *George Napier of the 52nd* (Leonaur reprint, 2012).
9. All three Napier brothers served in the Light Division.
10. Napier, Sir William, *The Military Career of Charles Napier* (Leonaur reprint, 2017).
11. Costello, Edward, *Adventures of a Soldier* (Colburn & Co., London, 1841). Extend the frontage from close order, normally to six paces between files.
12. Kincaid, Captain John, *Random Shots of a Rifleman* (Pen & Sword reprint).
13. Pelet (trans. Howard), *The French Campaign in Portugal, 1810–1811* (University of Minnesota, 1973).
14. Pelet gives a good account of the action, which accords with the salient points of Ney's report.
15. The 95th Rifles' best swimmers attempted to recover the eagle before they continued the advance. Later Wellington, informed of the eagle's loss, promised a substantial reward to the Portuguese villagers, who eventually recovered it on 15 June when the river level had dropped. Although not strictly captured by the Light Division, 'their eagle' resides in the Royal Hospital at Chelsea.
16. This biscuit was probably abandoned because the hamstringing of some 500 draft animals as a part of Masséna's 'lightening of the army's load' carried out during 15 March.
17. On the subject of supplies, Wellington reported to Lord Liverpool that 'I was obliged either to direct the British Commissary General to supply the Portuguese troops, or to see them perish for want; and the consequence is, that the supplies intended for the British troops are exhausted, and we must halt till more come up, which I hope will be this day.'
18. Noël, Colonel Jean, *With Napoleon's Guns* (Frontline, 2016).
19. Schaumann, Augustus, *On the Road with Wellington* (N&M reprint).
20. Schaumann.
21. Breaking the formation ordered by the divisional and brigade staffs was largely due to the disparity of knowledge, experience of working in a formation and fitness between the new arrivals and seasoned units.
22. Along with the Light Division the highly-experienced German Hussars were spared Wellington's censure over a lack of march discipline.
23. Letter in Robinson's *Life of Picton*, Volume II.

Chapter 6: Combat of Sabugal, 3 April 1811

1. Gurwood, *Dispatches*.
2. Eventually, as a result of sickness and casualties the 52nd's 2nd Battalion transferred its men to the 1st Battalion and was sent home to recruit; a fate shared by many 2nd Battalions.
3. Tomkinson, Lieutenant Colonel William, *The Diary of a Cavalry Officer, 1809–15* (Spellmount, 1999).
4. The sanctuary (Santuário da Sra. da Graça) is just above the modern Côa dam.
5. On the Napoleonic battlefield an aide-de-camp or staff officer spoke with the authority of his commander.

Notes   257

6. It appears that in the absence of General Merle the division was commanded by General of Brigade Sarrut, Braquehay's *Le General Merle*.
7. Cooper, Captain T.H., *A Practical Guide for the Light Infantry Officer* (Robert Wilkes, Chancery Lane, 1806).
8. Kincaid, Captain Sir John, *Adventures in the Rifle Brigade* (Pen & Sword reprint, 2007).
9. Strictly speaking, 'grape' was a form of naval ammunition. In land service it was light or heavy canister, the difference being the size/weight and number of lead balls in each light metal container.
10. With the arrival of the 2nd 52nd Light Infantry, the 2nd Brigade was some 500 men stronger than the 1st Brigade.
11. A horse prancing on its hind legs.
12. Donaldson, Joseph, *Recollections of the Eventful Life of a Soldier* (Spellmount, 2000).
13. Napier, William, *History of the Peninsular War*, Vol. III (Constable, 1993).
14. Oman, Sir Charles, *A History of the Peninsular War*, Vol. IV (Greenhill Books, 2004).
15. The debate between the 52nd and 43rd as to who captured the howitzer lasted, as these things do, until 1881 when the two regiments were amalgamated to form the Oxfordshire and Buckinghamshire Light Infantry.

Chapter 7: Back on the Border Lands

1. Gurwood, *Dispatches*.
2. Tomkinson, Lieutenant Colonel William, *The Diary of a Cavalry Officer, 1809–15* (Spellmount, 1999).
3. Oman notes that the army was deployed on the Côa in a 12-mile area where they could concentrate within a day if threatened by the Army of Portugal.
4. Today this is the ruined village of Molino de los Galanes.
5. General Jean-Baptiste Drouet, Comte d'Erlon.
6. There was always a tension in the relationship between Picton and Craufurd and the Light Division. This, however, did not at the time extend to the officers and soldiers of the 3rd and Light divisions, who held each other in high regard.
7. Waters had been given a lieutenant colonelcy in the Portuguese army, but in May 1811 he was given the same brevet rank in British service and a more closely-defined role on Wellington's staff.
8. Napoleon's son and heir, born to his new wife Marie Louise.
9. Ciudad Rodrigo was referred to as the 'Keys to Spain' and had to be in Wellington's hands before he took the offensive in 1812.
10. In modern terms this would be approximately a platoon in strength; that is to say +/- thirty men.
11. Moorsome, W.L., *Historical Record of the Fifty-Second Regiment (Oxfordshire Light Infantry) from the Year 1755 to the Year 1858* (N&M reprint).
12. 'Old Trowsers' or the *Pas de Charge* was a rhythmic drumbeat delivered with an increasing tempo as French infantry closed with the enemy.
13. Leach, Jonathan, *Captain of the 95th Rifles: Rough Sketches of the Life of an Old Soldier* (1831).
14. The leading correspondent in Salamanca was one Dr Curtis, principal of the Irish College, whose Catholicism and Irish birth convinced the French that he sympathized with them.
15. He actually reached Allamanda on the evening of 28 April and was at Vilar Formoso the next day.
16. Marbot, *The Memoirs of Baron de Marbot* (Kessinger Publishing).
17. Oman, dispatch from Bessières to Berthier, 6 June 1811.
18. When the Legion reached the borders of Portugal and Spain at the end of March 1811, the regiment had 19 officers and 254 men present and a further 128 men sick.
19. Village of the Pigs has unsurprisingly been renamed Puerto Seguro.

Chapter 8: Fuentes de Oñoro, 3–4 May 1811

1. Today it is called Porto de Ovelha.
2. General Erskine had been transferred to command the 5th Division, with the news that General Craufurd was shortly to rejoin the army and resume command of the Light Division.

258 Masséna at Bay

3. The 2nd Battalion 83rd (County of Dublin) Regiment was the only formed regiment in the defence of Fuentes de Oñoro village on 3 May.
4. Quoted by Griffith, Robert, *Riflemen* (Hellion, 2019).
5. Masséna contradicted the view that Loison and Ferey attacked without authority in his report: 'I hoped to enter Fuentes and stay there; I had it attacked, and it was soon occupied.'
6. 'Thomas', *Journal of a Soldier of the 71st or Glasgow Regiment* (Edinburgh, 1819).
7. Madder red was the traditional herb dye used for dying British army coats, which produced a dark brick red that faded rapidly to a pinkish-red. The far more expensive scarlet cloth was reserved for officers and sergeants.
8. Craufurd's harsh discipline from the retreat to Vigo onwards and the issue of his hated standing orders the following summer had been roundly resented, but having experienced the command of Erskine, the division appreciated that it was Craufurd who had forged 'The Division' into the elite of the Peninsular Army.

Chapter 9: Fuentes de Oñoro, 5 May 1811

1. Gurwood, *Dispatches*.
2. Brotherton (ed. Perrett), *A Hawk at War* (Picton Press, 1996).
3. It is arguably the case that Wellington's thin deployment on the right flank was a result of him also overestimating the marsh as an obstacle to serious French manoeuvre.
4. Wellington wrote in his report: 'I had occupied Poço Velho and that neighbourhood in hopes that I should be able to maintain the communication across the Côa by Sabugal, as well as provide for the blockade, which objects it was now obvious were incompatible with each other; and I therefore abandoned that which was the least important.'
5. Gordon, Lieutenant Colonel Alexander (ed. Rory Muir), *At Wellington's Right Hand, 1808–1815* (Army Records Society, 2003).
6. The light cavalry in the army at this time, especially the 1st Hussars KGL, were experienced and thoroughly professional units in the outposts. In this general action, Major Meyer seems guilty of what Wellington would describe as 'charging at everything'.
7. There is some evidence from the Light Division that Sánchez's men fought and Wellington reported the capture of Colonel La Motte of the 13th Chasseurs, but in any event, outnumbered guerrillas against regular cavalry in a straight fight would have been a rather one-sided affair.
8. The regiment's full title was the 85th (Bucks Volunteers) Regiment of Foot (Light Infantry). It had been converted to light infantry in 1808 and had served at Walcheren in 1809.
9. The diarists and authors of memoirs all come up with different figures for the strength of the French cavalry. The generally accepted number is approximately 3,500.
10. The inference is that Bull's battery was operating in support of the cavalry in three sections, each of two guns.
11. Wheeler, William, *Private Wheeler: The Letters of a Soldier of the 51st Light Infantry During the Peninsular War & at Waterloo* (Leonaur reprint, 2009).
12. The Chasseurs Britanniques were originally raised from the remains of French royalist units and *émigrés* in 1800, but by the time of the Peninsular War the ranks were increasingly made up with French deserters. The Chasseurs Britanniques had a fine reputation for fighting in battle but they were plagued with desertion, so much so that they could not be employed in the outposts. As a result of the battalion's action on 5 May 1811, Lieutenant Colonel Eustace was mentioned in Wellington's dispatches.
13. Wheeler recorded that they were only supported by a pair of Portuguese cannon, one of which was dismounted by enemy artillery at the beginning of the battle.
14. Colonel Neil Campbell, in his 1807 Instructions for Light Infantry and Rifles, states in the section on 'double quick time' that in a square '… it is difficult to move in that order, even for a short distance, the square should always be thrown into column.'
15. On this occasion the British cavalry's action in support of the Light Division was far from 'charging at everything'. It was both controlled and effective and achieved with remarkably little loss.

16. General Picton, no friend of Craufurd or the Light Division, presents a different view in a letter to his family: 'During these operations the Light Division, under General Craufurd, was rather roughly handled by the enemy's cavalry; and had this arm of the French army been as daring and active upon this occasion as they were when following us to the Lines of Torres Vedras, they would doubtless have cut off the Light Division to a man, and probably have destroyed our cavalry; but they let the golden moment pass.'
17. 'Hiving' or the command 'Rally orb' would see the skirmishers in extended order dashing to form a mini square around an officer or sergeant. Bristling with swords and bayonets, the enemy's horses would not press home their charge on the orb.
18. Donaldson is in error here: the riflemen were from the similarly green-coated 5th 60th Rifles.
19. Grattan, William, *Adventures of the Connaught Rangers, From 1808 to 1814* (London, 1847).
20. Nicknamed 'The Incomparable 9th' by Napoleon following their performance at Marengo in 1800, this was a 4th Battalion raised specifically for the Army of Portugal and had little of the depth or tradition of its parent regiment.
21. They attacked down the road on a narrow front of five or six men with the left flank company leading. In this case with the battalion's Light Company deployed, it would have been No. 9 Company in front. See diagram.
22. These would have been line infantry grenadiers distinguished, similarly to grenadiers of the Imperial Guard, by bearskins and red plumes and epaulets.
23. At the beginning of the campaign in 1810 Cardon wrote: 'The day after tomorrow we set off again to enter Portugal to join the army ... We burn to join our brothers and share the honour of chasing these hated English from the continent. If they are stubborn, we will show them the cost of resisting the victors of the Danube reunited with those of Burgos.'
24. Cowdry, T.E., *Incomparable – Napoleon's 9th Light Infantry* (Osprey, 2012).

Chapter 10: Aftermath

1. Small defensive positions, normally earthen, offering frontal and flanking cover.

Appendix IV: Wellington's Orders for Fuentes de Oñoro

1. Modern spelling: Nave de Haver.

Appendix VI: Order of Battle

1. There is a contention that by grouping the newly-arrived light battalions in the 7th Division, Wellington was attempting to form a second light division. The 68th Light Infantry had joined the division by the time of the 1812 campaign.
2. The majority were covering the line of the Agueda north of its confluence with the Azaba; i.e. a part of the blockade.

Index

Águeda, Rio   130, 153, 154, 161, 162, 167, 179, 171, 173, 223, 234, 241, 259
Alhandra   23, 28, 34, 41, 231, 232, 234
Allied Army
  1st Division   35, 40, 41, 50, 62, 64, 82, 91, 114, 127, 134, 185, 178, 182, 184, 194, 204, 208, 209, 210 236, 237, 238, 242, 243, 244, 245, 249
  2nd Division   33, 34, 100, 247, 250
  3rd Division   11, 33, 49, 66, 82, 83, 87, 89, 95, 96, 101, 108, 109, 110, 114, 120, 122, 125, 132, 134, 136, 146, 178, 181, 209, 212, 235, 236, 237, 238, 239, 242, 243, 244, 247, 249, 250, 255
  4th Division   41, 43, 82, 87, 91, 96, 108, 135
  5th Division   9, 17, 41, 134, 147, 149, 154, 169, 177, 217, 224, 236, 237, 238, 239, 241, 242, 243, 244, 249, 253, 257
  6th Division   41, 82, 101, 108, 165, 177, 223, 235, 236, 237, 238, 242, 243, 244, 254
  7th Division   141, 177, 184, 189, 196, 197, 198, 200, 203, 210, 236, 238, 242, 243, 244, 249, 255, 259
  Light Division   10, 11, 17, 18, 20, 22, 34, 46, 511, 52, 57, 59, 61, 52, 64, 66, 67, 69, 70, 81, 82, 84, 90, 91, 98, 101, 105, 106, 107, 108, 110, 114, 116, 118, 122, 123, 126, 133, 134, 142, 145, 146, 147, 151, 153, 154, 156, 161, 162, 169, 171, 173, 178, 134, 187, 192, 197, 203, 204, 205, 206, 208, 210, 218, 235, 236, 237, 241, 243
  Anson's Brigade (Light Cavalry)   18, 59, 62, 64, 65, 169 235, 236, 238
  Arentschildt's Brigade (Light Cavalry)   67, 86, 105, 123, 127, 153, 196, 244, 250, 255
  Slade's Brigade (Heavy Cavalry)   59, 61, 62, 127, 196, 206, 224, 250, 255
  Pack's Portuguese Brigade   17, 41, 59, 64, 67, 69, 105, 108, 125, 162, 165, 175, 223, 224, 242, 243, 244, 245, 259 255
  1st Royal Dragoons   81, 127, 128, 189, 206, 250
  14th Light Dragoons   62, 127, 189, 200, 210, 250
  16th Light Dragoons   61, 64, 67, 87, 124, 127, 134, 153, 172, 173, 178, 206, 250, 255
  1st Hussars KGL   67, 69, 71, 84, 86, 87 103, 104, 120, 127, 250, 256, 258
  A Troop RHA (Ross's Battery)   69, 86, 90, 91, 93, 105, 118, 127, 154, 250, 255
  43rd Light Infantry   17, 18, 20, 51, 91, 105, 108, 109, 135, 136, 137, 142, 148, 149, 151, 196, 204, 205, 250, 257
  51st Light Infantry   198, 200, 202, 203, 249, 258
  52nd Light Infantry   17, 51, 59, 62, 68, 91, 93, 105, 106, 107, 108, 110, 111, 114, 18, 133, 142, 151, 154, 162, 164, 165, 205, 250, 256, 257
  5th 60th Rifles   40, 146, 181, 209, 219, 255, 259
  71st Highland Light Infantry   35, 36, 38, 43, 44, 45, 46, 39, 50, 52, 57, 181, 182, 183, 212, 249, 254, 258
  88th Connaught Rangers   17, 49, 50, 53, 118, 209, 212, 213, 215, 254, 259
  94th Scotch Brigade   66, 72, 84, 98, 125, 147, 186, 209, 217, 218, 249
  95th Rifles   18, 35, 48, 49, 52, 54, 59, 81, 82, 89, 91, 95, 106, 107, 110, 126, 135, 136, 137, 139, 142, 143, 149, 154, 164, 165, 166, 204, 206, 208, 210, 250, 254, 256, 257
  Brunswick Oels   43, 50, 69, 70, 134, 249
  1st Caçadores   142
  2nd Caçadores   197
  3rd Caçadores   17, 22, 89, 93, 114, 118, 125, 135, 136, 137, 139, 144, 149 151, 205, 208
  4th Caçadores   96
  Chasseurs Britanniques   133, 198, 200, 201, 202, 249, 258
Almeida   10, 11, 12, 13, 76, 77, 127, 129, 134, 152, 153, 154, 155, 161–5, 167, 168, 173, 174, 175, 177, 179, 192, 194, 218, 221, 222–6, 232, 235, 241, 242, 243, 244, 249
Alva, Rio   13, 65, 120, 121, 122, 123
Arruda   34, 35, 41, 46, 51, 57, 58, 232, 234
Azaba, Rio   132, 154, 155, 162, 169, 173, 174, 221, 243, 259

262 Masséna at Bay

Barbra del Puerco 155, 172, 223, 224, 241
Beresford, Martial 4, 59, 78, 81, 127, 133, 148, 152, 165, 167, 168, 220, 221
Bessieres, Marshal 156, 168, 170, 171, 175, 203–4, 220, 248
Bevan, Lieutenant Colonel 224, 225
Brenier, General 165, 221, 222, 223, 224, 225
Brotherton, Major 189, 194, 196, 197, 258
Buçaco Ridge, Battle of 9, 10, 14–18, 23, 36, 121, 175, 179, 184, 208, 256
Bucelas 23, 28, 232, 233, 234

Cadogan, Lieutenant Colonel 36, 44, 182
Campbell, Major General 49, 82, 108, 162, 165, 223, 235, 237, 242, 244, 249, 254, 258
Casa Novo 101, 104–11,
Ceira, Rio 111, 113, 114, 115, 116, 117, 120
Ciudad Rodrigo 10, 11–14, 34, 77, 127, 134, 135, 153, 154, 155, 161, 162, 168, 173, 223, 227, 253, 257
Clausel, General 43, 46, 55, 57, 254
Côa, Combat on the 11
Côa, Rio 11, 59, 132, 133, 134, 141, 148, 151, 152, 159, 174, 177, 179, 192, 231, 237, 238, 256
Cocks, Captain 172, 173, 178, 179, 188, 192, 196
Coimbra 13, 14, 18, 19, 23, 49, 82, 84, 86, 89, 91, 98, 99, 100, 101, 156
Cole, General 41, 43, 91, 108, 133
Commissariat 9, 10, 18, 51, 84, 118, 156, 253
Concepción, Funte la 10, 154, 175, 177, 189, 223, 247
Condexia 18, 87, 98, 100, 101
Corunna 8, 13, 25
Costello, Rifleman 93, 95, 106, 118, 125, 187, 256
Cotton, General 9, 196
Craufurd, General Robert 10, 11, 18, 20, 34, 51, 52, 58, 59, 60, 61, 62, 66, 67, 72, 90, 126, 154, 187, 203, 204, 206–8, 250, 255, 257, 258, 259

D'Urban, Major General 27, 35, 49
Denial Policy 13, 49, 54, 55, 72
Donaldson, Private 72, 83, 84, 125, 147, 149, 179, 181, 186, 187, 209, 210, 217, 218, 221, 251
Dos Casas 153, 154, 171, 175, 176, 177, 178, 179, 183, 184, 188 192, 194 195, 217 219, 223, 241, 242, 244, 245

Drouet, General (Comte D'Erlon) 55, 66, 77, 134, 153, 155, 179, 210, 255
Drummond, Colonel 134, 141, 142, 250

Eagle, 39th Line 116
Elbé, General 69, 81, 210
Elder, Colonel 89, 93, 136, 139, 205, 254
Erskine, Major General 40, 43, 49, 50, 72, 82, 90, 91, 93, 105, 107 108, 111, 134, 135, 149, 151, 153, 161, 162, 224, 237, 238, 242, 245, 249, 255
Exploring officer 81, 114, 130

Fletcher, Colonel 23, 27, 28, 231, 233, 254
Forage 6, 8, 9, 13, 49, 53, 54, 57, 67, 72, 74, 123, 156, 162, 254
Foy, General 17, 76, 77, 227
Foz de Arouce 111, 120, 122
French Army of the North 156, 168, 171, 251, 255
  II Corps 13, 34, 62, 75, 123, 134, 137, 179, 185, 189, 210, 223, 250
  VI Corps 6, 10, 17, 36, 78, 79, 100, 101, 103, 105, 110, 111, 114, 122, 129, 130, 132, 134, 162, 179, 189, 192, 227, 250
  VIII Corps 6, 18, 34, 35, 37, 43, 57, 118, 132, 133, 179, 189, 250
  IX Corps 55, 66, 77, 134, 153, 155, 179, 188, 189, 210, 248, 255, 251
  Imperial Guard 6, 203, 215, 248, 251, 259
  Montbrun's Cavalry Division 34, 51, 95, 99, 100, 189, 203, 208 210, 248, 251
  Clausel's Division 43, 46, 55, 57, 254
  Ferey's Division 179, 183, 188, 189m 192, 210, 212, 217, 222, 247, 250 258
  Heudelet's Division 15, 17, 137, 142, 145m 149m 223, 224, 250
  Marchand's Division 17, 98, 107, 110, 114, 115, 116, 162, 183, 189, 197, 204, 247, 250
  Menard's Division 31, 43, 46
Funtes de Oñoro, Battle of vii, 183–220, 221, 229, 239, 240–5, 248, 249

Gallegos 154, 165, 173, 174, 176, 177, 179, 221, 241, 242, 247
Guerrillas 5, 155, 159, 161, 168, 171, 177, 188, 194, 253, 258

Harry Smith, Lieutenant 141, 142, 156, 157
Hill, General 6, 34, 59, 62, 65
Hopkins, Captain 137, 139, 142–3
Horse Guards vii, 72

Index   263

Houston, General 133, 189 192, 203, 238, 242, 245, 249
Howitzer 97, 139, 142, 148, 151, 255, 257

Jones, Captain RE 23, 27, 29, 30, 41, 43, 46, 105, 254
Julian Sánchez, Don 161, 163, 171, 177, 188, 189, 194, 195, 245, 253
Junot, General 6, 34, 35, 36, 37, 39, 43, 46, 61, 72, 78, 81, 86, 100, 179, 250, 253, 255
Junta 8, 16

Kincaid, Lieutenant 18, 20, 21, 49, 52, 57, 91, 97, 110, 114, 139, 253, 254

Leach, Captain 67, 165, 166, 178, 204, 205, 218, 257
Lebreton, Henriette 14, 15, 104, 253
Leira 21, 78, 790, 91, 92, 102
Leith, General 9
Leith Hay, Ensign 3, 4, 253
Lepic, General 203, 204, 208, 251
Line *v* Column 148–59
Lisbon vii, 1, 4, 9, 13, 18, 23, 25, 27, 28, 34, 36, 38, 39, 41, 49, 51, 52, 53, 57, 61, 64, 69, 71, 76, 84, 120, 151, 156, 161, 203, 210, 231, 232, 254, 255
Liverpool, Lord 25, 84, 93, 96, 108, 154, 159, 160, 162, 171, 189, 256
Logistics 6, 10, 126, 156
Loison, General 129, 132, 134, 181, 184, 203, 208, 247 250, 258

Magazine 6, 7, 9, 10, 13, 18, 34, 134, 153, 156, 158, 165
Mainwaring, Lieutenant Colonel 200–3
Marbot, Major 1, 4, 23, 36, 38, 39, 40, 51, 76, 78, 101, 104, 168, 176, 179, 181, 183, 188, 189, 192, 194, 200 203, 210, 220, 122, 223, 253, 254, 256, 257
Marilaba 162, 164, 169, 179
Marmont, Marshal 227
Massena, Martial vii, 1, 2, 6, 7, 9, 13, 14, 15, 17, 18, 19, 21, 23, 34, 36, 37, 40, 43, 46, 49, 55, 57, 59, 66, 67, 69, 70, 72, 76, 77, 77, 78, 79, 81, 87,, 90, 99, 101, 103, 104, 110, 113, 120, 121, 125, 127, 128, 129, 130, 132, 133, 134, 153, 155, 150, 165, 168, 169, 171, 173, 174, 175, 177, 179, 181, 183, 184, 188, 189, 210, 211, 217, 218, 220, 221, 222, 223, 227, 229, 247, 250

Mayor, Rio 57, 60, 62, 64, 66, 67, 69, 70, 71, 72, 75, 78, 82, 156
Memorandum on the Defence of Portugal 2, 231–4, 253, 254
Mondego, Rio 13, 18, 77, 79, 81, 86, 87, 90, 91, 93, 95, 99, 100, 101, 112, 120, 121, 132, 156, 158, 235, 236, 255
Montbrun, General 34, 99, 100, 203, 204, 208
Monte Agraco/Grand Redoubt 33, 41, 43, 50, 58, 232, 233, 234
Moore, Sir John 13, 208

Napier, George 105, 110, 256
Napier, William 78, 91, 93, 96, 104, 105, 108, 147, 151, 161, 176, 205, 255, 256, 267
Napoleon 1, 5, 6, 7, 8, 10, 38, 39, 76, 77, 125, 129, 132, 160, 161, 168, 174, 220, 225, 227, 229, 253, 254, 255, 256, 257, 259
Nava de Haver 171, 175, 177, 188, 189, 192, 194, 197, 204, 207, 241, 242, 243, 244, 245, 247, 259
Ney, Martial 6, 10, 11, 15, 17, 36, 49, 78, 79, 81, 86, 87, 89, 91, 92, 93, 96, 97, 98, 99, 100, 101, 103, 104, 105, 106, 110, 113, 114, 115, 117, 118, 121, 122, 128, 129, 130, 227, 229, 258

O'Hare, Captain 89, 208
Ordenanza, Portuguese 13, 30, 34, 100, 254

Pack, General 64
Pass of Matos 51, 52
Pelet, *Chefe de Battallon* 18, 36, 37, 51, 74, 112, 115, 117, 118, 129, 227, 253, 254, 256
Pero Negro 50, 58
Picton, General 4, 11, 15, 33, 49, 51, 91, 95, 96, 97, 101, 105, 108, 110, 111, 118, 120, 121, 122, 125, 132, 134, 146, 147, 149, 156, 177, 237, 242, 243, 249, 256, 257, 258, 259,
Piquets 15, 22, 34, 36, 43, 54, 57, 62, 67, 68, 69, 105, 111, 134, 135, 136, 154, 162, 164, 165, 169, 174, 184, 188, 194, 209, 221, 223, 235, 242, 243, 245, 255
Pombal 78, 83, 84, 86, 87, 89, 90, 100
Ponte d'Asseca/Hill 63, 74, 255
Ponte de Murcella 13, 101, 120, 122, 253
Porço Velho 175, 184, 188, 189, 192, 194, 196, 197, 205, 243, 245, 247, 258

Rally Orb 144
Ramsay, Captain 196, 197, 205

Regency Council, Portuguese 13, 14, 54, 72, 156
Rehdina, Combat of 91–100
Reynier, General 13, 15, 17, 23, 36, 62, 64, 75, 81, 133, 134, 135, 145, 146, 147, 148, 149, 151, 179, 189, 210, 217, 223, 247, 250
Royal Navy 31, 32, 52

Sabugal, Combat of 113–52, 153, 154, 159, 177, 192, 237–9, 256, 258
Saine-Croix 43
Salamanca 6, 7, 10, 14, 34, 55, 155, 161, 162, 168, 257
San Munzo 155
Santarém 10, 43, 55–80, 81, 83, 111, 156, 254, 255
Schaumann, Commissary 13, 20, 69, 70, 120, 123, 253, 256
Simmons, Lieutenant 54, 59, 61, 62, 64, 67, 81, 82, 84, 89, 114, 118, 126, 135, 136, 139, 148, 169, 220, 255
Sizandro, Rio 43
Sobral 28, 34, 35, 36, 40–9, 50, 55, 57, 58, 59, 232, 233, 234, 235
Soult, Colonel Pierre 34, 90, 142, 250
Soult, Marshal 8, 77, 78, 133, 165, 168
Spanish Army 8
Spencer, General 41, 59, 82, 87, 127, 165, 167, 249

Talavera, Battle of 1, 8, 23, 27
Telegraph system 31–3
Tomkinson, Lieutenant 61, 64, 87, 134, 153, 154, 256, 257
Torres Novas 81, 82, 175
Torres Vedras, Lines of vii, 4, 9, 10, 19, 22–54, 66, 79, 231–4
Trant, Colnel 19, 59, 89, 100, 101, 134, 153, 235, 253
Turon, Rio 153, 171, 241, 244

Val de la Mulla 153, 241, 242, 244, 245
Venda da Cruz 86, 91, 93
Vilar Formosa 153, 241, 242, 244, 245, 257

Walcheren Expedition 9, 25, 258
Wellington vii, 1, 4, 6, 8, 10, 13, 14, 15, 17, 18, 23, 24, 25, 27, 28, 30, 33, 34, 39, 39, 40, 41, 42, 43, 49, 50, 51, 52, 55, 58, 59, 61, 62, 64, 65, 66, 72, 76, 78, 79, 81, 82, 84, 86, 87, 89, 91, 93, 96, 96, 99, 101, 107, 108, 110, 111, 114, 120, 121, 125, 126, 127, 130, 132, 133, 134, 135, 136, 145, 146, 148, 149, 151, 153, 154, 156, 158, 160, 161, 162, 165, 167, 168, 171, 172, 173, 174, 175, 177, 179, 181, 184, 188, 189, 190, 192, 193, 199, 203, 204, 208, 210, 212, 213, 214, 217, 218, 220, 221, 223, 225, 231–4, 235–45

Zibeira Gap 34, 43, 50